INVENTING THE WORLD
GRANT UNIVERSITY

INVENTING THE WORLD GRANT UNIVERSITY

Chinese International Students' Mobilities, Literacies, and Identities

STEVEN FRAIBERG
XIQIAO WANG
XIAOYE YOU

UTAH STATE UNIVERSITY PRESS
Logan

© 2017 University Press of Colorado

Published by Utah State University Press
An imprint of University Press of Colorado
5589 Arapahoe Avenue, Suite 206C
Boulder, Colorado 80303

 The University Press of Colorado is a proud member of
The Association of American University Presses.

The University Press of Colorado is a cooperative publishing enterprise supported, in part, by Adams State University, Colorado State University, Fort Lewis College, Metropolitan State University of Denver, Regis University, University of Colorado, University of Northern Colorado, Utah State University, and Western State Colorado University.

∞ This paper meets the requirements of the ANSI/NISO Z39.48-1992 (Permanence of Paper)

ISBN: 978-1-60732-732-5 (paperback)
ISBN: 978-1-60732-733-2 (ebook)

Library of Congress Cataloging-in-Publication Data

Names: Fraiberg, Steven, author. | Wang, Xiqiao, – author. | You, Xiaoye, – author.
Title: Inventing the world grant university : Chinese international students' mobilities, literacies, and identities / Steven Fraiberg, Xiqiao Wang, Xiaoye You.
Description: Logan : Utah State University Press, [2017] | Includes bibliographical references.
Identifiers: LCCN 2017016849| ISBN 9781607327325 (pbk.) | ISBN 1607327325 (pbk.) | ISBN 9781607327332 (ebook)
Subjects: LCSH: Chinese students—Education (Higher)—Western countries. | Chinese students—Foreign countries. | Culturally relevant pedagogy.
Classification: LCC LC3057 .F73 2017 | DDC 371.829/951—dc23
LC record available at https://lccn.loc.gov/2017016849

Cover photograph © Kaidi Mao

To
Selin, Johsua, and Ari
Tianfu, Brooke, and Raina
Hsiao-Hui, Tianhuan, and Tianle

CONTENTS

ACKNOWLEDGMENTS

In order to study transnational and global issues across social and geographic borders, it takes, as Jay Lemke writes, "a village to study a village." This book has been a collaborative project in all senses of the word, and has included conversations with a wide range of colleagues, students, and family members. We would particularly like to thank Kevin Roozen and Brice Nordquist for their generous readings of this manuscript, and their advice has sharpened its aims and arguments. We are also grateful to Paul Prior, Tom Fox, and Tiane Donahue, who further engaged us in conversations and offered important feedback during various stages of this project.

In addition, each of us wishes to express our gratitude to a number of individuals.

Steve would first like to thank Yisi Fan for her four-year participation in this study and assistance with large and small aspects of this project. He would furthermore like to thank Xiaowei Cui, Shengxian Liu, Jianyang Mei, and Tunan Guo for their research assistance. Editor-in-Chief Zi'an Li at *Nebular* provided valuable support, and generously granted permission to use the image on our book cover. Steve would more broadly like to thank the colleagues across the Michigan State University campus who assisted him, including Charles Liu, Elizabeth Matthews, Desiree Qin, Joyce Meier, Bump Halbritter, Julie Lindquist, Rain Wuyu Liu, Regina Noto, Patricia Waters, Dwight Handspike, Kelly McCord, Larry Long, Saul Beceiro-Novo, Timothy Hinds, Nancy DeJoy, Matt Gomes, and many others. Numerous students also contributed in key ways to various aspects of this research, including Xutong Li, Shuning Liu, Tao Sun, Aiden Wang, Siqi Wang, and Taoli Zhang. The support staff at MSU, Melissa Arthurton and Diana Shank, has also been invaluable. Finally, Steve is grateful to Selin, Joshua, and Ari for their steadfast support. Where this book manages to succeed, Selin provided sound advice and guidance, a sharp editorial eye, and picked up slack (and Joshua and Ari) during many late evenings away from home. This book could not have been written without her support.

Xiaoye would like to express gratitude to his students at SIE for their participation in the study and to Melissa Butler, academic dean of SIE, for being supportive of his work. He used his time as a Yunshan Scholar at the Guangdong University of Foreign Studies to complete the last revisions of the manuscript. The Penn State Multilingual Writing Research Group provided an important forum for discussing his part of the study. Finally, he also wants to thank Hsiao-Hui, Tianhuan, and Tianle for being understanding and supportive while he worked in China during the last few summers.

A multitude of people have contributed to Xiqiao's field research, among them the students enrolled in her Preparation for College Writing (PCW) classes, members of the WeChat study groups who allowed Xiqiao to observe their learning activities, and a number of students who stayed in touch and provided continuous feedback to versions of the manuscript. Xiqiao would like to express gratitude to Ellen Cushman for being supportive of the various pedagogical and empirical research taking place in the context of PCW. Finally, she wants to thank Tianfu, Brooke, and Raina for being the first audience of her writing who always point out things that "do not make sense."

We would finally like to thank Michael Spooner at Utah State University Press for his strong support of this project. We are also indebted to Laura Furney who gracefully and expertly helped to shepherd us through the production process. We further thank the entire production and marketing team at the press, including Kami Day, Kelly Lenkevich, Dan Miller, Beth Sinavich, Charlotte Steinhardt, Dan Miller, Linda Gregonis, and, finally, Daniel Pratt for his design of the book cover. We additionally thank the reviewers and Chenchen Huang for helping with manuscript preparation.

The study has been supported by a Conference on College Composition and Communication (CCCC) Research Initiative Grant and by the project (17BYY110) A Comparative Study on English Writing Textbooks Published in China and the United States over the Last Century, funded by the National Planning Office of Philosophy and Social Sciences, P.R. China. This project further received support from the College of Arts and Letters (CAL) at Michigan State University through the Undergraduate Research Initiative (URI) and CAL Research awards. Finally, we would like to thank the Department of Writing, Rhetoric, and American Cultures for its generous support.

INVENTING THE WORLD
GRANT UNIVERSITY

INTRODUCTION

We begin this book with a scene that unfolded directly outside a first-year writing (FYW) classroom at Michigan State University (MSU), which is located along the banks of the Red Cedar River. The course was an honors section comprised of largely middle-class students from the state and surrounding midwestern region. It was themed around ethnographic approaches to writing, and on this day, the students were turning in papers on the analysis of a cultural artifact. Through the first-floor window overlooking a bridge were a number of other artifacts ripe for analysis: a row of US and Michigan state flags waving in front of the Old Auditorium building for Veteran's Day, the campus rock with Greek letters, graffiti underneath a bridge over the river running through the campus, and the street Farm Lane indexing the university's agricultural roots. This backdrop, however, went largely unnoticed by the students, who were silently typing in-class reflections on their laptops. However, their attention shifted as the scene was unexpectedly disrupted. Whispers began as an exotic white sports car slowed to a stop on the bridge and pulled to the curbside. Inside was a young Chinese student in sunglasses staring straight ahead, and beside him was a young female student. Directly across on the other side was a green-and-white SUV police vehicle with a policeman running the registration numbers and stepping out of the automobile to issue a ticket. Gazing out at the interaction, the midwestern students broke into peals of laughter at the incongruity of the scene. The sports car (and driver) seemed out of place on the midwestern campus, particularly in a state struggling from downsizing in the automotive industry. The social, cultural, and class divisions were intensified by the perception of international students as operating in ethnic enclaves.

Alastair Pennycook (2012) foregrounds the politics of mobility through attention to how and why objects and moments turn up in "unexpected places." The unexpected offers a window into social norms and forces regulating everyday interactions, practices, activities, and travels. The wholly unexpected scene outside the classroom brought these issues

DOI: 10.7330/9781607327332.c000

into sharp relief. The scene foregrounded how language and culture regulated the students' movements, with the physical separation of local and international students indexing a wider linguistic and social divide among the student population. Entirely absent from the honors FYW section (with the sole Chinese student dropping it after the first day), most Chinese international students were tracked into remedial courses while paying out-of-state tuition dollars for limited college credits. From the perspective of the international students, the vehicle indexed a sign of modernity and mobility in the context of rapid social transformations within contemporary Chinese society. Moreover, it signified efforts to get around the system and subvert institutional rules and authorities, an issue we will more fully discuss in relation to what we refer to as underground economies of learning on campus. Finally, from the perspective of the university, the scene symbolized the university's efforts to capitalize on international students while also policing them through policies of containment. It is this focus on fixity and flow that will serve as a framework for attending to complex movements of this student population across semiotic, institutional, and geographic borders. We will moreover attend to the ways these movements shape and are shaped by everyday practices as they co-constitute part of a wider transnational social field in which the higher education landscape is being reconfigured.

These moves extend the emergent mobilities paradigm (Blommaert 2010; Lorimer-Leonard 2013; Nordquist 2017; Pennycook 2012) within writing and literacy studies through foregrounding the complex interplay among lived literacy practices, student mobilities, and internationalization. Attending to the intermingling of geographic and social spaces, this framework focuses on ways power is reflected and reinforced (Massey 1994). Core to these issues are questions of travel and movement in higher education: who is able to move, how they move, when they move, and to what effect. In the following pages, this line of inquiry is taken up with respect to a largely privileged upwardly mobile class within Chinese society—stereotyped in the popular media as "second-generation rich"—and the role of higher education institutions (HEIs), languages, and literacies in this process. This analytic approach opens up for scrutiny ways educational programs and practices are embedded in wider global eduscapes (Luke 2006) as well as in how globalized power operates through a variety of linked scales (Dingo, Riedner, and Wingard 2013) that connect diverse regions, nations, and HEIs.

While international study is certainly not a new phenomenon, what is new is the scale and intensity of this process. International-student enrollment is part of a worldwide trend, with levels now at nearly 4.5

million (Institute of International Education 2014). With its rapid economic expansion and emergence on the world stage, China is the largest engine of this growth, with one out of every six international students now from the People's Republic of China (Institute of International Education 2014). These newly affluent and mobile students have become a cornerstone of an aggressive recruitment campaign as a means to offset decreased national and state funding in an era of neoliberal reforms and privatization. While the landscape is shifting as students discover the benefits of alternatives in European countries, and as China develops its own competitive programs, the largest players in this marketplace have been the English-speaking destinations of Australia, the United Kingdom, Canada, and the United States. More particularly, because the United States is the select destination for many of the students, there have been record numbers of international students in the United States every year, with the numbers increasing by 40 percent over the past decade. In 2014, the number of students from China totaled two hundred and seventy thousand, or 31 percent of the local international-student population (Institute of International Education 2014). While these students are enrolled in large and small public and private institutions across the country, the majority are located in major public state schools, whose total international enrollments have doubled or quadrupled within the span of a few years. On the whole, however, institutes of higher learning such as MSU have been unequipped to absorb such a large contingent of students from a single region or to accommodate sometimes wide cultural and linguistic differences. Surrounding these matters are questions about how and whether or not educators should accommodate cultural and linguistic differences. Critically, at the core of these tensions is a reconfiguration of "the power differences and structural relations" (Li 2006, 3) between international students and the educational system. Central to the issues are "who controls what is taught, who has access to what, and whose literacy is legitimatized in schools" (6). In this transnational study, we unpack these tensions in the context of writing and rhetoric programs and higher education institutions. It is our contention that the task for the various stakeholders is not to ask whether or not to change but rather to identify how HEIs are changing and the nature of these transformations.

Central to these moves is the need for closer insight into the ways that multilingual (translingual) and multimodal (transmodal) literacy practices of international students—inside and outside school-based contexts—mediate the development of their academic, disciplinary, and transnational identities. In a study of the rapidly growing immigrant Asian community in Vancouver, British Columbia, literacy scholar Guofang Li (2006) put forth educators' "need to find effective ways to collect student social and cultural data outside school, as we cannot teach when we do not know who we are teaching" (211). Though Li was referring primarily to the context of secondary education, her contention is equally relevant to higher education spheres. The need for a more in-depth understanding of students' values, worldviews, and literacy practices is particularly critical for writing, speaking, and language-learning classrooms that often work with the largest contingent of international students when they first arrive and are tasked with the responsibility of preparing those students for the work they will be engaged in across the university.

To capture the multidimensional nature of this phenomenon, we draw on a longitudinal study that maps out the transliteracy practices of undergraduates at a major state university in the United States and at a private study-abroad program in China. Crossing semiotic, cultural, and geographic boundaries, we trace students' literate and social trajectories as they traverse home and host cultures while attending to the ways this process mediates literacy practices, academic socialization, transnational dispositions, social and class identities, and the fundamental restructuring of higher education. Grounded in this frame is the sense that education is no longer solely a sovereign entity (if it ever was) but is increasingly "a shared, transnational phenomenon" (Meyers 2014, 7). Taking up this perspective, our project attends to the ways the intertwined issues of globalization, education, and economics reach into everyday life. The book speaks to issues of the ways globalization demands rethinking of educational inquiry, and also, by implication, educational practices. Hence, beyond a focus on understanding how students adapt and adjust to Western models of education, there is the need to conceptualize the ways increased student mobilities challenge the underlying assumptions surrounding these HEI models. In particular, this study is built around the following questions:

- How are transformations in HEIs shaping and being shaped by the transnational migration and movement of students in and across home and host culture(s)? What are the uneven local and global structural relationships and linkages mediating this process? How is this process bound up in the reconstruction of social, class, and national identities?
- How do the students transculturally position (Guerra 1998) themselves as they move across social and material spaces (distributed across temporal and spatial scales)?

- How does this process mediate students' socialization into the language, literacy, and disciplinary practices of the university? In reciprocal fashion, how does their academic socialization mediate their identities and literacy practices outside classroom contexts?
- How can a more complex and in-depth understanding of these processes help us develop culturally responsive and reciprocal pedagogies (Li 2006) and research practices in writing, public speaking, disciplinary literacies, and global citizenship?

TRANSNATIONAL SOCIAL FIELDS

Our study takes up these questions through attention to the ways everyday literacy practices of Chinese international students are shaping and being shaped by the global higher education landscape. To perform this work, we bring together individual case studies of transnational literacy practices as the students traverse home and host cultures in and across two primary locations. The first is at Michigan State University. Originally a land grant founded on the Morrill Act in 1863, the university has been traditionally focused on agriculture and engaging the local community with a strong outreach agenda. More recently, however, President Lou Anna Simon has expanded the mission of the university in a shift from a land-grant college to what is labeled as a *world grant*. Currently, MSU is one of the top ten universities recruiting international students, and the number of Chinese students at MSU has increased from 2 percent of the population in 2007 to 10 percent of the population in 2014 (MSU Office of the Registrar 2014). One of the unintended consequences has been that the large number of international students has enabled those students to self-segregate and form a rich, complex subculture, or sense of a "college within a college," that remains opaque to many local students and faculty (Fraiberg and Cui 2016). Despite a need for a much more in-depth understanding of this population's linguistic and semiotic repertoires, cultural practices, and motivations, there remains limited research in this area or in the ways these students' literacy practices afford and constrain the formation of their academic or global dispositions and learning. This data is particularly critical in the composition program, in which two of the scholars involved in this research project teach, where it is not uncommon in basic writing courses for 80 to 90 percent of the students in each classroom to be Chinese. It is moreover essential for those in writing across the curriculum (WAC) and writing in the disciplines (WID), as well as for other instructors intersecting with literacy studies, to attend to the ways students traverse the curriculum. Most broadly, this in-depth portrait is critical for making sense of processes through which wider transformations in higher education are shaping and being shaped in the context of everyday literate practices. Even while MSU brands itself as a campus grounded in ideals of global diversity and social justice, its current recruitment practices, as well as other global strategic initiatives targeted at China, index a wider set of tensions as the university attempts to penetrate new markets. Pressured by current shortfalls in state funding, academic capitalism is playing an increasing role in the reproduction of social divisions on a global scale and in the construction of a transnational social class.

The second site serving as a focus for this research is called the Sinoway International Education (SIE) Summer School in China, which has a complex relationship to Michigan State University and the broader area of higher education within the United States. Indexing ways schools such as SIE are both a recent product of the higher education system in the United States and, in key respects, a challenge to its dominance, the SIE school itself was founded in 2009 by a Wabash College student and his friend from Harvard Law School after the former realized Chinese students returning home had little opportunity to take the same kinds of summer credit-bearing courses that were available to their North American counterparts. Modeling itself on the North American educational system, the SIE Summer School opened on the campus of East China Normal University in Shanghai and hired thirteen faculty members. As of 2015, the school has received financial backing from Renren (equivalent to the Facebook of China) and employs 250 faculty, with more than five thousand students enrolled in the program. The SIE program, as the first of its kind within China, has moreover engendered an array of competitors that have also recently opened their doors in a dynamic and rapidly expanding educational marketplace. In this fashion, the focus on this site and its relation to MSU serves to foreground a dynamic, shifting socioeconomic structure in which the Chinese middle class is not only reproducing but is also contesting and appropriating an educational model based on North American and US-centric hegemonic practice related to teaching and learning.

Together, these sites comprise new transnational circuits (Rouse 1992) shaping and shaped by the flow of pedagogies, ideologies, practices, teachers, and, of course, international students. Forming complex networks that stretch across borders, these sites serve to co-constitute what Levitt and Schiller (2004) define as a "transnational social field." The term characterizes the manner in which transnational actors frequently live out their lives across borders as they cultivate multilayered and multisited identifications in and across local, regional, and national spaces. These varied spaces consist of "differing forms, depth, and breadth" as "a set of multiple interlocking networks of social relationships through which ideas, practices, and resources are unequally exchanged, organized, and transformed" (Levitt and Schiller 2004, 1009). This conceptual framework is grounded in Pierre Bourdieu's (1986, 1991) notion of field as a structured space of relationships that determines people's position and movement within it according to the relative distribution of resources or capital (economic, social, cultural). Within these social spaces, literacy serves as a form of capital production and exchange through which actors are variously able to attain positions in and across various fields. In order to map out this process, we theoretically and methodologically bring together a number of key theoretical strands as part of a more holistic approach that links local literacy practices to wider social, cultural, and economic mobilities.

LITERACY IN MOTION

Our "mobile literacies" approach (Lorimar-Leonard 2013; Nordquist 2017) centers on how literacy affords and constrains movement of actors, identities, and practices across geographic and social structures. Closely aligned with a rich body of work in academic socialization in writing and literacy studies over the past thirty years, research in this area has largely focused on ways students learn to "invent" (Bartholomae 1986) the university. This work examines ways students acquire academic and disciplinary identities as they learn to adopt the ways of speaking, being, and knowing in the academy (Casanave 2002; Ivanič 1998; McCarthy 1987; Prior 1998; Russell and Yañez 2003; Sternglass 1997; Zamel and Spack 2004). Moreover, emergent scholarship (Prior 1998; Roozen and Erickson 2017) has challenged models of disciplinary enculturation grounded in structuralist assumptions focused on container metaphors of "going into" disciplines. This is parallel with a recognition that the university is not a homogenous space but is rather co-constituted and dynamically comprised of multiple and competing discourses (Harris 2012). This scholarship breaks from a classroom-as-container model that conceptualizes educational spaces as bounded and discrete (Leander, Phillips, and Taylor 2010).

Concurrent with this shift is a broader move in transnational studies away from container models of the nation-state and what has been referred to as "methodological nationalism" (Shahjahan and Kezar 2013; Wimmer and Schiller 2002). This transnational optic indexes how transnational actors frequently live out their lives across borders as they cultivate multilayered and multisited identifications in and across local, regional, and national spaces. This framework links local practices to networks of power and the material and political effects of these relationships (Dingo 2012; Hesford 2006; Hesford and Schell 2008). These moves align with research in New Literacy Studies (NLS). NLS has generally argued for a conceptualization of literacy as ideologically produced within social and institutional settings (Barton and Hamilton 1998; Gee 1996; Heath 1983; Street 1993) as opposed to a universal set of skills linked to individual cognition. This social-literacies approach conceptualizes reading and writing as situated practices whose values and meanings shift according to specific purposes in various contexts of use. Whereas this generation of literacy studies, however, focused predominantly on local communities and relatively bounded contexts, a new wave of research (Berry, Hawisher, and Selfe 2012; Brandt and Clinton 2002; Bruna 2007; Baynham and Prinsloo 2009; Duffy 2007; Kang 2015; Lam 2009; Leonard, Vieira, and Young 2015; Pahl and Rowsell 2006; Vieira 2011, 2016; Yi 2007) is moving toward investigating literacy practices within local and global, or translocal, contexts. As Lam and Warriner (2012) write, "It is mostly within the last decade that studies of language and literacy have begun to explore the relation between communicative practices and the multilayered relationships that migrants develop across geographical borders" (192). Key to this research is attention to the interplay between the local and distant (in space and time), with participants conceptualized as "bricoleurs" (Black 2009). Engaged in a process of "layered simultaneity" (Blommaert 2005), transnational actors draw on multiple resources from home and host cultures as they construct polycultural identities and traverse multiple lifeworlds. Through these practices, actors transculturally position (Guerra 1998) themselves as they develop multilayered affiliations, or "multiple reference points in the position of the self" (Black 2009, 378). It is within these spaces that actors negotiate and develop bifocal perspectives (Vertovec 2004) or a transnational habitus (Meinhof 2009) in which actors view the world from the perspectives of home and host cultures.

Stemming from this perspective, educational contexts are viewed through the lens of a wider transnational social field—comprised of complexly interlocking sets of campuses, classrooms, peripheral institutions, educational policies, neoliberal regimes—that mediates the complex flow of students, teachers, and curriculum across borders. Taking up this broader focus in a study of educational spaces across the US-Mexico border, Susan Meyers (2014) adopts a comparative approach to explore the spaces between sites and the ways they "cross over, combine, intersect, and influence each other" (7). Further focusing on transnational connectivities, scholarship has begun to study the social effects on writing programs as they are increasingly entangled with other near and far-flung institutional practices and spaces (Donahue 2009; Kang 2015; Martins 2015). This scholarship includes attention to the complex linkages with international branch campuses (Wetzel and Reynolds 2015) and intensive English programs (Rounsaville 2015) as components of a relational network mediating international-student mobilities and identities. Overlapping with this focus has been increased attention to globally networked learning environments (Starke-Meyerring 2015) and cross-border and cross-national collaborations and partnerships (O'Brien and Alfano 2015). Finally, as part of an effort to challenge hegemonic US disciplinary and monolingual assumptions, writing scholars have begun to examine the socially and historically situated nature of writing programs beyond North American borders (Anson and Donahue 2015; Ayash 2014; Muchiri et al. 1995; Foster and Russell 2010; Thaiss et al. 2012; You 2010). Nevertheless, much of the literature remains focused at the level of individual actors and the ways they learn to invent the university as opposed to a broader focus on the ways the higher education landscape is being reinvented. Moreover, transnational studies that challenge narrower frameworks generally adopt a bird's-eye perspective of transnationalism (e.g., broad-based policies, discussions of statistical trends). This view is in contrast to a grassroots focus on transnationalism (Smith and Guarnizo 1998) that attends to local and material processes of actors and literacies "on the move."

Finally, dovetailing with this focus, we foreground the embodied nature of local and material processes by incorporating the literature in spatial theory (Latour 1999, 2005; Lefebvre 1991; Massey 1994, 2005; Reynolds 2007; Soja 1996; Thrift 2006). This scholarship broadly attends to the intersections of real and imagined spaces and ways they shape and are shaped by social relations. In a shift from neutral understandings of context, space is not a backdrop or stage against which activity takes place but is dynamic, changing, sedimented with ideologies, and co-constituted by the participants. Opening up relations of power for scrutiny, this analytic lens highlights ways spaces mediate uneven and differential flows of actors and objects. In making this move, it attends to the politics of mobility, or "how people move—why, with whom, and under what conditions" (Nordquist 2014, 18). In education and literacy studies, this analytic frame has been leveraged to examine the production of spaces and identities in classrooms (Leander, Phillips, and Taylor 2010; Leander and Rowe 2006; Leander and Sheehy 2004; Nordquist

2017). More broadly, Nedra Reynolds (2007) has looked at the social geography of the university and the ways it is bound up in geographies of difference and the production of social class. Despite the spatial turn, however, most studies in transnational higher education remain at the policy level, with more limited work (Brooks and Waters 2011; Sidhu 2006; Singh, Rizvi, and Shrestha 2007; Waters 2012) on the uneven and messy ways the educational landscape is being reconfigured in the context of everyday practices.

In sum, this book brings together scholarship in mobility studies, transnationalism, spatial theory, and disciplinary enculturation. In making these moves, we explore the intersections among social, geographic, and educational mobilities while attending to the complex manner in which everyday literacy practices are bound up in a wider shifting educational landscape. While individual strands of these issues have been taken up within writing and literacy studies, there is little research that brings these areas together as part of a less bounded approach. To accomplish these aims, we focus specifically on the Chinese international-student population, whose rapid and large-scale movement onto Western campuses serves to foreground key theoretical, methodological, and pedagogical issues.

MOBILE LITERACIES FRAMEWORK

Grounded in our mobile literacies framework, educational structures are imagined as physically and symbolically transporting students, teachers, administrators, policies, textbooks, and other actors across social and material landscapes. Operating as what Nordquist (2017) has identified as a mobility system, HEIs afford the movement of some actors while constraining the mobilities of others. This process is part of an ongoing struggle as actors continually shape and are shaped by these systems. Urry (2007) compares the emergent and dynamic nature of mobility systems to walking through a maze whose walls rearrange themselves as one travels. Useful for conceptualizing the fluid, dynamic, co-mediated nature of this interplay is "knotworking" (Prior and Shipka 2003). This process entails the complex orchestration of activity or the tying and untying of actors and objects distributed across near and far-flung spaces. It is this process that shapes the alignments of the participants, the coordination of activity, and the fluid ecologies co-constituting the dynamic and emergent pathways through which signs, symbols, and actors circulate. While the concept has generally focused on organizational contexts, scholars (Fraiberg 2010; Prior and Schaffner 2011) have argued that knotworking is a long-standing feature of all literate and place-making practices. Taking up this frame, space itself is imagined as a knotwork or complex entanglement of densely knotted streams of activity. Challenging bounded container models, this analytic lens foregrounds how the mobility system is "enacted, maintained, extended, and transformed" (Spinuzzi 2008, 16).

Methodologically applying this perspective to international student mobility forces one to attend to the various material resources that afford and constrain "how they come to travel, how they travel, how often, and to what effect" (Brooks and Waters 2011, 130). Consequently, the mapping of literate identities necessitates the tracing of "trajectories of participation" (Dreier 1999) across scenes of writing, as actors draw on a diverse array of heterogeneous resources distributed across space-time. This approach provides the rationale behind our unit of analysis as mediated action (Wertsch 1991), serving to link situated practice to transnational social fields. The tracing of mobile practices further necessitates attention to how social objects and meanings on-the-move hold or lose their values as they travel from place to place (i.e., as they move through the world and move/are moved by the world). This movement includes not only the corporeal and physical travel of people and objects, but also imaginative and virtual travel (e.g., on the Internet).

In order to map out this process as we examine how students learn to "invent" the university (Bartholomae 1986)—and ways it is being reinvented—we engage in what has been characterized as multisited (Marcus 1995) and global (Burawoy 2000) ethnographic approaches. Dovetailing with this framework is the argument that global mobilities have transformed the traditional social fields and objects of education:

> If people and objects are increasingly mobile, then, Gupta and Ferguson argue, ethnography has to engage these movements and, with them, the ways in which localities are a product of the circulations of meanings and identities in time-space. Research must become embedded self-consciously within the world systems, changing its focus from single sites and local situations to become multi-sited and multi-local, responsive to the networked realities. (Rizvi 2009, 279)

Critically while we have characterized this study as focused on two key locations, in the midwestern United States and southern part of China, these are not conceptualized as bounded or static spaces, as opposed to densely interrelated spaces that are continually under (re)construction. In mapping out activity in and across these sites, we are not only attending to actors and objects' traversals between them, but the ways that they are densely intertwined with other regional and globally distributed spaces inside and outside our specified "sites."

Positions

Arjun Appadurai (1996) describes the various dimensions of "scapes" characterizing globalization as "not objective given relations that look the same from every angle of vision but, rather, . . . deeply perspectival constructs inflected by the historical, linguistic, and political situatedness of the various actors" (33). In this fashion, the various subjectivities of the authors of this project offer multiple perspectives on this process. In the chapters that follow, we present individual case studies conducted by the authors. The first two authors, Steve and Xiqiao, are located at Michigan State University, where they teach in the composition program. Steve was born in Michigan and speaks English as his home language; Xiqiao is originally from Lanzhou, China, and received her PhD in the States. While Chinese is her first language, she is for all intents and purposes bilingual and biliterate. As the case studies show, these differences mediated their individual studies and served to surface important "rich points" (Agar 1994). The third researcher, Xiaoye, is a professor at Penn State University but has taught in the SIE international program for several summers and, similar to Xiqiao, is biliterate. In similar fashion, his positioning among the summer-school students from various US colleges and universities is central to the story as it unfolds. Indexing the significance of the positioning of the researchers, we shift between *I* and *we* as part of an effort to capture the multiauthored and multivoiced nature of the book. Furthermore, as the process of globalization is driving new forms of subjectivity and hybrid identities, this move serves as an acknowledgment of ways the researchers' positions have not only afforded a study of transnationalism within educational settings but have also been directly a product of them. Summarizing the motivation and necessity for a multiresearcher approach in the study of complex ecological systems, Leander, Phillips, and Taylor (2010) write as part of an argument for mapping mobilities and the changes in social spaces of learning,

> Lemke (2000), among others, considers how historical and contemporary methods of research very often index what is reachable by a single researcher (in place and time), and how it may well "take a village" to study a village (275), or ecological system of learning. (343)

In this respect, the varied positions of the individual researchers have allowed for a richer and broader mapping of a transnational higher education field. Each of our case studies foregrounds different aspects of our analytic frames and methods based on our respective positons as researchers.

In key respects, we have leveraged our differing subject positions to make sense of our data. For instance, in an analysis of the social and class positons of the students in his class, Xiaoye focused on a debate over a film celebrating the lifestyle of a group of post-nineties-generation new rich. At the center of the tensions was a student's contention that the controversial film did not accurately represent the "real" lifestyles of average Chinese citizens. At first perplexed by the discussion and the use of the term *real*, Steve shared his confusion with Xiaoye. Unpacking the term, they jointly uncovered that missing were unshared assumptions linked to differences in their socialization into Chinese and American national discourses. Influenced by Xiaoye's upbringing in the People's Republic, the term "real" indexed the socialist-realism movement grounded in the notion that art should celebrate the working class. As a result of the interaction, Xiaoye incorporated additional historical context into his analysis. In this fashion, our social backgrounds and orientations served as a means to a fuller understanding of linguistic and cultural distinctions.

Mobile Methods

In locating situated moments of practice within a wider transnational social field, we were presented with a number of methodological issues related to global scale and complexity (Blommaert 2013; Urry 2003). Working across two different institutions including a major state university, we were tasked with trying to capture an entangled network of teachers, administrators, policies, regulations, digital networks, events, media reports, departmental units, a myriad of spaces, and four thousand Chinese undergraduates. Without a single fixed location as a starting point, we followed the advice of Bruno Latour (2005) to "begin in the middle of things" (27). Latour notes that starting almost anyplace will provide traces, vestiges, and linkages to other nodes or actors in the network. More particularly, he argues for a flat ontology to ensure that the establishment of every link in complex interlocking sets of associations—stretching in and across near and distant spaces—is visible. In order to achieve these aims, he offers three analytically separate but deeply related moves: localizing the global, redistributing the local, and connecting the sites. In the following section, we will identify more closely how these moves framed our methodological choices. However, first we articulate key assumptions undergirding these moves.

Grounded in conceptions of place as continuously in the making, our questions focused on what social or political forces render this process invisible or naturalize it as fixed. As Pennycook (2012) has suggested, disruptions (as well as contradictions and breakdowns) in everyday scenes can help uncover hidden power geometries (Massey 1994), or the politics of mobility mediating who/what moves, when they move, how fast, how far, and to what effect. With these questions in mind, we began to register things turning up in unexpected places. On the MSU campus, this was not difficult: Chinese signs across campus; MSU workshops in Chinese (e.g., how to use library resources); large lecture halls filled with predominantly Chinese speakers; name-pronunciation workshops; underground economies for everything from delivering food to selling spaces for a course filled to capacity; media reports of a Chinese student gang; vandalized cars in a campus parking lot with the message "Go Home"; and the largest football half-time show in the school's history directed by a planner of the Beijing Olympics. Identifying such moments as starting points, we interrogated wider social, cultural, and political forces mediating the construction of space and place.

As a flip side to looking at contradictions and breakdowns, we also identified moments of development and change over time. These moves were similarly premised on the assumption that fully developed and stabilized human practices, scripts, routines, and rituals are difficult to study because they are "so fast, fluent, dense and condensed" (Prior 2008, 3) that little is visible. Tracing the development of people (e.g., disciplinary identities and practices) and things (e.g., academic policies) offered glimpses into mechanisms through which they became "black boxed" or stabilized, as various actors recruited and were recruited into wider social and semiotic systems.

Attending to these areas, we focused on three specific moves.

Localizing the Global

Latour's first move in keeping the analysis flat is to localize the global. The point is to make visible extended chains of actors (humans and non-humans) without jumping, breaking, or tearing. In this case macro no longer contains the micro; that is, no place can be said to be larger or wider than any others, "but some can be said to benefit from far safer connections with many more places than others" (Latour 2005, 176). As a result, what was above or below now remains on the same focal plane. This is not to suggest a lack of hierarchies or scales, but instead that one should not presuppose these in advance. To connect one site to another, the researcher needs to pay the full cost of the relation without shortcuts. Keeping this principle in mind, we charted transnational flows of people, imaginaries, and things in motion as they were translated or recontextualized across space and time. In making these moves, we drew on a number of traditions related to tracing chains of activity (Kell 2009; Latour 1999, 2005; Leander 2008; Norris and Jones 2005; Prior 2004; Prior and Hengst 2010; Silverstein and Urban 1996; Spinuzzi 2003; Wortham 2006) across people, genres, languages, modes, and spaces. This process attends to the complex manner in which objects and meanings are translated, rearticulated, and transformed as they migrate across near and distant contexts. These unequal encounters across difference are sites of struggle and friction shaping and shaped by material and social structures. This framework foregrounds a historical-developmental view of actors and objects as they accumulate meanings and become stabilized-for-now structures mediating everyday activity. Localizing the global, this methodology never makes a "jump" with a "yawning break" between scales (Latour 2005, 173).

Redistributing the Local

Second, we redistributed the local to show how single sites and moments are relationally linked or folded into other times and places. Scale then does not depend on the absolute size but on the number and durability of the connections. Relevant to inquiry in higher educational spaces, Latour offers the scene of a university lecture hall that was planned fifteen years ago and two hundred kilometers away by an architect who drew up the blueprints. These plans provide a wider blueprint or social script shaping how loud the lecturer will need to speak, the arrangement of and number of students in well-ordered tiers, and the teacher located behind a podium. In this fashion this physical space is sedimented with orientations and meanings linked to other times and spaces that have been rendered invisible or black boxed. These structures both shape and are shaped by everyday interactions, so it is no longer only the teacher giving the lecture, but the teacher-lecture-hall-university delivering it. The question then is, who is carrying out the action? The answer is always at least two actors (or actants). In this fashion, we focused on such questions, asking who/what was acting (translating) and who/what was being acted on (translated). Extending Latour's examples, we traced complex webs of activity in our own educational institutions across near and far-flung contexts.

Connecting Sites

Finally, we looked for the links, relations, and connections in the networks (see also appendix I). This entailed identifying events, objects, and people that were drawn together in various trajectories. Through tracing chains of activity across multiple sites we were able to identify complex connections between them. For instance, on the MSU campus an MBA student established a for-profit Chinese college program for cheaper transferable college credits in less time. The school itself was a copy of another school, SIE, that was the focus of Xiaoye's study. Moreover, affecting these locations was a report published in *The Chronicle of Higher Education* interrogating the quality and legitimacy of growing numbers of for-profit Chinese higher educational programs. Following the report both schools suffered drops in enrollment and triaged in various ways. In this fashion, we began to trace complex linkages across the sites and the resultant reconfiguration of the higher eduscape. This was done without scaling or "zooming" (e.g., from micro to macro). Latour uses an accounting metaphor to ensure that the development of analytic frames or scales have been paid in full through fine-grained tracing of chains of associations. To carry the metaphor forward, we paid the "transaction costs for moving, connecting, and assembling" (Latour 2005, 220) these various streams and threads of activity forming part of a transnational social field.

In order to accomplish these aims, we traced various actors, imaginaries, and objects across contexts. First and foremost this entailed the tracing of students in and across classrooms, bar rooms, and online chat rooms as they developed language and literacy practices and identities. Core to this focus was attention to translanguaging centered on questions such as, When did they use Chinese? When did they use English? How and why did the languages mix? In making these moves, we further focused on how students wrote and developed papers and oral presentations along with the various scenes and moments that went into developing them. For example, we attended to the ways a conversation out of class (in English) was translated into student jottings (in Chinese and English), later discussed (in Chinese) with a classmate back in China on a social media platform, and finally translated into a draft (in English) brought to a student-teacher conference. In this fashion, we linked students' local transliteracy practices to near and far-flung contexts distributed across a transnational social field. By following the students beyond the classrooms and into their everyday lives, we further attempted to understand how their extracurricular literacies and activities were deeply woven into this process. We additionally collapsed an array of binaries: virtual and real; in-school and out-of-school; text and talk; and local and global. Beyond a focus on international students' social and literate trajectories, we lastly traced the planning, development, and histories of things in the making, such as university policies, international student events, translingual pedagogies and curricula, and university marketing materials.

DATA COLLECTION TOOLS

To gather data, we drew on an array of data-collection tools based on our subject positions and local contextual factors: computer screen recordings of writing sessions, still photographs, audio and video recordings of activity, participant observation, field notes, focus groups, retrospective and elicited interviews, literacy narratives, and the collection of artifacts (e.g., student papers, social media posts, syllabi). When possible, we used simultaneous and multiple means to provide optimal data sources (Leander 2003) for complicating our analysis. Assembling our data sets to map out relational networks, or knotworks, we adopted a critical perspective on how our data-collection methods framed our analysis grounded in the assumption that each method narrows down the field of view in its privileging of certain aspects of activities while limiting or omitting others. Reflexively attending to these issues, we focused on tracing multiple interlocking mobilities (embodied, imagined, virtual).

Tracing these complex entanglements, our study argues for a more holistic approach to writing and literacy studies, with attention to global complexity (Urry 2003). Core to our argument is the necessity for fine-grained tracing of mobile literacies across space-time while connecting moments of everyday practice to wider distributed networks, or knotworks, of activity. While in many respects these mobile methods have been firmly established in literacy studies, what is new is the scope of the analysis and their application to the study of transnational social fields in higher education. Over the past ten years, composition studies has experienced a translingual turn (Canagarajah 2006, 2013; Horner, Lu, Royster, and Trimbur 2011), with much of the conversation tending to focus on classrooms and pedagogical practices related to leveraging difference as an asset for learning. Our study is a call for an expansion of this focus in a shift from tranlingualism to transliteracy (You 2016) and from single-sited analyses to multisited approaches. Dovetailing with a shift in writing and literacy studies toward a less bounded framework, it situates local classroom practices in the context of the world grant university.

CHAPTER OVERVIEW

The following chapters map out key issues shaping the students' movement across transnational HEIs. The first half of the book looks at the cultural, social, and linguistic landscape at Michigan State University while situating broader social shifts within the context of a rapidly increasing Chinese international-student population. In performing this work, chapter 1 offers a broad overview of the ways the recent influx of

Chinese international students is reshaping the social, geographic, institutional, and linguistic landscape on the MSU campus. It maps out the ways the university and local community are repositioning themselves in a globalized marketplace while simultaneously trying to capitalize on and "contain" the Chinese international students. Untangling this process, the university is conceptualized as a complex mobility system (Urry 2007; Nordquist 2017): that is, one open and unfinished and in which several apparently unrelated forces operate simultaneously without being centrally controlled or planned. Bringing together several disparate strands of activity, the analysis attends to the ways the reconfiguration of the university is bound up in the construction of pathways regulating movements of students in and across the HEI landscape.

Chapter 2 examines ways international students' grassroots literacy practices are complexly entangled in this process as students take up, resist, and transform institutional structures. To analyze this interplay, the chapter attends to the ways grassroots activities are mediated by students' *guanxi* networks. *Guanxi* is a key term in Chinese society referring to a complex system of exchange mediating the construction of social networks. The chapter examines how this trope is bound up in the ways students leverage transnational resources across home and host cultures. In particular, the analysis focuses on the ways two transnational entrepreneurs mobilized a deeply distributed array of social and material resources as a process intertwined with the reconstruction of identities and the HEI landscape. The first case focuses on ways a student who served as the "poster child" for the university leveraged his official status to develop an array of side businesses, including the establishment of the Summer China Program (SCP) International School. The chapter then turns to ways another student's efforts to start an international student magazine, *Nebular,* was deeply linked to the production of emergent social and class identities in China. Together, the telling cases foreground the complex ways students were reconfiguring both social space and the social imagination.

Chapter 3 focuses on how the students' social networks afford the development of disciplinary, academic, and transnational identities. To conduct the analysis, the chapter offers a fine-grained account of how a first-year English major similarly leveraged guanxi networks across campus, the United States, and China. Drawing on this trope—conceptualized as fluid, dynamic, contested—the analysis attends to the ways this process became densely intertwined with this student's everyday literacy practices and academic trajectory. Tracing this English major's movement in and across various courses—astronomy, Arabic, composition, and English literature—the longitudinal study identifies ways her guanxi networks scaffolded her literate activities and afforded the manner in which she learned to write and "invent" the university. Linked to the previous chapter, the analysis furthermore attends to the ways her in-class collaborations and out-of-class participation in *Nebular* became densely intertwined. The chapter broadly argues for attention to ways unofficial literacy practices can serve as a powerful—and often over-looked—resource in teaching and learning. It also suggests wider ways the international students complexly positioned themselves both inside and outside the university as official and unofficial literacy practices spun off from one another.

Chapter 4 offers a contrastive case that indicates how the students' social networks not only afforded but also *constrained* learning and the development of bifocal identities (Vertovec 2004). This chapter specifically examines the ways Chinese international students' underground literacy practices in a basic writing course allowed them to self-segregate and to collectively circumvent assignments and find loopholes in the system. The analysis specifically attends to the ways the students organized themselves according to popular social and national identity types (typifications) related to educational status within mainland China. It particularly focuses on how the students collectively used a social media application, WeChat, to collaborate and exchange course information. The analysis further attends to the ways students' underground networks extended into other spaces across the university, with a specific focus on ways one student established a strong standing within the community through exchanging online assistance in economics courses in return for other forms of social capital. The findings problematize discourses of diversity and multiculturalism perpetuated by the university while foregrounding not only the possibilities but also the significant challenges of recent translingual approaches.

Chapter 5 begins the next section of the book in turning to a study of the Sinoway International Education (SIE) program in Guangzhou, China. This chapter offers a broad overview of the program itself while conducting a spatial analysis of the social and linguistic landscape that situates the program within a complex and contested HEI marketplace. Central to this focus is the linking of material structures (buildings, computer networks, textbooks) to wider social, economic, and political structures. The chapter pivots around a key debate related to the status of for-profit Chinese summer college programs that was published in *The Chronicle of Higher Education* and the ways the arguments were taken up, resisted, and transformed locally at the SIE school. Central to the analysis is attention to how educational institutions are bound up in a struggle for legitimacy, authority, and status within a contested and shifting globalized marketplace. The analysis itself is also situated in relation to the earlier discussion of SCP from chapter 2 in a move that serves to foreground the deeply relational and contested nature of the higher education landscape within and across national borders.

While the previous chapter maps out the social and linguistic landscape at SIE, chapter 6 turns to a fine-grained analysis of ways these structures shape and are shaped by everyday classroom practices. In the history of English-language teaching in China, while writing has been a college course for a long time, public speaking was seldom offered in Communist China (You 2010). When students participated in debates sanctioned by the university, both their topics and arguments had to conform to the Communist Party ideologies and government policies. This chapter attends to how the students took up a public-speaking model focused more squarely on Western as well as cosmopolitan frames related to civic engagement. In making this move, it focuses on the ways the students took up the curriculum in general and more particularly on debates surrounding social and class mobility within Chinese society. The chapter interrogates the ways the students and instructor were complexly positioned in relation to the discourses and roles in these debates as they struggled to reconfigure their literate, class, and national identities. The analysis illustrates the ways the social spaces of the classroom are densely intertwined with wider institutional, national, and international contexts. Our attention to this process foregrounds the need for a closer focus on ways writing and speaking—in both Chinese and English—are densely intertwined in students' rhetorical processes and practices.

Chapter 7 continues to map out the complex links between the students' literacy practices inside and outside the classroom and the ways these are bound up in their shifting academic as well as national identities. Whereas, however, the previous chapter primarily traces the students' activities within a classroom setting, this chapter extends the analysis through a close tracing of the students' literate activities across bars, hot-pot restaurants, and social media. Through situated observations of these practices—primarily focused on gaming (video games, television games, board games)—the chapter illustrates ways these scenes became densely intertwined with the students' in-classroom presentations. One key finding is that students' academic socialization inflects the *shanzhai* tradition in China. In this tradition, individuals or marginalized communities, who are often portrayed as outlaws, learn the rules and ideas formulated by dominant groups and rewrite them for survival, for resistance, or for creativity. Attending to students' gaming practices, the analysis points to how students' dispositions, literacy practices, and identities are cultivated through weaving and reweaving bits and pieces of texts, objects, and ideologies from near and far-flung spaces. Attention to these translocal practices is conducive to understanding how middle-class mobilities mediate the reproduction of social inequality in China.

The conclusion synthesizes the various themes across the chapters while identifying the complex manner in which pedagogies, tropes, ideologies, languages, and actors travel across the various scenes of literacy. Implications are drawn for tracing the links between literacy and mobility across multiple sites and scales. In making this move, the chapter articulates methodological challenges in performing this work. More broadly, the chapter reflects on what this study suggests for both teaching and research in the fields of composition, second-language and literacy studies, and Chinese rhetorics while also drawing implications about HEIs more generally.

1

FRICTION IN THE EDUCATIONAL MARKETPLACE

I, Steve, drive past the state capitol toward the Michigan State campus, where I teach a composition course filled with Chinese international students. One of my Taiwanese colleagues jokes that an outsider visiting these basic writing courses on the MSU campus might think they were outside the United States. As I continue down the Michigan Avenue corridor past strips of dollar stores and boarded-up buildings, I pass a modern urban apartment complex with a Chinese character on the side of the rental office. Disrupting the midwestern landscape, the character *jia* (家), or "home," suggests the complex ways notions of home are being remixed on the local campus and in the surrounding area. This sign in the middle of a rustbelt town is disruptive, with the tensions indexing how the university and local community are entangled in a globalizing marketplace. Michigan State University is a major land-grant institution located in the heart of the Midwest in the state's capitol region. The college has grown into a sprawling campus over a 153-year history, with its core values centered on service and engagement in the wider community and the state of Michigan. Historically, the college has sought to provide educational opportunities to the local community, especially to those from the farming and working classes. Over the past ten years, however, in response to declines in state funding and in the face of sharply decreasing number of high-school graduates in the state (National Center for Education Statistics 2013), the student demographic has begun to shift. While in 2006 the number of Chinese international students at Michigan State was 2 percent, by 2014 the figure had increased to 13 percent (MSU Office of the Registrar 2014). These rapid changes are transforming the local cultural, economic, and linguistic landscape. Evidence of these transformations is found across campus and along the main city street dividing the university and the wider community, where one finds a wide array of Chinese posters, flyers, bookstores, educational centers, hot-pot restaurants, apartments,

DOI: 10.7330/9781607327332.c001

and oriental markets. These constellations are entangled with the academic market, where language and literacy are key forms of capital. As a writing instructor, I am densely enmeshed with students in networks, or knotworks, of activity.

Arriving in the parking lot across from the Agricultural Engineering Hall, I pull up directly in front of a yellow sports car driven by one of my students. I enter the overheated class filled with Chinese students, three African Americans, a Nigerian, and one Latino from Texas. With most of the background discussion before class in Chinese, I try to imagine how to balance the needs of the different populations. The unevenness within my own classroom indexes wider messy and highly uneven shifts at the university as instructors, departments, and units adjust to a new set of dynamics. At the center of these tensions are questions about who changes, how much, and to what effect. These struggles are unfolding in moments of everyday practice as the influx of students is destabilizing the everyday norms of campus life. Anna Lowenhaupt Tsing (2005) refers to friction as the process of messy and unequal encounters across differences through which cultural forms are continually coproduced. As she further argues, the metaphorical image of friction reminds us that "heterogeneous and unequal encounters can lead to new arrangements of culture and power" (5). Indeed, the Chinese students' presence on the MSU campus has been accompanied by increasing friction between the students and the university administration. In this chapter, I attend to how these messy and unequal encounters mediate how the world grant university is being invented.

Grounded in our analytic frame is the conception of the university as a mobility system (Nordquist 2017; Urry 2007) mediating who moves, how they move, when they move, and to what effect. This analytic optic foregrounds how the university disciplines the traversals of international students as students are regulated through visas, language requirements, tuition fees, residential-hall living arrangements, and grading policies. However, I further attend to how the transnational movements of the students are in similar fashion reshaping the university as part of a complex and dynamic struggle. Aiwa Ong (1999) writes that transnationalism refers to moving through space and across lines "as well as the changing nature of something" (4). In this chapter, I look at the changing nature of the social, cultural, and linguistic landscape on the MSU campus. Grounded in our mobile-literacies framework is a shift from spatial container models toward a less bounded approach, with the university conceptualized as shot through with multiple and competing trajectories knotted into everyday activities. As Stephen J. Rosow (n.d.) argues, higher education is not an ivory tower walled off from the uncertainties, tensions, complexities, and ambiguities of economic, social, and political life. Rather, the university exists in deeply interwoven contexts with different intersecting forces comprising multiple positions, ideologies, and motives of diverse actors. Turning to the knotty nature of this activity, this analysis uncovers wider sets of contradictions, and things turning up in unexpected places. Leander and Sheehy (2004) argue that the purpose of a spatial analysis is not to reduce space to a fixed map but instead to show how space is always changing and to question how, when, and into what. Posing these key questions about the higher education landscape, such moves allow us to glimpse wider power geometries (Massey 1994) and the politics of mobility.

Attending to the convergence of multiple spatial trajectories, I survey these complex entanglements in and across local, regional, national, and international scales of activity. I wish to emphasize that the concept of scale (Nespor 2004) is not imagined as static but as dynamic, emergent, constructed, and bound up in a wider struggle. To offer a fine-grained account of this globally complex system, I draw on data gathered through linguistic and semiotic landscaping (Blommaert 2013); the collection of artifacts (posters, flyers, websites, white papers, social media posts); participant observation on university committees, meetings, and activities and events aimed at international students (full-day workshops, documentaries, coffee hours); and semistructured interviews with approximately twenty-five administrators, instructors, and students. Assembling this data, I sorted and traced the networked connections among people, practices, objects, and locations to identify relations between near and distant social spaces. Through tracing these networks, or knotworks, I uncovered forces mediating the politics of mobility (Cresswell 2010), or the rhythms, velocities, routes, turbulence, and sources of friction. In making these moves, I first turn to a broad-brush sketch of the restructuring of the linguistic and social landscape off campus in the local Lansing economy. I then focus more fully on structural shifts on the MSU campus as it repositions itself both at home and abroad, with attention to transformations in missions, policies, administrative and departmental units, and, finally, classroom practices.

GLOBALIZING THE LOCAL LANDSCAPE

Entangled in a globally complex network, or knotwork, the influx of international students is impacting the shifting structures of the state. The economy in the state of Michigan has been struggling due to the decline of manufacturing and automotive industries. In an effort to retool, the local capitol area has formed a consortium identified as Global Lansing. One of the aims of this group is to "utilize the valuable international resources and talent available in the greater Lansing area including *international students* [emphasis added], businesses, and international relationships" (LEAP 2015). In this manner, the city and state are moving to reposition themselves within a wider global marketplace. The state is moreover leveraging international investment through the Michigan EB-5 program, which is intended to stimulate job creation and capital investment from outside the United States in exchange for permanent residence for participants, with more than 25 percent of all inquiries about the program originating from local Chinese students. Directly stemming from this program, a pair of Chinese international students have been involved in the creation of Port Lansing, or a foreign trade zone, at the Capital Regional International Airport to provide a competitive advantage to companies doing international commerce. The port entry is intended to make it simpler for goods to clear US customs, with reduced, deferred, and eliminated customs fees. The Port Lansing website includes a picture of the city pinned to a world map and the tagline calling it a "Gateway to the World." Contributing to the construction of this space, the international students located investors from China and have been involved with the architectural plans for two cargo spaces estimated at $2.5 million total. In this fashion, the movement of people and things across borders is reshaping the local landscape.

Further evidence of these transformations is an urban mixed-use residential and commercial development project on a lot purchased from the county land bank. Mentioned at the beginning of this chapter, the symbol on the rental office, 家 (jia/home), serves as a linguistic branding strategy further articulated in the marketing materials.

> You will notice a Chinese character, 家, pronounced "Jia" and translating to "home." The intention of the logo is to start a conversation with our community about the value of engaging international students at MSU in order to expand on the shared idea for a global Michigan. (Gillespie Group 2015)

Part of a global strategic plan, the vision is to rebrand the region as a new cosmopolitan center. Further, on the website is a map (Figure 1.1) illustrating the proximity of the apartment complex to the MSU campus, with a Chinese character 家 on one side of street (the housing complex) and again on the other side (the MSU campus), under which is written the slogan "Creating Global Experiences." The map is an act

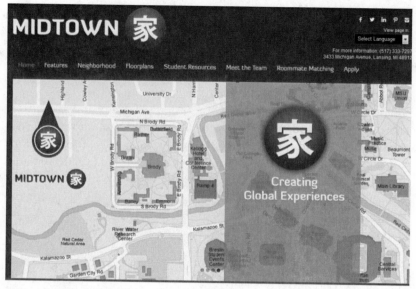

Figure 1.1. Map of midtown and MSU campus

of placemaking reconfiguring the relationship between the university and the global economy. In this context, the map is a political and interpretative act disrupting current material and cognitive maps of the local physical and social landscape. Central to these moves is a commodification of culture with a cosmopolitan sense of place, or "home," densely intertwined with marketplace forces. The merging of these geographic and social spaces indexes ways the university is increasingly entangled in a wider economic restructuring mediated by flows of actors, objects, and ideologies across a transnational social field.

THE WORLD GRANT UNIVERSITY

In this section, I continue to explore these complex and messy entanglements and the ways that marketplace and neoliberal logics are bound up in the reconstruction of the MSU campus. In parallel with the urban developers, the university is engaged in moves to reposition itself as it shifts from a land-grant to a world grant university. This is represented as an effort to "establish a new twenty-first century framework" (Simon 2013, 49) that extends the university's "traditional values" of community engagement to a global frame. As officially articulated by the university president, central to this strategic shift is the creation of global linkages to infuse international and comparative perspectives throughout the mission of higher education. An extension of the ideals of the land grant created under the Morrill Act, the world grant ideal is an effort to "reinvigorate the public trust" (Simon 2010, 42) and expand the notion of the common good on a global scale. In a white paper articulating these basic tenets, the university president (Simon 2009) says, "At its core, the *World Grant Ideal* is not about dominance or status. . . . It is about helping people and communities—local, national, ad global—to realize their dreams and to make their dreams bigger" (15). Motivated by a belief in the common good, the aim is to create a "sustainable global prosperity that goes beyond the finances and fortunes of any single institution, state, or nation" (19).

Forced to confront state disinvestment in higher education, however, this vision of education as a public good conflicts with wider shifts toward a degree as a private good measured in terms of market logics (Giroux 2010). Evidence of these contradictory knots are found at administrative and structural levels at the university, including the president's establishment of the China Initiative, which targets the People's Republic of China (PRC) as a strategic partner. Central to this initiative is the Office of China Programs, which is tasked with expanding the university's presence, alliances, and outreach in the PRC. Framed squarely around academic capitalism, a white paper found on its site argues for strategic global outreach to help the university maintain its reputation and "market share in international higher education" (MSU China Working Group 2005). These moves are "informed by economic imperatives," with China identified as central to its plans. Posing the question "Why China?," it argues that a "combination of economic drivers" creates a competitive advantage for US-branded degrees. Listing key elements of its strategic approach, it identifies the need for MSU to partner with Chinese universities while working to assure MSU "will not be 'traded' by China partners for more prestigious US university partners at a later date." Debating the tradeoffs of maintaining the current tuition "sticker price" abroad, the paper also raises the need to explore whether China can serve as a foundation for recruiting in the broader Asian market, which is referred to as "MSU Asia." Outlining a long-term plan, it finally suggests a feasibility study on building a "21st Century MSU campus in China to achieve economies of scale." In this fashion, the document is framed by colonizing and expansionist rhetorics as the university tries to claim territorial space.

Overall, the university's global expansion and outreach agenda is shaping and being shaped by two competing discourses. One underlying narrative is linked to the world grant ideal grounded in notions of the common good and engagement in addressing global issues. The other stance is more squarely situated in marketplace logics and the production of a global educational regime. Rather than singularly providing access to knowledge and economic opportunities for a broader proportion of the population, the university's rapid expansion into the global marketplace is tied to the construction of new networks of power and geographies of difference (Harvey 1996). As the entangled narratives illustrate, the invention of the world grant university is a deeply disjunctive and contested process bound up in multiple and deeply knotted threads of activity.

UNEQUAL ENCOUNTERS AND NEW ARRANGEMENTS OF POWER AT THE WORLD GRANT UNIVERSITY

While the previous section primarily attended to the ways that the university is trying to extend its reach beyond state and national borders, in this section I more fully trace flows in the opposite direction as international students arrive in increasing numbers to the state university. Bound up in a relational interplay, the rapid social and structural shifts on the MSU campus are entangled with the higher educational landscape in China. The Chinese school system is a highly competitive and structured space with students in class ten-hour days followed by protracted hours of study after school and on weekends. With education as the primary mechanism for social mobility and limited slots available in China's universities, the majority of students' lives are structured around preparing for the national college entrance examination, the *gaokao*. The social and economic control exerted through this apparatus is evident in images in the popular press of students in study halls with intravenous (IV) drips of amino acids to keep them alert for extended hours of study. Infiltrating almost every corner of the society, the educational regime is further manifested in scenes of city lockdowns, banned honking horns, rerouted traffic, and throngs of parents pressed against school gates manned by security guards as they anxiously wait for their children to complete the two-day exam. In this fashion, parents and students are negotiating mobility regimes (Schiller and Salazar 2013) that have become deeply embodied in their everyday lived experiences.

As a consequence of these social and material forces, many families have increasingly turned to Western universities as a means to circumvent this system and achieve upward mobility. To bolster chances of admissions, those with financial wherewithal frequently enroll their children in a rapidly expanding network of international programs and schools that adopt Western curriculums intended to equip students for international academic life. With many parents lacking English or knowledge of the American educational system, such programs further provide advising and assistance on a complex and foreign application process. Part of an expanding educational marketplace, the leading educational corporation, the New Oriental Education and Technology Group, is listed on the New York Stock Exchange at more than $6 billion (Stecklow and Harney 2016). Stemming from this fierce marketplace competition and pressure to place students, many organizations have been implicated in falsifying transcripts and credentials, composing student essays, forging letters of recommendation, and providing answers to standardized tests. As reported by a former MSU graduate student at a leading test preparation center, for example, teachers and students routinely memorize and share computerized tests questions that are later recycled. A published report issued by Zinch China, based on 250 interviews with Beijing high school students, their parents, and agents and admissions consultants, further found that "90 percent of Chinese applicants submit false recommendations; 70 percent have other people write their personal essays; 50 percent forge their high-school transcripts; 30 percent lie on financial-aid forms; and 10 percent list academic awards and other achievements they did not receive" (Wilhelm 2010). Though less prevelant, there is also a black market of gunmen (Tyre 2016), shorthand for test-taking proxies, who impersonate their clients using fake IDs to obtain high scores on standardized tests. Through such mechanisms, this underground network is disrupting higher educational structures that enable and constrain the mobilities of different sets of actors in different ways.

These processes are further densely entangled with a shifting higher education system in the United States, where divestment in education has increasingly forced universities to make up cost differences by seeking international student tuition. In response on the MSU campus, the university doubled its international student enrollment in a ten-year span (from 2004 to 2014) with the admissions office inundated with applicants from China. In 2014 more than 7,000 of its 9,000 international student applicants were Chinese. The large influx of students was coupled with language and culture differences, distinctions in educational structures and approaches, and the manipulation of applications (as aforementioned). The result was an admissions office and administration left largely unprepared for the rapid changes that rippled throughout the university. The university structure is loosely coupled, decentralized, and diffuse, and as a result, the influx of the students affected the departments in multiple and varied ways that were complexly intertwined. At the center of these struggles were questions bound up in who changes, how much, and into what.

On campus were efforts to control and contain disruptions through narratives of inclusivity and diversity that portrayed "the global university as a conflict-free space" (McNamara 2016, 34). Marketing the educational benefits of internationalization, the university promoted diversity as a value or resource that could be materialized into a "cohesive and synergistic community" (Tardy 2015, 253). These rhetorics and ideologies circulated across an array of programs, events, media, and artifacts: names pronunciation workshops, seminars on culturally sensitive pedagogies, multilingual welcome signs on posters and free t-shirts distributed across campus, documentaries and movies intended to foster dialogue about the integration of Chinese international students, and a yearlong celebration of Chinese arts and culture.

In 2015 one of the most elaborate productions was a halftime show at a Michigan State football game dubbed the "Art of the March." Directed by the creator of the opening ceremonies in the Beijing Olympics, the production was the largest and most complex in the school's history with more than 600 performers, 1,500 audience members performing "card art," and 1,000 free tickets given to Chinese international students. Drawing from the ancient Chinese classic *The Art of War*, the performance drew parallels between football and the military. The message underlying the spectacle was a celebration of cross-cultural mixing and exchange. Yet the sheer size of the event devoted to a single student population also drew attention to a wider gap that failed to neatly fit the university branding message or marketing materials.

Starkly calling attention to these disjunctures was a program called "Live It" intended to encourage racial harmony and tolerance in the residence halls. Echoing the rhetorics from Art of the March, a widely distributed poster (Figure 1.2) marketing the program displayed the slogan "All the World on One Campus," along with a mosaic of multicultural artifacts and ethnically diverse students from around the world. In making these rhetorical moves, the university occupied the position of the dominant center, "inviting difference into the academic community, and controlling the ways in which diversity would impact the university itself" (Tardy 2015, 253). Through such framing devices, MSU sought to legitimize a set of normative assumptions and ways of representing the world. Tellingly the Asian figure in the center of the frame signified how the Chinese student population had become central to everyday life on campus. In this scene, the university was literally positioning the student on the marketing materials as a way to promote and control the story.

29 08月
2013   📍 在 巴音郭楞蒙古自治州和静县

ALL THE WORLD ON ONE CAMPUS

即使我走了，我也会在MSU的各个角落默默的注视着每一个学生。回
国倒计时：10天

🌐 照片   👍 赞(11)   ❮ 分享   💬 回复(31)

Figure 1.2. All the World on One Campus poster

Yet a more fine-grained look at the Asian student who is also the subject of chapter 2 serves to complicate the narrative. A public figure on the campus who also worked as an Intercultural Aide—a position intended to foster student mixing and diversity—he posted a wholly unexpected profile picture (Figure 1.3) on his Chinese social media account. On it was an image of him in an American marine's uniform saluting with a clean, white glove along with a swastika on a Nazi flag posted prominently behind him on the dorm wall above his bed. Placed side by side with the university poster, the contrast makes visible the social cleavages between the institutional rhetorics of diversity and the more messy and complex realities on the ground. Even as the university was trying to

Figure 1.3. Profile picture with Nazi flag

manage and discipline the student body, it was unable to contain the narrative frame.

Further bringing to the forefront the university's inability to fully control or contain the narrative was a widely publicized incident surrounding a Chinese student "gang." The scene centered on a fight in a local karaoke bar involving a group of friends that put on their automobiles decals of a local police force in China, the Chengguan, known for their brutal and brazen tactics enforcing city ordinances. The story served to perpetuate negative stereotypes of the Chinese international students on the campus with the event seeming to suggest how the university's admissions policy was threatening the fabric of the university.

The story was initially picked up by the local *Lansing State Journal* with circulation of 65,000, and turned into a series covering a complex and murky courtroom trial that resulted in one student's sentencing to a year in prison. Foregrounding these tensions (Ma 2015) was a column in the *Lansing State Journal* on Sunday, February 8, 2015, featuring the MSU president expressing her vision for the state. The article laid out key projects that were transforming the social and economic landscape of the Midwestern state. That same day, an article was featured in the side column that related to the alleged intimidation and bullying tactics of the Chengguan group. The two articles side by side again foregrounded the university's inability to contain the narrative about the international student population as it traveled across global mediascapes. The university was losing control of the social imaginaries circulating about the MSU brand, as the story traveled across national and international contexts.

Published by the major media outlets in China, the story went viral with more than 7,000 comments posted by midday on *Chinese Headline News*, with some representative posts below ("Chinese Students Built 'Chengguan Gang' in the US, Violation and Fight" 2015).

一看两人不是官二代就是富二代。

(These two guys just look like the second-generation rich or kids of government officials.)

查这些人的父母一定是贪官或奸商。

(Do a background check on those guys' parents and we will find them either corrupt officials or unscrupulous merchants.)

恭喜中国城管享誉海内外。

(Congratulations, Chinese Chengguan, you finally have become well known around the world.)

真TM丢人啊,赶快滚回国来吧。

(How fucking shameful is this, get your ass back to China.)

As a broad social critique, the comments indexed social tensions surrounding China's second-generation rich (fuerdai/富二代): that is, the children of the wealthy in Chinese society labeled as possessing a sense of entitlement while operating outside and above societal boundaries and laws. The incident triggered a crisis for both the international student population and the university, both of whom were concerned not only about student well-being but also the potential damage to the MSU brand.

To address and contain such issues as they unfolded on the ground one of the university's signature initiatives was a group called Project Explore (PE). Sponsored by the Office for International Students and Scholars (OISS), the group comprised seven select Chinese students who served in an advisory capacity on issues related to the international student population. It furthermore spun off into a larger community of students on campus (called Project Synergy). The Taiwanese-American-born founder had formerly served in the Marines and referred to his group as the university's "eyes and ears." While such initiatives were part of community-building efforts, the comment also suggests how the programs simultaneously functioned as instruments to surveil and contain any problems. Serving as linguistic and cultural translators for the university, PE met with departments across campus on a range of issues, such as cafeteria rice cookers, academic dishonesty, two Chinese student fatalities, and the rumors of the alleged Chengguan gang.

In an effort to further manage the MSU brand identity, the university used PE to plan and run a pre-departure meeting in Beijing and Shanghai for both parents and students. As one of the administrators involved explained, the meetings were intended to help ensure the university achieved its yield, or the percentage of students who enroll after being offered admission. The students from PE spent the second part of the semester and several weeks during the summer preparing for the event, including being coached on how to answer sensitive questions related to negative publicity. They furthermore coordinated with other Chinese student groups. One of the key struggles, however, was ensuring that the groups remained "on message," because in the past conflicts had arisen between the factions as each vied for attention to attract more members and social capital. For instance, in the pre-departure meeting in 2015, a number of student associations produced their own Chinese handbooks for campus orientation (replete with university policies, procedures, and campus life information) while competing to have theirs selected as the officially sponsored university welcome guide. However, after some wrangling each of the groups ultimately distributed their own handbooks, causing administrative concern that multiple versions and lack of vetting could lead to confusion or even misinformation delivered to the incoming class. Drawn into such controversies, the university struggled to contain and manage the student body and delivery systems used to regulate and control information flow.

In addition to overseeing and coordinating the different student organizations, one of the key roles of PE was to provide translators and cultural brokers for campus administrators during the pre-departure meetings. One of the students recalled a high-pressure situation in which a parent demanded to know why the ranking of MSU in *US News & World Report* had fallen from 75 to 82. The question itself foregrounded how global university rankings functioned as part of a wider educational regime influencing an institution's world reputation and the attitudes of parents and students (Yang 2016). As a result, the room began to fill with the murmurs of other concerned parents. Thinking fast on his feet, the student offered an explanation of how the rankings were tabulated. He explained that parents should concern themselves with not only the overall rankings but also the rankings designated for specific majors and programs. He proceeded to discuss in more detail how the rankings were calculated while offering examples of unexpected factors that could impact the numbers. To emphasize his point, he noted that one key metric was the endowment generated for the football team and asked parents if this was really a matter of serious concern. The response placated the parents, who were unfamiliar with football or the university system and imagined this explanation as quite plausible. The student was mistaken, however, because the *US News & World Report* does not in fact use sports endowments as part of its formula. This information gap highlights how meanings travel across contexts in complex and often messy ways.

On the ground the university suddenly found itself with a myriad of unexpected issues. Rather than increasing diversity on campus, the large number of Chinese students enabled the creation of ethnic enclaves and increased segregation of the student body or the sense of a "college within a college" (Fraiberg and Cui 2016, 84). These social divisions were exacerbated by policies and practices at the university. The MSU residence hall complex, for example, is divided into five different areas across campus referred to as neighborhoods with the majority of international students placed in the East neighborhood. The physical separation, which one international student referred to as a "ghetto," was in part due to a residence hall policy of keeping only a few dorms open during holidays and breaks. This policy resulted in these dorms being populated by international students, who often remained on campus or were not able to return home during holidays. As a consequence, Chinese students who had come to MSU for a study-abroad experience found it difficult to immerse themselves in English or the local culture. In this case, even as the university promoted cross-cultural mixing and diversity, its policies were bound up in the construction of geographic and social divisions. These divisions were further the product of academic and curricular structures that sought to contain and regulate the international student population.

A set of pamphlets in one of the neighborhood centers foregrounded the academic dimensions of the problem. Targeted at students who found themselves on academic probation, the flyers were intended to provide information on the consequences and how to return to good standing. Intended to capture students' attention, the pamphlet cover highlighted key questions in a large red typeface: "What? I'm on Probation? What does that mean?" Tellingly set beside the English version was another stack of the same flyers translated into Chinese. With more than 19 percent of first-year Chinese students at MSU on academic probation in 2014 (Mei and Qin 2015), the two versions foregrounded a broader set of tensions and the contradictory position of the university toward the Chinese student population. The materials, which presupposed Chinese probationary students might lack the capacity to read English, exposed the university's own ambiguous stance and uncertainty about how to respond to the language and cultural divisions.

REGULATING STUDENTS THROUGH ENGLISH WRITING

At the administrative level one of the key sites where these issues played out were language and writing programs that typically serve as first responders to pedagogical and institutional challenges. While they are traditionally intended to prepare students for writing at the university, they also serve as mechanisms for regulating and disciplining the student population. Officially tasked with testing and providing instruction to international students, for example, the English Language Center (ELC) found itself inundated with more than 25 percent of the international student class at its height in 2011 who were admitted under provisional status. This designation prevented students from enrolling full-time in university courses until they had met a basic proficiency requirement in English. Faced with a staffing crisis, the associate director half-jokingly recalls that she found herself pulling adjuncts off the streets. If she by chance met someone such as a retired high school teacher in a bar, the conversation would turn to a vacant position. Due to these pressures, the faculty rapidly increased from six to thirty-six full-time members, sixty-seven adjuncts, and fifteen teaching assistants. The rapid changes further necessitated new administrative structures for training, standardizing curriculum, and assessing instructional practices. In this fashion, the globalization of the university was a deeply uneven process affecting various faculty, staff, and administrative units in differing and often unpredictable ways, as part of a wider set of networked relations that were more or less intense, mobile, and at a distance from each other (Urry 2007). More broadly, the ELC served as an apparatus through which the university could charge students tuition while simultaneously limiting access to mainstream courses, with language and literacy regimes bound up in these mechanisms.

Another area deeply impacted by the shift in the student population was the first-year writing program. Even after completing the ELC, most students were required to enroll in a basic writing course referred to as Preparation for College Writing (PCW), with many classes frequently populated with as many as 80 to 90 percent Chinese international students. The course name itself suggested that the classroom was preparation for the real work done at the university. As a remedial course aimed at removing student "deficiencies" (MSU Office of the Registrar 2016), it served as yet another apparatus to regulate and contain the student population. The remedial designation further required students to enroll in five hours of class time and pay four credit hours of tuition dollars, but granted only three credit hours toward a degree. The course was referred to as *keng die* (坑爹) in Chinese social media circles. The term itself is Internet slang used to describe a situation when one does not receive what is expected (i.e., one has been cheated or deceived), and in this case students felt that they were "cash cows" who were not receiving credit in exchange for their international tuition dollars. As a result of receiving complaints from a disgruntled student and learning of wider grievances circulating among the student body, the writing program director began to put in motion the complex bureaucratic machinery of altering what he felt was an inequitable system that levied an "international tax" on the students. After a yearlong process, however, the first attempt failed after a procedural breakdown as it passed through various committees. Although the writing program director will try again, the incident foregrounds the difficulty of resisting and transforming wider university structures that seek to regulate and contain the student body.

This shift in the student population affected different colleges and departments in highly uneven ways. The majority of incoming students listed business as their preferred major with more than 60 percent of the population attending the business school orientation upon their arrival. With the college needing to reserve its largest lecture hall to accommodate the cohort, the business school struggled to locate a space that could literally contain or hold the student population. With specialized Chinese tutoring and testing centers further emerging that targeted business school applicants—advertising tutors regarded as business school "study gods" (see chapter 4) who had effortlessly sailed through the core courses and exams—the proportion of international students admitted to the college reached 30 percent of business school enrollment. One of the administrators overseeing business school admissions explained that the number had become "too many." Serving as a shorthand for a complex number of factors affecting the college, this included the fact that the large number of students in part worked against the college's mission of fostering a diverse environment and maintaining space for other marginalized populations. As a result, the business school rethought its selection process. Underlying the new admissions procedure was an increased emphasis on language and communication skills. Revising the set of core courses for admissions, the college designated first-year writing as a central component and simultaneously removed two quantitative accounting and economics classes in which Chinese students had tended to perform well. The business school also required two separate writing samples, including a proctored case study. Though in place only a single semester as of this writing with perhaps not enough data to establish a trend, the number of Chinese international student admits immediately fell to 18 percent. More broadly the policy shifts foreground how language and literacy were regulating the access and pathways of student trajectories.

RECONFIGURING THE CLASSROOM WHEN THE MINORITY BECOMES THE MAJORITY

Continuing to map out the complex ways multiple and competing trajectories were knotted into the higher education landscape, I turn more closely to the disruption of classroom life as teachers struggled to adjust to the shifting classroom dynamics. These tensions were driven by the fact that many of the Chinese international students had not been socialized into a Western educational system and lacked the linguistic abilities to participate in discussion-style classrooms. While most had studied English in junior high school and high school, the focus had primarily been on grammar, vocabulary, and reading-comprehension questions. This stemmed from a national educational testing regime privileging these areas over speaking, listening, or writing skills (Fong 2011, 105). As a result, even top students who had studied English for many years in China experienced difficulty with writing university-level papers or in-class written exams. Comparable to Vanessa L. Fong's (2011) long-term study of a Chinese international-student population, lower-achieving students also "had great difficulty understanding and communicating with instructors and participating in class discussions" (105). Presented with this situation, instructors found themselves uncertain as to how to respond. An MSU survey (University Committee on Faculty Affairs 2013) found that only 24 percent reported being completely prepared to teach and evaluate "international students." This characterization was a thinly veiled code for the Chinese population in their classes.

To further examine how such struggles were manifested in everyday instructional settings, I focus on how the rapidly shifting educational landscape was reshaping the pedagogies, practices, and social dynamics in three different classrooms. This focus provides a window into the shifting power dynamics and structural relations mediating everyday higher educational spaces. The teachers selected for the study were part of a faculty learning community (FLC) focused on international students and displayed a vested interest in this area.[1] More broadly, the creation of the FLC itself points to the dynamic and shifting nature of the campus as it responded to the influx of students. The classes I selected to study fulfill MSU's general education requirements, and I selected them because of their diverse disciplinary approaches (physical sciences, social sciences, composition) and because they tend to enroll the largest number of international students. As such they serve as telling cases foregrounding the cultural conflicts and contradictions between teachers on the ground and the student population.

International Students in the Physical Sciences

A primary area affected by the shift in population was general education courses in the sciences required for nonmajors. These courses were large lectures combined with smaller lab sections with a more hands-on component. One of these courses, Integrative Studies in Physics 209: The Mystery of the Physical World, was taught by Manuel Antonio, who had completed postdoctoral work in nuclear physics and had developed a deep interest in education. As one of the largest classes at the university, with approximately 250 students, it enrolled one of the highest percentages of international students. While the percentages tended to fluctuate, Chinese international students numbers frequently approached 90 percent. The instructor believed the reason for the high enrollment was that students in China had a relatively solid physics foundation coupled with the fact that the course required less facility with English than did other options. As a result, these factors helped ensure a high grade. His assumptions were supported by personal observations that undergraduates widely shared information about course difficulty levels and instructors through their online social media circles.

The course comprised weekly lectures and recitation sections. In the lab sections, Antonio relied on group-based projects to support active engagement but struggled with balancing the makeup of the teams. The following is an exchange from an interview in which he articulated his struggle:

> MANUEL: Not always but in some sections, I have 90% of Chinese students. Out of 27, I have 3 Americans and then that is an extra challenge. I don't even know if there is research about that. I know there is research about females in groups and research says that when you only have one female in a group with all male that female typically works worse . . . let's say if I have 27 students and only 3 are females, I would put the three females together. And that is supported by research. Now I don't know if the same applies when the minority becomes the majority.
>
> STEVE: Or the majority become the minority.
>
> MANUEL: Say I have three Americans in my classroom, what do I do? Do I put one in each group of Chinese? Or do I let them [choose]? Typically I let them do the groups, and what happens is the three Americans sit together.
>
> STEVE: Automatically?
>
> MANUEL: Automatically.
>
> STEVE: They just self-select?
>
> MANUEL: And actually the Chinese self-select too, they sit together because they can speak their own language.

In this lab setting, the uneven ratio of domestic to Chinese students disrupted the balance of the classroom. With respect to pedagogical interventions, Antonio was no longer clear whether the traditional rules applied when the minority had become the majority. Rooted in his uncertainty was a destabilization of classroom norms, such as who, how many, and what languages one would naturally expect to find. Though English was the standard language of university instruction, Chinese had gained force and power, particularly in a relatively contained lab environment. Upending a dominant linguistic order, the traditional position of English speakers was unsettled. Reflecting on these shifting norms, Antonio wondered if it was necessary to create a safe space (Pratt 1991) for this unexpected minority. Traditionally reserved for underrepresented and marginalized populations, the inverted classroom dynamics were linked to new arrangements of culture and power.

Even in situations in which Chinese and Americans were seated at the same table, the groups often separated into distinct teams. Attempting a social experiment to destabilize this social dynamic, Antonio decided to ask students to work in groups on the final exam.

> This year I made an experiment . . . I give a final exam, which is only fifteen percent of the grade. And it is a general overview of what you have been doing, and this year, I did it in groups. So you can work in groups for the exam, too. You have worked in groups all year—so why not. And you saw that [in] those mixed groups, they were not working as a group in the exam—they were doing the exams individually. Whereas those groups that were actually working well and had the roles in the groups, you would see . . . they can bring a cheat sheet. So see, they coordinated their cheat sheets. They were not four identical sheets.

Antonio's experiments to destabilize the fixed social and physical locations of the class uncovered the powerful forces that established, reinforced, and maintained social and linguistic boundaries. Even in the context of a high-stakes final exam standing to benefit all interested parties, mixed groups continued to splinter. In contrast, the Chinese teams coordinated their activities by delegating different responsibilities to different members, as each prepared cheat sheets on their designated topics. These patterns, however, were not completely entrenched. One exception included a mix of students that had purposely self-selected into a diverse group: an American-born Chinese, two Americans, and two Chinese women.

> The two Chinese girls are very Americanized, they are very open and they want to stay in the United States. So they came from China, they are first generation of immigrants, but they are those that are really open. And they really want to get into the culture, so they self-selected themselves into going into an American group to have that experience. Which I feel that that should be, it's like if you are going to an American University that's what you would want, I would think. But that is the exception. Like most of them is like, I come to here get my degree in an American university but I want to have as little interaction as I can with the American reality.

Contributing to the group's productivity was the diversity and openness of its members. Motivated to work across borders the bilingual US-born Chinese male student could traverse languages and cultures. The female international students had also been immersing themselves in US culture. But Antonio found such students were an exception as opposed to the rule.

Antonio also adapted to the students' linguistic backgrounds and repertoires through other strategies and tactics, including the hiring of Chinese-speaking learning assistants to facilitate interactions and tutor in the lab. One drawback, however, was that he himself was not always privy to the Chinese conversations between the assistants and lab groups. This gap constrained his ability to monitor and train the undergraduate assistants. Antonio also modified his lectures to adjust to students' needs. He shifted from PowerPoint presentations after discovering that students were generally unable to simultaneously process both his lecture and the written content on his slides. As a result, he developed an alternative approach that involved working through problems step by step on an overhead computer projector.

> This gives them time to process the information, to copy it. They are reading while you are saying the same thing so they can follow. That helps a lot with international students because you are giving two supports, you are talking and you are writing at the same time. That is kind of like having subtitles, which is extremely useful.

Despite such adjustments, however, he estimated 10 to 20 percent of the class still struggled due to their level of English proficiency. For example, one student did not know the term for the metal lead. In this scenario, while the instructor tried to imagine creative ways to explain it, the concept proved ultimately too fundamental. As a final resort, Antonio turned to a Chinese classmate to translate. Engaged in these types of large and small acts, the instructor continually sought out ways to balance an assortment of needs and bridge social and linguistic differences. While these adjustments were sound pedagogical practices standard in any well-managed classroom, they were distinct in Antonio's class because of the size and scale of the shifts.

Suggestive of the scale was a moment during Antonio's first iterations of the course when he discovered after running out of examination copies that thirty extra students had shown up on exam day. Many of the students enrolled in the class had brought in proxies or stand-ins to take the exam, thinking no one would notice in the context of a large lecture with two hundred students. As a general policy, the instructor now makes it a habit during the first days of class to have a learning assistant publicly tally the students in the class with a counter, as an explicit message that they are being surveilled. This public performance is bound up in an emergent set of rules and practices that were being negotiated, enacted, and established on the fly.

As these scenes illustrate, Antonio aligned his classroom instruction in relation to the international-student population. Inventing a range of creative methods, he was a dynamic instructor highly attuned to students' needs as he engaged in culturally sensitive and reciprocal pedagogies. Yet even in the context of such ongoing practices, a wider web of complexities resulted in often partial and fragmented solutions. Part of a dynamic and emergent process, the story further illustrates how such issues were entangled in a range of institutional factors, such as class size, disciplinary subject matter, and the format of the course (lectures versus lab sections).

International Students in the Social Sciences

Another large social sciences course, ISS 210: Society and the Individual, calls attention to an intersecting but disciplinarily distinct set of issues. Taught by an archeologist, Abigail Richards, the large lecture of approximately 200 students was made up of 30 percent Chinese internationals. Her class focused on the history of social issues in the United States, and she faced a different set of challenges linked to the diverse backgrounds of the students and their historical knowledge of the country. Central to the course material, for example, was a study of the history of race relations between whites and African Americans in the States. Pointing to the students' lack of historical knowledge, she noted many Asian students were unaware of the significance of the United States' having its first black president. Conceptualizing this piece of knowledge as fundamental for engaging with the broader concepts in the course, she stated, "If you are trying to come to a country and you have no concept that you are in a country where there are issues between black and white people, it would be difficult to teach you issues of racial inequality when you have no clue what is going on."

This was one key reason for choosing *The Myth of Individualism* (Callero 2009) as the course textbook.

> Partly I chose that really because I have Chinese students, because when Peter Callero brings up anything, as an example, like he brings up Rosa Parks as an example, or he brings up Martin Luther King as an example, he takes the time to explain who that is and why it's important.

Even with such materials, they failed to completely bridge wider social and cultural divides. This disparity extended to knowledge of laws such as "the one drop rule" as a social and legal principle of racial classification. Originating during slavery and later codified in the Jim Crow laws, it legitimized racial segregation and defined the criteria for who could "pass" as white. Richards felt that without a certain level of knowledge about the American South and the Civil War, however, it becomes difficult to engage in the complex social and ethical issues surrounding these histories. Complicating these tensions were additional social and political divides: for example, most of the Chinese students in her classes were products of the one-child policy, were from mega cities, and were unfamiliar with Western religions. From her perspective, such gaps made it more challenging to address issues related to kinship, small-town America, and how Catholicism and Protestantism have been foundational in forging an American worldview. Widely embedded in these perceived barriers was the belief that students need to share a basic cultural literacy as a reference point. The instructor maintained: "I cannot explain everything that is going on in the class . . . cultural literacy is gone." Echoing arguments of E. D. Hirsch (1987), the reference to cultural literacy indexed fixed notions of language and culture. Grounded in container metaphors, such a view of cultural literacy assumes that the goal was to fill students with a circumscribed set of content. Embedded in this pedagogical framework and approach were also deficit models—conceptualizing students' lack of social and cultural knowledge as a hurdle to be overcome or an impediment to learning.

International Students in First-Year Writing

Finally, as a contrastive case Assistant Director for the writing program and instructor Janet Munson taught the first-year writing course Preparation for College Writing (PCW). Concurrent with the sharp rise in the number of Chinese international students at the university was a dramatic increase in the number within the course. Capped at twenty-four students, the course (as previously mentioned) was typically comprised of about 80 to 90 percent Chinese international students. The remainder were typically a mix of African American, Hispanic, Saudi Arabian, African, or Korean students. In contrast to a cultural literacies model, central to her approach was a translingual framework (Horner et al. 2011) that conceptualized linguistic and cultural differences as resources for learning. In this asset-based approach, differences served as ways into understanding the dynamic and constructed nature of culture.

In counterpoint to the example from the social science course, Munson related a story about an assignment in which students brought in cultural artifacts. In the context of these discussions, one of the Chinese women brought in a parasol. A black Dominican Republican student residing in Detroit inquired as to why Chinese students walked around with umbrellas even when the sun was out. The woman's response was, "Well, because I want my skin to be as white as possible." This led to a discussion of race, nationality, and the significance of whiteness across different cultures. The wide-ranging conversation included a discussion on women at the turn of the twentieth century who also wanted white skin because it signified membership in a leisure class. Echoing the social science course, the discussion further turned to the history of racial relations in US society, the one-drop rule, and the phenomenon of "passing." In this fashion, the class opened up a space for a conversation on the privileging of white skin in two very different cultures. In making these moves, the students' own cultural and linguistic backgrounds served as a focal point of the course and a way to engage with other perspectives. In contrast to the archaeology professor, who viewed cultural divisions as barriers to domestic discussions about race, in this scenario the students' different worldviews served as a site of inquiry and a way to challenge their naturalized worldviews.

These interactions, however, were not perfect. One problem that, again, presented itself was finding balance.

> JANET: The problem is I get so predominantly Chinese students. Even when I do the culture panels which are all mixed up in the class itself, it's sort of tricky to do because I've got like five people from Beijing and six people from Shanghai or Guangzhou. They'll come from similar places, so I don't want them to be close. I want them to represent the Mongolian student, the whatever, to mix them up in as many ways as I can so that they're learning about each other somehow. I just don't have enough, I wish they were more diverse, the classes. Truly diverse.
>
> STEVE: Right. So balance, then?
>
> JANET: Yeah yeah yeah, yeah. Like, the best classes I've done have had more Arabic students, more, maybe an Indian from India, you know student. Two or three from South American, the Venezuelan student was great. I had a Venezuelan and a Japanese-Brazilian student in that class. And then I had a couple of Americans, and one from CAMP [program for student migrant workers] who was very pro-Mexican-American. I mean, I had enough variety in that class, so it made it more interesting.

Another classroom activity Janet used to leverage difference was through setting up culture panels in which students from different parts of the world interviewed partners. In this scenario, however, exchanges across difference were narrowed by the relative lack of diversity. To compensate, Munson mixed students from different parts of China, a strategy premised on the notion that cultures are not homogenous and diversity exists within nation-states. Despite these adjustments, however, the more effective courses were "truly diverse," or made up of students from diverse regions of the world. The constraints suggest tensions linked to the university's rhetorics of diversity. Even for instructors who squarely focused on such issues in everyday classroom contexts, the administration's policies were putting into play forces militating against these efforts. Similar to the issues in the general physics lab were tensions about how to handle a situation in which the minority had become an overwhelming majority.

As a writing program administrator (WPA), Munson was interested in how a translingual approach might work across the university. While she did not want to minimize the challenges or problems, she saw the influx of international students as an opportunity to shift mindsets.

> I've thought about this and I think the idea of doing an individualized workshop or things with these other teachers to help them invent ways of thinking about how to rethink their learning goals . . . I mean it's hard to think of how this might look, but I do think our instructors here are smart. They just need to have time to think about how to invent this. . . . not just an occasional lunch once a month, but, real time to sit and invent ways to make this happen . . . if we had five hours and our goal was to think within each discipline different ways of constructing activities, exercises, assignments, etcetera, that would be around the idea of using students' languages and cultures as assets rather than deficit. What would that look like, in each of our fields? Where we could brainstorm.

Drawing on an asset-based approach in which language and cultural differences serve as a focal point for teaching and learning, this WPA sees the current influx of international students as an opportunity for reinventing the curriculum. Thinking in relation to writing across the disciplines, she imagines the possibilities as highly contextual with differences a product of disciplinary and institutional constraints. From her perspective, this shift is hard but doable. At the same time, she also recognizes this process has been largely ad hoc and unplanned, noting that it has been ten years since the university started upping the number of international students, with the people on the ground still working it out. She believes the university opened its doors without fully thinking through the ramifications. This has left the burden on other people's shoulders—and most of the time those people have been the teachers and students.

In this fashion, a comparative analysis foregrounds the complex ways the social dynamics in the three courses are localized in individual classroom settings based on factors such as the individual instructors' teaching and learning orientations, disciplinary subject matter, course size, and distribution of students. At the center of each was a struggle based on who changes, how much, and into what. While instructors modified their styles to accommodate students, their underlying frameworks varied, with some focused on students' lack of linguistic and cultural literacies as a learning constraint, while others sought ways to leverage the students' backgrounds as learning resources. In each case, however, the solutions were partial and part of an ongoing struggle. These messy engagements across difference were densely bound up in the production of new social arrangements of culture and power.

CONCLUSION

Tracing movements of people and things across wider global eduscapes, this chapter focuses on global complexity. Shot through with multiple and competing threads of activity distributed across near and distant spaces, the higher education landscape comprises networked, overlapping, and circulating social and semiotic systems. These interlocking webs are deeply relational, as elements in one location have effects in very different locations. This process is refashioning social relations and geographies extending across a wider transnational social field. Uncovering these messy and unequal encounters across difference, this chapter revealed mechanisms through which a public university is trying to contain international students through the production of social spaces and educational imaginaries. The university is unable to fully tame the student population as their traversals across the higher education landscape are also reterritorializing the university. This shift is destabilizing classroom orientations and social norms. Teachers are densely entangled in these processes as their classrooms and practices are shaping and being shaped in the context of everyday struggles. In line with Li's (2006) observations, the challenge consequently for teachers and scholars is not "simply about understanding cultural differences, but about reconceptualizing power differences and changing structural relations" (3). The analysis thus far has primarily attended to these issues from an institutional perspective. In the following chapter, we more fully turn to the ways the invention of the world grant university is intertwined with the underground literate economies of the students as they weave and are woven into the HEI landscape.

Note

1.   Pseudonyms are used for the instructors in these cases.

2

GEOGRAPHIES OF DIFFERENCE
Underground Knotworks and Transnational Social Fields

The analysis has thus far adopted largely an institutional perspective with a focus on how the state and university implement policies of containment to regulate student mobilities. In this chapter, I, Steve, turn to how the international students draw on complex underground literacies and economies to negotiate these mechanisms of control. I further uncover how their dense networks, or knotworks, of activity serve to disrupt, subvert, and resist higher educational regimes. This process is central to not only the mediation of students' geographic and social trajectories but also the reconfiguration of a global eduscape. Describing her train ride from London to Milton Keynes, Massey (2005) illustrates how space is a product of social relations.

> Since space is the product of social relations you are also helping, although in this case in a fairly minor way, to alter space, to participate in its continuing production. You are part of the constant process of making and breaking of links which is an element in the constitution of you yourself, of London, of Milton Keynes (which will not have the pleasure of your company for the day), and thus of space itself. You are not just travelling through space or across it, you are altering it a little. Moreover, this movement of yours is not just spatial, it is also temporal. The London you left just half an hour ago (as you speed through Cheddington) is not the London of now. It has already moved on. Lives have pushed ahead, investments and divestments have been made in the city, it has begun to rain quite heavily (they said it would); a crucial meeting has broken up acrimoniously; someone has caught a fish in the Grand Union Canal. And you are on your way to meet up with a Milton Keynes which is also moving on. Arriving in a new place means joining up with, somehow linking into, the collection of interwoven stories of which that place is made. Arriving at the office, collecting the post, picking up the thread of discussions, remembering to ask how that meeting went last night, noticing gratefully that your room's been cleaned. Picking up the threads and weaving them into a more or less coherent feeling of being 'here', 'now.' Linking up again with trajectories you encountered the last time you were in the office. Movement, and the making of relations, take/make time.

DOI: 10.7330/9781607327332.c002

> At either end of your journey, then, a town or city (a place) which itself consists of a bundle of trajectories. And likewise with the places in between. You are, on that train, traveling not across space-as-a-surface . . . you are traveling across trajectories. (118–19)

Analogous to Massey's train ride, international student travels from China to the United States similarly entail the act of tying and retying a bundle of trajectories or the "simultaneity of stories so far" (9). Conceptualized as a process of educational placemaking, I consider how this phenomenon is bound up in new power geometries, geographies of difference (Harvey 1996), and structural changes in HEIs. Attending to this asymmetrical and relational interplay, I map out not only students' traversals from home to host cultures but also a wider web of activity that extends back to China as part of "a complex array of transnational networks and connections linking home and host societies" (Brooks and Waters 2011, 134). These messy and unequal encounters across difference are structuring international student identities, mobilities, and practices as they traverse a shifting transnational social field. It is this process through which the world grant university is being reinvented.

UNDERGROUND NETWORKS

To map out how students' mobile practices are bound up with the construction of new linkages and power relations, I turn to the ways their complex underground networks, or knotworks, mediated their social, cultural, and geographic trajectories. Key is how the students' grassroots literacies were entangled with wider constellations of practices, people, and technologies fluidly dispersed across near and distant contexts. In order to uncover this process, I turn to *guanxi* as a key cultural frame within Chinese society. This concept characterizes a complex system of exchanges through which one leverages a relationship with the purpose of gaining a personal advantage (Lu 2000): for example, a job, acceptance to a school, preferential treatment, and so forth. A guanxi relationship can involve, for instance, a friend, a friend of a friend, a former classmate, a current associate, and so on. As Xing Lu (2000) argues the ability to establish guanxi is considered the most important quality in any social encounter in modern China:

> In describing the success of Bo Feng [a venture capitalist] in doing business in China, David Sheff (1999) comments that "Guanxi wang (the network of connections) is the crucial social structure in China and runs deeper than Silicon Valley has ever known. Guanxi—the connections he makes and the rapport he establishes are his currency." (15)

As a form of social currency linked to Bourdieu's social capital and habitus, it is a resource that can be converted into "personal power, thereby supporting one's life chances or social trajectory" (Ong and Nonini 1997, 22). Densely entangled with the students' social trajectories, this process was one that started from the moment that students were accepted to the university, as they quickly formed social circles and connections in online forums, including one sponsored by a key figure in this chapter. It is through these online exchanges that the students found roommates, booked flights together, and established bonds and friendships (Fraiberg and Cui 2016). In this fashion, the students' digital and social spaces became inextricably intertwined— forming part of a global assemblage—mediating their movements across borders, as they accumulated social and cultural capital. This process of networking, or knotworking, moreover extended into students' arrival onto the MSU campus as they established tightly knit underground communities and economies. As part of this dense ecosystem, they purchased used automobiles, dined in student apartments turned into Chinese-style restaurants, acquired Chinese cigarettes and designer handbacks, formed study groups, and accessed an array of other resources. In this chapter, I will broadly attend to this process as a way to understand how it brokered students' mobilities (social, economic, geographic) as they traversed home and host cultures. Before proceeding to the study, I first provide additional context for guanxi, which will also serve as a key conceptual frame for the chapters that follow.

Looking at how an elite transnational social class blends strategies of migration and capital accumulation, Aiwah Ong (1999) studies how guanxi relations are linked to actors' capacity to flexibly move across the globe. Leveraging their ability to simultaneously draw on resources from home and host cultures (as well as an array of other contexts), they accrue capital and power as they take advantage of complex webs of relations in and across local, regional, and national boundaries. Dovetailing with these cultural and marketplace logics, this chapter examines how parallel processes amongst international students were bound up in their underground literacies and economies. One MSU student joked that her mother said that when Chinese are involved "it's complicated." Turning to the local entanglements of the students, I map the complexity of their social webs of activity and the ways that they are economically, socially, and politically linked to other "people, places, and institutions crossing-nation state borders and spanning the world" (Vertovec 2009, 1). As the data will show, this process was intertwined with the construction of the world grant university. However, in making this move, guanxi is not conceptualized as static or essentialized, but instead as dynamic, contested, and co-constituted in the context of mobile practices.

To more closely attend to the participants' complex networks, and knotworks, I turn to the stories of two public figures in the international student community. These widely known individuals complexly orchestrated a rich social web of relations that mediated their geographic and social movements across a transnational social field. As such they serve as telling cases for studying this social dynamic. While there was certainly a wide range of variation amongst the Chinese international student population and far from everyone engaged in forming social webs to the degree of the focal participants, it is the exceptional nature of their stories that offers key insight into this grassroots mobility system. Notable in these analyses, English language and literacy is backgrounded similar to the ways that it was frequently relegated to the backdrop of students' everyday lives at the university. (Some students in the study reported that they often went for days without ever speaking a word of English.) Yet as the analysis will show, the students also selectively poached and appropriated cultural and institutional discourses, and translated them into a form of transnational capital that structured their social and geographic mobilities.

The analysis traces the focal participants' tangled pathways across media, languages, modes, and spaces. Following these relational networks across both near and far flung contexts, I draw on the notion of a flat ontology (Latour 2005) by collapsing the local-global binary or localizing the global.

> As soon as the local sites that manufacture global structures are underlined. . . . Macro no longer describes a wider or large site in which the micro would be embedded like some Russian Matryosha doll, but another equally local, equally micro place, which is connected to many others through some medium transporting specific types of traces. No place can be said to bigger than any other place, but some can be said to benefit from far safer connections with many more places than others. This move has the beneficial effect to keep the landscape flat . . . What is now highlighted much more vividly than before are all the connects, the cables, the means of transportation, the vehicles linking places together . . . It is a landscape which runs through, crosses out, and totally shortcuts the former loci of "local interaction" and of "global context." (176)

Attempting to trace activity without jumps or "breaking or tearing" (173) between scales, the analysis serves as an argument for a less bounded and relational approach to the study of how students learn to invent the university. It moreover illustrates the processes through which the world grant university is being reinvented.

THE DIRECTOR

The first case foregrounds a grassroots analysis of the complex struggle between the university and students. Even as the university implemented policies of containment (chapter 1), the students were taking up, resisting, and transforming these institutional and regulatory regimes. To frame this struggle and the ways it was bound up in the construction of a global eduscape, I return to the profile picture (Figure 1.3) of the public figure featured in the university diversity campaign. In contrast to the university marketing materials, his profile showed him dressed in an American Marine's uniform with a Nazi flag in the background. Underneath was an MSU slogan celebrating the school colors, "Go Green, Go White." Disrupting official and institutional narratives, the scene highlights the social distance between the administration and student population. Still, in unpacking the story of this figure in the analysis that follows, I downplay the notion he was a neo-Nazi or extremist. The student was glaringly unaware of the image's significance, and the flag is part of an Asian fashion trend characterized as "Nazi chic" (Hay 2015). Lacking the same powerful associations with white supremacy commonplace in the West, the role of Nazis in World War II is typically given minimum treatment in the Chinese educational system. Drawing on his social history, I offer an alternative read related to the Director's broader identification with the military and a display of masculine cool, as his father had in fact wanted him to enlist in the People's Liberation Army after his decision to quit his Chinese college. His alignment with America and MSU (as indexed in the slogan and US uniform) further points to his weaving a complex constellation of histories, structures, actors, and ideologies as part of his academic and transnational identity. This was a messy and highly fragmented process.

To reconcile these discrepancies, I bring together the two contrasting narratives in a more detailed account of this key public figure. Due to his profile image and rumors of his backstage activities, I expected resistance to efforts to recruit him into the study. In my role as an English speaker and instructor at the university, I was in fact part of the networks and institutional processes in which the students were implicated. Moreover, as an American who spoke no Chinese, my positioning made my task even harder. Yet when I finally approached him through another Chinese student, I was surprised that he was open and even eager to talk to me. As an indication, he posted the IRB form that I had sent him to his WeChat microblog as a source of pride and evidence of his storied legacy at MSU. Equally if not more surprising was that the profile picture he used to communicate with me was the same as the one in this book. These tensions point to the wider gap that I begin to uncover in this study. Offering a fine-grained account of his social trajectory, this narrative will provide insight into a complex social world often less visible to administrators and instructors. Largely beyond the university's purview, it uncovers a rich set of underground economies and literacies mediating the complex ways that students organize and structure their activities. More broadly, it provides key insights into the ways that space and place are remade in the higher educational sphere.

One of the key hubs of the students' social networks was a legendary figure on campus known as *daoyan* (导演), or the Director. Though he departed the campus in 2014 without his degree, he is still widely remembered, celebrated, and—in some cases—maligned within Chinese student circles. A graduate student assistant on our project, for example, recalled upon her arrival to the MSU campus that she had asked about who would be good to know for making connections, and the Director's name was immediately mentioned. In fact, a phrase still circulates about this well-known public figure: "如果你有问题,导演会帮你解答" ⟨If you have a question, the Director will answer it⟩. This phrase is typically uttered when students have questions they need answered or problems solved, including getting a phone plan from the local ATT store, finding a used microwave oven, and filling out an I-94 form. Proud of his reputation, the Director boasted that to this day students will still contact him with questions, even though he is now residing back in Beijing, China, where he owns an upscale apartment, several businesses, and an Cadillac XTS. As a marker of his financial achievements, he further proudly serves as the founder of the Cadillac XTS car club, which he claims is the largest online automotive community in China.

It is because of his reputation at the university and posters of him on the main city street next to campus (as part of the university residence housing campaign) that I sought to establish contact. Flattered that his name still reverberated throughout the campus (as previously mentioned) and that I wanted to contact him for academic research on the Chinese student population, he agreed to audio interviews on the social media platform WeChat. As a result, I set up two separate times to speak with him with the aid of a research assistant who conducted most of the exchanges in Chinese. The interviews were recorded, translated, transcribed, and analyzed using a grounded theoretical approach. I further collected stories about him circulating on campus and examined hundreds of posts from his social media accounts (Renren, WeChat), which offered lengthy and detailed historical records of his social trajectory dating back to his first arrival at the university in 2010. Using these different data points, I cross-checked and triangulated the claims in his story (Charmaz 2014).

Though his story was rich in particulars about his wide-ranging entrepreneurial enterprises, noticeably absent from his account were details about his academic life. By his own admission, he was a poor student with limited English, a factor that in all probability impacted his decision to drop out of MSU. Not proud of his performance, he was reluctant to speak about this aspect of his university experience so the data on his academic and language learning was decidedly thin. As he reflected, "虽然有点小遗憾,没有拿到文凭,但我觉得这是另外一种人生,就像比尔盖茨和扎克伯格一样"(Although it's a pity that I didn't get a degree, I think it is just another way of life, like that of Bill Gates and Mark Zuckerberg). Drawing a parallel with his own entrepreneurial activity, he framed his situation in relation to two American entrepreneurial legends who had similarly dropped out of university. The comparison is suggestive of how social imaginaries and bits and pieces of his experience became entangled with his identity and practices in fragmented, partial, and messy ways. Indeed, as his story will show, despite his general malaise for his studies, he creatively leveraged his institutional positioning at the university and translated it into an upwardly mobile lifestyle and affiliation with a transnational capitalist class.

This public character, Xubin Ning (a pseudonym), arrived at the university in 2010 on the cusp of the large wave of Chinese students that began arriving at Michigan State.[1] In China, he was a struggling student who, in his own words, was a *xue zha* (学渣) or scumbag of learning. This is Internet slang that refers to a social matrix of categories (see chapter 4) indexing informal student rankings in a hypercompetitive educational marketplace. Xubin Ning stayed an extra year in high school and then attended a mediocre college without much of an imagined future other than being a courier (i.e., truck delivery service). Deciding to quit college in China, he calculated that the best alternative route was to study abroad. He took the TOFEL and calls it a "miracle" that he was accepted to MSU under provisional status, where he enrolled as a student in the English Language Center (ELC). In our first interview, he began in English, "I'm not from a rich family in China, just-a-so-so family." He then stopped before continuing: "Ah . . . can I speak Chinese right now? Sorry, I haven't speak English for three years." His switch to

Chinese indexed a linguistic struggle that had mediated his social trajectory at the university.

Initially after arriving to the program, he found himself in a clique of second-generation rich that made him feel poor. These ELC classmates drove Porsche Cayennes while taking weekend shopping trips in Chicago for Gucci and Louis Vuitton brands. Out of his element, he then switched to another friendship circle comprising a key entrepreneur in the local community—who has since opened two markets, two pastry shops, a bookstore, and an educational tutoring service, with further plans to extend his activities across other Big Ten university campuses—and a group of others with an entrepreneurial drive. These were students who relied on themselves and did not waste their parents' money. Discussing his newfound motivation and energy, he described the social dynamic among this circle of friends: "天天比较你赚了多少钱,我赚了多少钱。你睡了多少个小时,我就一定要比你睡得少。这个圈子给我提供了很好的平台" ([We] competed everyday about how much money you made and how much money I made. If you slept for this many hours, I had to sleep less than you. This circle provided me with a very good platform [to realize my dreams]). The comment about working hard to achieve social and financial status is one that surfaces across a number of the other chapters in this book, and marks a shift within Chinese society as it moves from a socialist working class aesthetic to a new national narrative more firmly entrenched in the capitalist logics of the American dream. Influenced by the American films and television shows back in China, this social imaginary swayed his decision to study in the United States. Even so, nationalistic and collectivist frames were still deeply embedded in his identity, as suggested by the Director's close-knit relations with a set of like-minded conational entrepreneurs.

This complex mixing extended into an array of other social contexts, as part of a process through which space and place were being remade. Documenting his travels on his Renren account, he began a countdown to his arrival in the United States, recorded his first days of life at MSU, and posted several images of his dorm room. One from his blog (Figure 2.1) was of a workspace in the corner of his room: his desk with a MSU Spartan hat beside a laptop, a poster of the football stadium on an adjacent wall, and a campus map pinned on a bulletin board over his desk. Suggestive of a natural order or backdrop for college life, the arrangement of these materials was complexly located in a wider social order. Such everyday mundane and routine artifacts are ideologically charged and bound up in social-control mechanisms linked to power and authority (Barton and Barton 1993). The map on the bulletin board of a student's dorm room

Figure 2.1. Director's dorm room workspace

in particular serves to legitimize certain orientations and worldviews of higher education at this Midwestern state university (classroom schedules, pathways and walkways, designated study areas). Operating as a "technology of power" (Harley 1988, 1996), it orders and regulates everyday habits of mind. Bourdieu (1977) refers to culture itself as a map or "the analogy which occurs to an outsider who has to find his way around in a foreign landscape and who compensates for his lack of practical mastery, the prerogative of the native, by the use of a model of all possible routes" (2). Maps moreover not only reflect specific representations of the world, but are also bound up in the production of those representations while serving as a proposition for how a landscape ought to be read. Yet as Wood (2010) argues, maps need not be accepted and, in fact, are almost always contested (2). Xubin Ning was involved in this complex process of remapping a university's social and institutional structures.

This activity was on full display under the welcome sign on his door with a dragon in the shape of an "S" (for Spartan) cut from a poster of the Michigan State Spartan football stadium (Figure 2.2). The remix foregrounds ways that Xubin Ning was rearticulating various lifeworlds. The dragon itself was the symbol for a student group, the *Long Teng* (Jumping Dragon) Crew, which he had started with some friends after receiving a cold shoulder from the Chinese Student and Scholar Association (CSSA), which seemed unresponsive to new ideas.

our door, i made this dragon which i cut it down form a spartan poster

Figure 2.2. Director's door with dragon in shape of Spartan "S"

The establishment of the student association and efforts to affiliate with CSSA also foreground how such groups served as a primary vehicle for networking. As part of his organization's mission, he began an online student forum to answer questions for other incoming students. Though the fledgling organization quickly folded, with its most memorable activity being the painting of the campus rock on China's National Day, the list itself continued on and established him firmly within the international student community.

Central to the construction of his guanxi networks was a first chance encounter with a like-minded student, Baiwei Kong, who had shown up at his door in Hubbard Hall working as an Intercultural Aide. This position is intended to help foster inclusivity in the residence halls with Chinese international students increasingly sought for these roles in response to the population shift. Upon learning that the job would connect him to other international students, he inquired about open positions and, when finding none available, volunteered. Becoming actively involved with the program, he offered help in whatever ways possible, including serving meals and collecting trash at international student events. It is this work ethic that led him to a chance introduction to the leader of the Intercultural Aide team, Marion, who subsequently hired and assigned him, along with Baiwei, to a new initiative, the Chinese Culture and Academic Transitions Team. As a member of this team, he quickly developed a strong reputation for his service. This included his administration of the QQ forum (online chat), which had grown to over 600 members. This work gained him widespread notoriety with both the student community and the MSU administration, and he literally became a "poster child" on the university branding materials for residence hall living.

One of these was posted on main campus street displaying his image and a large caption that read, "It's where I made 600 friends . . . and counting." Underneath a story of his transition to MSU read:

> With a room on campus, Xubin "Sab" had a roommate to help him with English. He had a dining plan to taste authentic food from back home or a cheeseburger with fries. He had a fast commute to class without a car. Sab found what he needed on campus and he decided to help others. He found a way to connect with aspiring Spartans in China to get the answers they needed. Corresponding regularly with 600 members, he's even had to start blogging to answer all their questions. Like where you live next year.

In this marketing material, the university was constructing a message of diversity and cross-cultural mixing through the appropriation of the Director's story. At the same time, however, the Director was also leveraging his official endorsement and position at the university to build his own personal brand and burnish his standing within the Chinese international student community. Part of a complex transaction, even as the university was leveraging the Director's storyline, so too was he leveraging the resources of MSU as he moved between home and host cultures to accumulate material and social capital.

A letter posted on his Renren account pointed to his growing standing in the community.

写给我敬爱的导演

作为一名msu 2011 fall freshmen,我们都是幸运的宠儿,因为我们有一个叫宁旭斌(sab),当我们还一无所知的时候,新生群诞生了,同时导演来了,然后群里的人数呈飞跃式的增长。因为我们有导演。

每当我们有问题时,导演都会义务的为我们解答,不管你什么问题,他都会细心的给你解答,知道你完全弄懂为止,有的时候刚刚回答完问题之后另一个新人没有看到或者刚刚入群,会再一次的问,而导演依旧是很耐心的解答,一次又一次的解答,牺牲了自己的时间。回答一次不是难事,一天内回答一个问题无数次就不是每个人都能做的,而导演他持续了8个月。有的时候新人的问题是非常让人无语的,即使如此,导演还是会解答,即使他自己有学校的事情,要上班,要开书店,要收旧货,但导演依旧会抽出时间来给我们解答。还有的时候导演的qq都要爆了,因为很多人但m他,同时导演还是很多群的管理员,要在不同的群里穿梭,为我们解答。

导演仅仅是比我们大一届而已,但他为了我们做了很多铺垫,众所周知,外国的大学教材是很贵的,但在他的书店里却可以买到6折的书,在他的二手货店里可以买到生活中必须的电器,都是以低价出售给我们,而且导演还经常推荐我们别的可以买到便宜东西的商店,可以说为我们节省了很多钱

导演辛苦了!!!!

(Written to my dear Director:

As a member of the msu 2011 fall freshmen [cohort], we are lucky to have someone named Xubin Ning(Sab). When we struggled in ignorance, the cohort QQ group emerged and the Director arrived, and the exponential increase of membership followed. [It's all] because we had the Director.

Whenever we had questions, the Director was there to volunteer his answers; whatever our questions were, he would provide detailed answers until you fully understood; even if someone asked exactly the same question because he/she missed it or just joined, the Director still answered with patience, over and over again, sacrificing his time. It is not hard to answer one question, but not everyone would care to answer the same question over and over. The Director, however, persisted for eight months. A newcomer's questions could render anyone speechless, but the Director answered them despite his own school work and his obligations to his job, the book store, and his recycling business. He always found the time to answer our questions. Sometimes his QQ group exploded with so many messages directed at him; he shuttled across multiple groups as a moderator, answering our questions.

The Director was only one class senior to us, but he had made tremendous contribution to facilitate our transition. It is widely known that textbooks in U.S. universities are quite expensive, but we could buy textbooks at forty percent off at his bookstore; his used-goods-store offered electronic appliances at discounted prices; he also referred us to other stores where we could buy cheaper goods. He saved us plenty of money.

Thank you for your hard work, Director!)

The letter from a first-year student expressed the widespread sense of goodwill and respect that the Director had generated. Stemming from his moderation of the QQ forum, Xubin managed activity and fielded questions every day from at 8:00 a.m. or 9:00 a.m. to midnight. As a result almost the entire Chinese freshmen class knew him, with the well-known slogan beginning to circulate, as indicated in the letter: "Whenever we had questions, the Director was there to volunteer his answers." Also indexed in the letter were all of the Director's other side businesses, such as running a bookstore and selling secondhand items. In fact, the Director was always doing something on the side, so that it became almost impossible to trace his trajectory in a linear fashion.

One of his jobs mentioned in the letter was working in what was known as the Straight A Bookstore. The bookstore was a company started by Baiwei Kong, who had hired the Director to help with moving and carrying boxes. Similar to Xubin's rapid rise as an Intercultural Aide, he started at the ground level and quickly began to move up the ladder. Quantifying the benefits of his labor, he packed and mailed packages twice as fast as his boss and invented a packaging solution that saved $10.00 on each mailed item while increasing earnings tenfold. As the bookstore expanded, so too did his responsibilities as he transitioned into sales, where he again distinguished himself. Whereas most sales associates would just hawk books on the corner or send out flyers, he checked the schedules of all classes and with textbooks in tow (in a suitcase) would sell to the students on-site. The strategy worked well and he was soon promoted to Sales Director. Because the students knew him from his work as an Intercultural Aide and with the QQ lists, they often asked him where to purchase books. He related, "我说买二手的便宜,来我店里买,提我的名字打折" (I said it was cheaper to buy used [books]. Come to my store, mention my name and you would get a discount). This information was further advertised on his Renren social media account (a Chinese Facebook), where students would frequently seek out information posted in the context of his role as an Intercultural Aide. The bookstore earnings increased exponentially to the point where they were making $50,000 to $60,000 per month. In this fashion, he was converting social capital from the university into financial gain.

Entering into other entrepreneurial ventures, his business partner Baiwei opened two Chinese markets and appointed him as the manager responsible for the stores. In parallel, he simultaneously started selling used furniture and electronic appliances as part of his own business venture. At the time, there was no simple way for graduating students returning to China to sell their items. Taking advantage of a market niche, he purchased their items typically after bargaining down the price. To cement the deal, he would offer to take care of cleaning up the apartments after they departed.

同时我告诉他们,走的时候全家所有东西我给你个总数,你把钥匙给我。你也知道有些学生把宿舍弄得巨脏,还有什么呕吐物啊,虫子之类的。你什么都不用管,给我个总数,我帮你保证apartment不会charge你任何的钱。

(I told them, leave everything [furniture and appliances] in the apartment for me and I will give you a price for everything. You leave me with the key. You know some students made their apartments really messy. You don't worry about anything, even vomit and bugs. Pay me and I guarantee your apartment [leasing office] will not charge you any fees.)

Afterward the Director was able to flip the items for a profit by selling them to other international students. This process required moving and storage with a U-Haul costing him $40 for each trip. Since he was running the market, however, he was able to use its truck. As it was only used on Tuesdays and Fridays, he could drive it other days while only paying for gas. Still, storage space presented another obstacle due to the high cost and limited amount of space. As a result, he found a creative solution:

那时候我正准备出去住,所以我联合10个中国人,在Old Farm 租下来5间townhouse。我和他们商量,每户的第一层家具由我来提供,当作样板间,不用花任何钱。但他们有可能某天突然发现什么都没有了,被我卖掉了。因为我们关系都挺好的,所以他们同意了。所以我把收来的家具都放在他们的第一层,他们可以用,只要不破坏就可以了。我把床垫什么的都放在我房间了,相当于我那里做了一个储藏间。

(At that time, I was planning on living off campus. I teamed up with ten Chinese students to rent five town houses at Old Farm. I struck a deal with them, where I provided furniture for the first floor, [which served] as my showroom. [They could use this furniture] for free, but they might wake up to discover that everything has been sold. They agreed because we had a good relationship. I stored all the furniture I collected on the first floors [of their town houses]. They could use them as long as they didn't break them. I also put all the mattresses in my room. It was like I created a small storage there.)

Central to this narrative was the focus on his interpersonal relationships and ability to sell the other apartment residents on his plan. The Director noted that he could in fact sell anything: "所以我最后买什么都行,卖蛋糕、卖大闸蟹" (At the end I can sell anything, like cakes, crabs). Further taking pride in his ability to improvise and problem solve he foregrounded his strategic and creative repurposing of resources as he mobilized, orchestrated, and knotted together a complex array of social spaces and relations, with his work in the grocery market intertwined with the housing rental market. He further leveraged his position as an Intercultural Aide to cultivate a steady customer base.

因为新生都认识我,每年我都会建新生群。只要他们想出去住,都会找我。你也知道新家具很贵,而我只收新家具40%或者50%的钱。他们来我的仓库来看,订好家具后,我在规定的时间用超市的车给他们送过去,给他们布置好。

(I created a new QQ group every year for the incoming cohort of students, and they all knew me. They came to me if they wanted to live off campus. You know brand new furniture is expensive, but I only charged 40 or 50 percent of the price. They would come to my warehouse and order furniture. I would use the market's truck to deliver and arrange the furniture at a designated time.)

The Director thus designed a complex system while employing a staff to help run the operation: marketing his services online, bringing customers to his showroom, offering showroom discounts, delivering furniture to apartments, and helping students settle in. Even as he managed this business, however, he still moderated the QQ forum as a tool to drive sales. As he reflected, "因为大家都认识我了,所以生意越来越好" (My business prospered as more and more people came to know me). In this fashion, he was complexly knotting together an array of technologies and social spaces. From the money he earned, he managed to fund his tuition, living expenses, and finally, a black Saab that he purchased secondhand for $18,000. Proud of his achievements, he posted a picture of the car at the top of his Renren social media account, where he also wrote his nickname Sab. The nickname was borrowed from the characters of his Chinese name and also sounded like Saab. Not content to stand still, he started a number of other side businesses, including selling Amway products. Central to his sales strategy was again leveraging his status as an Intercultural Aide. "后来还有些小生意,比如安利。那时候我做 Intercultural Aide 的时候,问他们有什么问题需要帮忙,然后买不买安利,再问想不想上暑校" (I then started other businesses, such as Amway. When I was an Intercultural Aide, I would ask them if they had problems I could help with; [I then] asked if they would buy Amway products; then [I asked] if they were interested in attending summer school).

As his reputation continued to grow, he joined a more ambitious business venture as part of a for-profit educational summer school referred to as the Summer China Program (SCP). SCP was a privately owned institute in higher education in China catering to international students. Part of a new wave of privatized higher education programs, it offered transferable credit-bearing college courses at rates far below international student tuition during the summer. The program itself was founded by a recent graduate from the business college at Michigan State University, Yin Yu, and her husband, Xianwei Meng, a Wabash

College graduate. Meng had in fact been at the same school as one of the founders of a rival and the first school of its type called the SIE International Summer School (see chapter 5). The couple had moreover employed the Director as a recruitment coordinator—capitalizing on his dense network of connections—who was responsible for first finding customers for the school and later managing what were termed "student ambassadors." These were students on campus who received commission for recruiting fellow students. Together these various actors formed part of a transnational circuit structuring the "flow" of international students back to China.

Discussing how he became affiliated with SCP, the Director articulated a general philosophy for finding employment: "我从来都不找工作, 都是工作找到我" (I never look for work; work always comes to me). Further expounding on how this approach related to SCP, "因为他们知道我在MSU很有名,也是个很好的销售,所以他们问我要不要加入" (Because they knew I was well-known at MSU and was a good sales person, they asked if I was interested in joining them). Carefully evaluating the offer after surveying the market, he decided to join as a student ambassador. Assigned the task of recruiting students for the summer study abroad program, he marketed to them on his routine visits in his role as an Intercultural Aide. As a result, he enrolled 100 students on his own during his first year. Even though the company has now been in existence for six years, this figure still serves as a recruitment record. Quickly demonstrating his value to the company, he was appointed as the Campus Coordinator with the responsibility of managing other student ambassadors. Upon his return to China (as later discussed) he was promptly promoted to Sales Director and then to Vice President in charge of American and Australian liaisons. Through these networks the Director and SCP not only leveraged the resources of the university (i.e., student connections and institutional knowledge) but also established an educational operation that was in direct competition with it. This process was linked to the reconstruction of a global eduscape, complexly linking China and US campuses.

While the Director touted his business and sales acumen in his personal interviews, complicating his account was a controversy over the recruitment of students linked to a report in *The Chronicle of Higher Education* titled "Chinese Summer Schools Sell Quick Credits" (McMurtrie and Farrer 2013). The report questioned the credentials of a burgeoning number of private schools in China, with SCP as one of the programs singled out. Though the schools employed American university professors who taught similar curriculum in the United States, the investigative article suggested that these educational startups lacked proper oversight or the official authorization of the Chinese Ministry of Education. This groundswell of criticism reached its peak in 2013 after many SCP students found that their credits would not transfer to MSU. Though the program sold students on the promise that they could receive cheaper credit in less time, the school had not received approval from the Ministry of Education and was caught off guard when MSU and a number of other universities refused to accept transcripts. The tensions were linked to a struggle over legitimacy and control over the education marketplace. As part of this process, the Director was entangled in a deeply contested higher educational marketplace made up of multiple and competing actors dispersed across a transnational social field. (See chapter 5 for ways that this played out at SIE program.)

Ultimately, the Director decided to return to China in 2014. He explained that after four years, he had grown weary of school and was a poor student uninterested in academics. He conceded that while scientific knowledge might be relevant for students of engineering, for business school students (such as himself) it was better to leave the confines of the classroom and enter the world of practice. In terms of his local entrepreneurial operations, the Director found himself limited in the Lansing marketplace and faced rapidly growing competition from other student groups, which provided a wide range of their own services, including online forums, trips to banks to set up accounts, shopping discount cards, and a range of other services that had largely been his domain. Perhaps the most popular of the student groups to emerge was MSUwe54, named after a historical political youth movement aimed at protecting the national interest. In this case, the organization marketed itself as protecting the student interest in response to incidents such as the one surrounding SCP with the Director accused of taking advantage of the student population. In this fashion, the Director was complexly positioned in relation to both the university and international student community.

A product of the one-child-only policy, he was also positioned within state and familial structures. Consulting with his mother about leaving school, she asked: "你能养活你自己吗?你能养活我吗?" (Can you support yourself? Can you support me?) When he said "yes," she endorsed his decision. On his Renren site, he began to count down the days to his departure, leaving a dedication to his business partner, Baiwei Kong, in a photo of the two close friends standing in front of the Chinese market. Underneath the Director wrote: "我最好的搭档,或许正是因为三年前你敲响了我的门,才会有我今天的成就。为人不识孔白伟,拿到绿卡也

枉然"([To] my best partner: it was probably because you knocked on my door three years ago that I achieved all my accomplishments today. A green card would be of no use if I didn't come to Baiwei Gong). Embedded in this dedication to his closest friend, mentor, and business associate was the key role that Baiwei played in the Director's relationship web, and, as a result, the accumulation of capital. Central to his social mobility, this key figure was characterized as opening up more doors and opportunities than a green card. Ultimately, the parallel points to how Xubin was bumping up against institutional and national regimes regulating policies of containment, with his guanxi networks serving as a way to navigate these social spaces.

Nostalgic about his final days on the MSU campus, he posted the Live It poster (Figure 1.2), where he was featured as part of the university branding materials, as he wrote: "即使我走了,我也会在MSU的各个角落默默的注视着每一个学生." (Even after I leave, I will be watching every student quietly at every corner of MSU). With such artifacts and stories still circulating across MSU, the Director continued to be densely woven into the conversations on the campus long after his departure. The Director further left parting words of wisdom with a final farewell: "我叫宁旭斌,我是导演,我是商人,我是斯巴达人" (I am Xubin Ning, I am the Director, I am a business man, I am a Spartan). These four phrases indexed a complex blending of cultural roles into a transnational identity.

Back in China now for three years, the Director continues to extend his social networks (knotworks). Promoted to vice president at SCP, he runs the sales and marketing division where he recruits and manages student ambassadors in the North American and Australian markets. An extensive operation, a 2014 post on his social media account solicited student ambassadors from seventeen US universities. SCP is further looking into plans to expand business to the United Kingdom. The Director is also checking into the viability of exchange programs with local East Lansing, Michigan, high schools.

Beyond the educational realm, his entrepreneurial ventures have spun off into an array of other areas, as a stakeholder in six different businesses with three more to be launched by the end of the year. His long-term plan is to own fifteen businesses by the time he reaches twenty-eight years old. In addition, Xubin Ning started a Cadillac XTS owners club with 8,050 members. The group is organized on a WeChat list where he answers questions about automobiles similar to the way he used to answer questions about the university at MSU. He has established fifty local auto clubs while appointing the presidents, which has made it convenient for him to travel across China, where he is hosted by sponsors.

The club itself provides a platform for its members to meet mid- and upper-level business executives. At the same time, the Director uses this network to sell car accessories, decorations, food, and drinks. With 5,000 friends on his WeChat microblog (the maximum permitted) where he advertises various items, his sales are brisk as he continues to accumulate friends and social capital.

Recently, on April 22, 2016, the Director organized a public benefit activity picking up trash in a park with a group of Cadillac owners. He believes that the donation system in China has a lot of problems with the local government and agencies pocketing the money. As a result, a trash pick-up in the park is more feasible and practical. A lot of pass-ersby were influenced and also picked up trash, which he found very meaningful. He says: "当每个人把身边的垃圾捡起来后,慢慢的,越来越多的人就会养成这个良好的习惯。公益是会传染的"(When everyone picks up the trash, more and more people will gradually form the good habit. Public service is contagious). This shift in his own worldview was culti-vated during his participation at MSU as an Intercultural Aide through doing public service. He still proudly retains a social justice award for his service. In this fashion, these material and social artifacts traveled with him as they were rewoven into local contexts. Another story that he posted on his WeChat publicized an experience watching fireworks at Shanghai Disneyland. Afterward he got angry at all the trash littered on the ground and started to pick it up. However, this time people only took pictures in response to the novelty of the situation. He believes Chinese people need to improve themselves and get rid of bad habits. This perspective is a product of his complex and shifting habitus. Set in the Disneyland theme park the story foregrounds a broader reweaving of geographic and social spaces in Chinese society as it is increasingly enmeshed in a transnational social field. The Director's networking, or knotworking, is deeply intertwined with this process. Through this rela-tional interplay the world grant university is being reinvented.

ZI'AN

The second case study traces the social trajectory of another focal student, Zi'an, and the way he mobilized his guanxi networks.[2] I first learned of him through another focal participant (chapter 3) in my study, Yisi, who had befriended him. Having lived in Jordan for a num-ber of years, Zi'an was fluent in Arabic and began to tutor Yisi in her Arabic courses. Forming a friendship, he invited her to write articles for a local social media site he had started called Humans of East Lansing.

He and Yisi subsequently decided to start an international student magazine together, and they organized a number of friends to help with its founding. The group initially communicated by Skype from different cities, different time zones, and different parts of the world. When I asked for permission to collect data from these meetings and trace their activity, I was initially refused. Following from afar, I saw how the publication quickly expanded, changed, folded, merged, and spun off into other genres. From these glimpses, I further became increasingly interested in how the production of the magazine was mediated by complex social networks, made up of writers, editors, photographers, graphic designers, public relations specialists, budget officers, human resource managers, all distributed across near and distant spaces. These intricate webs further began to reveal how the complex production of the magazine was densely entangled with the reconstruction of social space and the social imagination.

While initially limiting my access to the inner workings of the journal, Zi'an enlisted me into his guanxi network after eventually deciding to pursue a master's degree in communication with hopes of entering the Columbia journalism program. The expectation was that our research project might assist him with his application. As a result, he granted me three one-on-one interviews over a period of years, and then he finally agreed to show me his "office" or the computer from which he managed the operation. Sitting with me for a period of several hours, he walked me through the various files and the ways that these mediated the production of the magazine itself. The video-recorded session foregrounded the material nature of this process, and the ways the structure of information on his computer was complexly tied to the ways he structured his editorial work. Transcribing the interview, I engaged in a process of open and focused coding in an effort to trace his network. This information was supplemented with the other interviews and a rhetorical analysis of approximately fifty articles, a task completed with the aid of three research assistants who coded for markers of international student identity. Overall, as suggested, the analysis reveals how the magazine was complexly bound up with the wider production of social relations and geographies.

Indexing these tensions is the cover (Figure 2.3) of the first print edition of his magazine, themed around "Labels." The black-and-white glossy image displays a bare-chested male whose face remains half-hidden. His torso, arms, and neck are further inscribed with labels written in a mixture of traditional Chinese characters, simplified Chinese, and English. The blending of languages and scripts indexes the complex

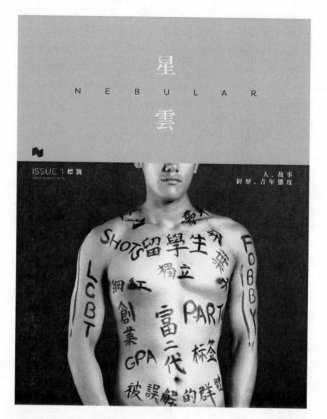

Figure 2.3. Cover of Nebular *print issue*

rearticulation of international student identity. Turning to look more closely at the image, the Chinese on the male figure's body includes an assortment of terms: "創業" (entrepreneurship), "獨立" (independence), "豪車" (luxury cars), "被誤解的群體" (misunderstood group), and "富二代" (second generation rich).[3] The term "second-generation rich" (see also chapter 1) on his abdomen serves in particular as a keyword embodying social and class tensions within Chinese society. In response to the stereotypes often placed on the international students both in China and the United States, the image as a whole might be read as an argument against being labeled or put in a box.

Yet the image also marks the current obsessions in modern China with brand-name labels. These contradictions surface on the inside back cover (Figure 2.4) of the magazine in an advertisement for a Chinese auto dealer (owned by a family member of the magazine's president) that resells used luxury cars with a picture of a $400,000 gullwing

Figure 2.4. Automotive dealer advertisement in Nebular

Lamborghini. The fact that both images appear in the themed issue indicates a wider tension related to international student identity. Even as the students were challenging stereotypes or labels, they were drawing on and reproducing them. In this fashion, the tensions embedded in the production of the magazine embodied wider contradictions in a shifting social landscape. In this case study, I explore these contradictions more fully and the ways that they are bound up in a contested process through which social spaces and geographies are being reconfigured. Turning to this analysis, I trace the literate trajectory of the focal participant, Zi'an, and the ways that the production of the magazine was bound up in these social and economic shifts. This focus on the production, distribution, and reception of this literary-style publication reveals the ways that writing is a complexly coordinated act. It entails the orchestration or tying and untying of an array of resources distributed across near and distant spaces. The case study further illustrates how wider cultural ecologies are densely intertwined with this process. Finally, it reveals literacy as a deeply political act bound up in the construction of identity and far-reaching geographies of difference. Dovetailing with the case study of the Director, it demonstrates how guanxi networks were deeply embedded in these processes.

Almost immediately upon his arrival in 2013 at MSU at the age of twenty, Zi'an was searching for ways to seek out and establish connections with leaders in the international-student community. His approach was grounded in the idea that "if you want to meet someone great, first you need to be someone great. So if you talk to a leader, first you need to be a leader." For Zi'an, that meant establishing his own group: "If you are still leading something, that is your chance to meet better people." The question, however, was what type of organization to establish. Zi'an had attended an international high school in Jordan, where he had received a broad-based humanities education and had made friends with people from across the globe. Visiting one of his friends who was now in Manhattan, he was introduced to Humans of New York. This social media site was started as a photography project in 2010 with the goal of photographing ten thousand New Yorkers on the street to create an exhaustive catalog of the city's inhabitants. When Zi'an traveled back to East Lansing, Michigan, the idea also traveled with him, as he established a local site called Humans of East Lansing. The concept for this site was the same as the concept for Humans of New York but on a smaller scale, focusing on the lives of everyday people in the local community. To help him realize this vision and assist him, Zi'an enlisted the assistance of an American friend from his dorm and a photographer, and they began to interview and photograph people on the street while posting their stories to Facebook. Over a period of six months, they gained a strong local following. Through their activity, wider transnational flows of media were rewoven into local contexts.

However, growing restless and feeling the limitations of the genre, Zi'an decided to expand and develop a new version of Humans of East Lansing for the Chinese international-student community. Zi'an migrated the version to an increasingly popular social media platform, WeChat, and it included three weekly columns released on alternate days during the week. This format entailed a major feature story every week, with the first on the local entrepreneur Baiwei Kong, who (aforementioned in the previous section) had opened up two Chinese markets, a bookstore, an online market, and a local pastry shop. Because Baiwei was a folk hero in the community—and a close friend of the Director—the article went viral in the international-student community. These intersections index the ways the students' social networks and knotworks become densely entangled. The publication of *Humans of East Lansing* generated more than five thousand hits and more than fifty international-student applicants interested in joining the publication staff. Because one room was not big enough to interview them all at once, the founder met ten people at a time and ultimately accepted about thirty photographers, editors, budget officers, and marketers. With a large number of cultural resources at his disposal, Zi'an reduced his efforts on the English media site while redoubling them on the Chinese iteration. In this fashion, wider language regimes structured his literate activity and trajectory.

Yet even as the Chinese version became an established brand in international-student circles, Zi'an had already decided to expand yet again. In coordination with his partner, he and Yisi planned a Chinese publication extending beyond the confines of East Lansing, aimed at the wider international-student community. To establish the core team, they turned to their friendship circles. One was a friend of a friend going by her English name, Sarah, who would be attending New York University in the fall as a marketing major. She had taken marketing classes during high school and attended a Harvard summer business program. Another was a high-school friend of Zi'an's from home, who was talented in design. Yisi further recruited a talented writer with whom she had developed a long-standing virtual friendship in an online forum—which also produced an online magazine—celebrating a famous Japanese filmmaker. Finally, they invited a local videographer. During that summer, the team collaboratively developed a strategic plan on Google Docs and held regular Skype meetings. With the group located in different parts of the world and time zones, they slowly learned to coordinate across deeply distributed geographic and temporal borders. Intertextuality is grounded in the notion that all texts are from a sea of other texts (Bazerman 2004), and in this situation we find the complex movement of texts (entextualization) across space and time as they were continually taken up, resisted, and transformed. Moreover, as the texts traveled, so too did other actors and objects move with them as part of a complex reconfiguration of social spaces.

The magazine, *Nebular*, was finally launched on February 1, 2014. Though the magazine was in Chinese, the English title indexed a complex blending of western culture and Chinese Society.[4] This mixing was further on display in its premier feature-length article on Zihao Song, who was a rapper, serial entrepreneur, and student at New York University. The story covered a range of his activities, including the composing of a rap song about his transition from Beijing to New York.

The feature article furthermore discussed his trip to the North Pole, the founding of a clothing line, and the establishment of an organization called The Blastoff Crew. This was an alliance of international students across seventeen US colleges and universities, with high-class cocktail parties hosted for them in Beijing. The first party had several hundred attendees as the organization gradually built up its social network and influence. This project then spun off into The Dream Connection. This was a program that organized tours to bring Chinese high-school students to Ivy League schools with promises of providing insights into the application process and connections to faculty and admissions officers. The story served as a template for other articles that would appear in the magazine, typically centered on leading student entrepreneurs and personalities. The publication both borrowed from and reproduced narratives surrounding an emergent upper class, with stories often focused on the processes through which they established their social networks. In key respects, moreover, the pattern of networking paralleled Zi'an's own efforts to establish the magazine and his own social networks. In this fashion, the broader reference to the "dream" (see also chapter 3 and chapter 5) was bound up in the production of a wider set of social imaginaries mediating new social divides and geographies of difference.

The initial story was a success, with more than ten thousand hits, and not unlike the experience of Humans of East Lansing, *Nebular* received requests from applicants from across the country wanting to join the magazine. During this time period, the *Nebular* staff turned over many times. It further merged with a student publication from Purdue, *Voice*, that resulted in an acrimonious split (see also chapter 3). In this fashion, the students' social webs continually formed, folded, and spun off from one another. Included among the flood of interested applicants was a student at Northeastern University in Boston. Originally, Zi'an was so busy he ignored or missed the e-mail. However, the student Naomi Mei subsequently sought to establish contact with him through a friend to express interest in joining the magazine. Socially well connected, she joined the public relations (PR) team, swiftly became head of PR and marketing, and then president, with Zi'an assuming the role of editor-in-chief. Beginning with the assumption of her new position in September 2015, she leveraged her green-card status to officially register the magazine as a nonprofit. Reflecting on her role, Zi'an said, "She has a lot of connections and is able to bring in and grow the business." She began to access her "really good sources of celebrities, of events, of partnerships." The magazine covered an ongoing series of high-end mixers, parties, conferences, and summits. Obtaining a press pass through a connection in the fashion industry, *Nebular* started what became a series of articles on high-profile events by covering Fashion Week in New York City. The coverage included an interview and video of a famous Chinese actress, Jiang Xin. The stories were quickly followed the next month by coverage of the Victoria's Secret fashion show in New York and a photograph of the Chinese supermodel Liu Wen. Next, *Nebular* served as the media sponsor (responsible for covering activities) for an elite social networking event billed as Empire Connect.

> #TheEmpireConnect 是一个联结学生领袖,社会机构,商业精英和知名企业的高级社交活动,将通过营造轻松愉快的氛围来帮助参与人员拓展人脉以及促进各方合作。11月14日,全美最受瞩目的Networking Event—The Empire Connect 社交派对将在纽约Empire Hotel隆重举办。这次派对会邀请17所名校学子,华尔街20家公司精英,百亿Fund管理者以及最炙手可热的创业领军人物。还在犹豫什么,这是一个让你走上人生巅峰,迎娶白富美,嫁给高富帅的难得机会,11月14日,成功的大门为你打开。

> (#TheEmpireConnect is a high-level social gathering that connects student leaders, social organizations, business elites, and well-known companies. It will help participants grow their network and foster collaboration by creating a relaxed and pleasant atmosphere. On November 14, the nation's most watched networking event—The Empire Connect social mixer—will be held in New York Empire Hotel. The party will invite 17 elite students, 20 Wall Street company elites, fund managers of tens of billions, and the hottest entrepreneurial leaders. Don't hesitate. This is a precious opportunity for you to reach the pinnacle of your life, and to meet up with a *gao fu shuai* or *bai fu mei*. This November 14, the door to success is open to you.)

Posted on *Nebular*, the promotion promised the opportunity to network with business and social elites. The marketing material further suggested the prospect of securing not only important business connections but also long-term-relationship partners and spouses. This suggestion was indexed in the words *bai fu mei* and *gao fu shuai*. These slang terms (see also chapter 6) are translated as "rich, white, and pretty" and "tall, rich, and handsome." Grounded in Western and capitalist ideologies, the labels are part of shifting social and class structures in Chinese society. The widely used terms suggest the ideal female as possessing beauty, money, and white skin, while males should be rich, tall, and handsome. It was through the coverage of such events that the editors of *Nebular* were engaged not only in the production of the magazine but also in wider social forms of identification. It was this process that mediated social and geographic mobilities in and across a transnational social field.

Through its coverage of a range of events, *Nebular* developed a growing reputation and secured an invitation as the chief media partner covering the Penn-Wharton summit. This summit would bring together a range of key Chinese journalists, ambassadors, photographers, actors, directors, and businessmen at the University of Pennsylvania. To prepare for the event, the team decided it would produce its first glossy print publication to distribute to the participants. The preparation for the event included managing approximately sixty-five staff workers distributed across New York, Illinois, Boston, Lansing, and California. The magazine cover itself, for instance, was largely created in an online conversation lead by Zi'an, who sketched out ideas and displayed them on Skype. This conceptual meeting was followed by a photoshoot in New York, with the image subsequently sent to the designer in California. The final product was published by a print house in Boston, and forty-five boxes were shipped by UPS (United Parcel Service) to the summit, as documented in Zi'an's microblog (Figure 2.5).

Arriving from various parts of the country, a fifteen-member team carried, unloaded, and distributed the magazines to the participants. In this fashion, complex social networks mediated the production, circulation, and distribution of the magazine. The event served as a key platform for the magazine launch, as an opportunity to market it to key players within Chinese society. More broadly, the students were producing not only the magazine but also a complex set of social relations.

One of the relationships was formed during an interview with well-known investigative reporter turned social activist, Deng Fei. At the beginning of the interview, Zi'an provided him with a copy of the magazine, but instead of a conversation about Fei's current work in social activism, it turned into a discussion about the magazine. Taking a strong interest and perusing its contents for about fifteen minutes, Fei began to inquire about it. He posed questions about the rationale for the selection of the medium (print magazine), the overall aims and audience, the processes through which it was produced, and finally, its plan for long-term sustainability and generating revenue. As Zi'an noted, "I went to interview him, and then it turned into a lesson." The advice he received about generating revenue and developing the magazine's young writers would subsequently shape the direction of the magazine and help Zi'an sharpen its focus. The interaction points to unofficial ways that the students sought out others to sponsor their learning in classroom and non-classroom contexts (Brandt 2001; see also chapter 3). Deng noted that when Zi'an had clarified some of Deng's questions, the aspiring editor-in-chief could contact him. According to Zi'an, Deng said, "I have good

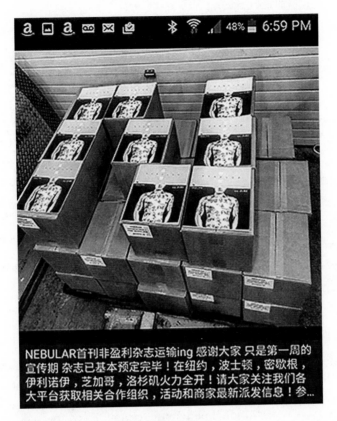

Figure 2.5. Packages of Nebular *magazine*

friends and if you want a connection I can tell you [make it]." In this fashion, the production and distribution of the magazine was bound up in the wider production of social connections.

Meeting with other writers and magazine editors was a networking strategy central to Zi'an's weekly activity. Each week, he regularly sought out social media sites and initiated at least two or three meetings. He explained, "When I see a good WeChat platform, when I see good journalism—a journalist, writer I'm interested in—I just approach them, set up a meeting. Maybe there's nothing much [there], maybe we—I don't have anything in mind, I just want to talk to you. Let's see what we can do together." One was Chinese-student-run magazine, *Weekend*, located in Seattle, Washington. Zi'an reached out to the president to let them know he would be soon publishing a magazine. Finding that they shared much in common, they had two- to three-hour conversations regularly by phone, and, finally, met face to face in Beijing.

ZI'AN: He gave me a book as a gift, I gave him a book as a gift. We didn't actually, we didn't actually talk to each other and then we did the same thing. SO that was amazing! [laughs] I give him a book, he give me a book. So actually—

STEVE: You just thought to do it yourselves.

ZI'AN: Yeah, yeah. And then, actually, so, so before that, before that, last semester we, we sent our magazine like, his magazine to us, and our magazine to him. Yeah. That was last, last . . . I, I mailed him our magazine.

Zi'an in fact regularly interviews editors-in-chief of other magazines, and they, in turn, regularly interview him as a form of promotion.

I think that's a really good promotion too. So like me as an editor-in-chief, just finished my first issue of magazine, and go out to reach out to some of the magazine editor-in-chiefs, I appreciate it. And then I interviewed them, about, like, talk together like, how hard it is to make a magazine? Or what's the fun things, interesting facts about making magazine? And also at this day magazine is going down, no one's looking at it, why we are still making it? And just want to find some similar viewpoint, I did some interview on them. So that was one of the promotion, period for the magazine. For our first issue.

Through such exchanges, their social networks were embedded in the student magazines and stories, as they reproduced and circulated social identities and capital. Reflecting on the all-consuming nature of his online social networking, he felt increasingly disconnected from the MSU campus: "Last year, I had nearly no friend in everyday reality. I had almost no interactions with people at MSU. People at MSU think I am not studying at MSU. I just made phone calls every day. I would make five or six phone interviews every night, talking with people . . . not friends but relationships and connections." As evidence of the rapidly increasing size of his network, his WeChat contacts grew from nine hundred to more than two thousand over the course of a single year.

In parallel his partner, Naomi Mei, was focused on forming connections related to PR and marketing.

ZI'AN: PR has a lot, like the head of PR, the president, she has a lot of people to deal with too, every week. Because with like different organizations, she needs to deal with like CUSA [Chinese Undergraduate Student Association], CSSA [Chinese Student and Scholar Association]—you know CSSA right?

STEVE: Yeah.

ZI'AN: From Boston University, Northeastern, NYU, Columbia, UCLA— she needs to deal with all of the associations and, ah to hear their proposal of different events and to, to, make a decision whether we should take the deal to cooperate with them and what's our benefit. They have a lot of those kind of things. And she also, you know she does a lot of personal connection with celebrities, and organizations that's how she can get more, better, do a better connection with people. So she does a lot of those kind of jobs.

His partner was engaged in lining up events and partnerships with a range of student organizations, such as the Chinese Undergraduate Student Association, for events and sponsorships. Her work furthermore involved coordinating with other professional organizations, including industry leaders such as the Internet giant Ali Baba, for whom *Nebular* was writing a promotional story about a new app for online payment. The story—as well as the *Nebular* logo—would be featured in the app banner. There were also plans to work with the national Chinese television station CCTV, with *Nebular* slated to promote and participate in an event billed as the Media Dream Academy, a summer event in Beijing in which the television station would bring together key social media organizations and personalities. Notable is how dream discourse continued to circulate across social and geographic spaces. Similarly, *Nebular* was involved with the popular reality singing competition show, *The Voice of China*, as part of an effort to produce a season of the show held in the United States. They also wrote a high-profile feature story featuring several of the international student contestants (see chapter 7 for how this show circulated into a classroom).

Zi'an managed much of this activity in what he referred to as his "office," or a Google Drive space. This space contained dozens of folders used to coordinate, write, and manage the magazine. The various folders included groups in Boston, New York, Illinois, and Michigan. There were furthermore folders for various departments. Because he was head of content, Zi'an's own folders contained an assortment of directories linked to his seven divisions and approximately twenty staff (writers, designers, photographers, editors, videographers, and social media specialists). The "office" also housed directories for a newly created human-resource department. Among its responsibilities, this department was charged with hiring new staff. As the magazine continually received a steady stream of applicants attracted by the opportunity to interview celebrities as well as make key connections themselves, the human-resources department screened candidates and set up online interviews. The department further conducted detailed monthly performance reviews of the *Nebular* staff, with forms listing number of meetings attended, reposts of *Nebular* articles, and an array of other details. Finally, the department "hired" a personal assistant for Zi'an who sent him a weekly agenda. In this fashion, Zi'an was emplaced in a relational network of actors distributed across near and far-flung spaces.

In addition to his online interactions, his activities further included offline face-to-face meetings, both in the United States and China. Meetings included regular gatherings of the leaders along with other staff. Explaining the process, he noted how they let all the staff know of upcoming gatherings.

> ZI'AN: So like, this summer we met twice. Once in New York for ten days, once in Beijing for five days.
>
> STEVE: Ah!
>
> ZI'AN: And then also for the [Wharton] Summit we were together, the whole time. And then whenever there's a big event—
>
> STEVE: But you met in New York and Beijing just to meet? Or you had an activity there planned anyways so you—
>
> ZI'AN: Um so, first we meet the leader team, we're gonna have like meetings together.
>
> STEVE: Ah, so you do meet face-to-face.
>
> ZI'AN: Yeah, but also, we gonna gather all the people like, "Hey everyone, the leader team is in New York this week and anyone want to come." Basically, we have a lot of people in New York and then some of the people can travel here. And then people probably just want to gather. And then we gonna plan some events together. Activities together. And then like Beijing, that's the same. Beijing—
>
> STEVE: You were home anyway in Beijing, is that?
>
> ZI'AN: No.
>
> STEVE: Are you, are you from Beijing? You're from Shang—
>
> ZI'AN: No, I'm from Shenzhen. South part of China.
>
> STEVE: Right, right.
>
> ZI'AN: Yeah. It's far.
>
> STEVE: So you flew back to Beijing?
>
> ZI'AN: Yeah. I flew back to Shenzhen and then I, I flew to Beijing.

Traversing the United States and China for professional-development meetings and activities, the staff of *Nebular* was also engaged in building a fan base. This was both through the establishment of online WeChat fan forums and through offline activities. The latter included gatherings and happenings in places such as New York, where fans would meet at locations such the Museum of Modern Art. One planned activity was for *Nebular* readers to meet in black masks and clothing and then see if they could form friendships without being able to judge based on appearances or labels. Labeling was a theme deeply embedded in the construction of the magazine and framed many of its stories.

Characterizing a reworking of Chinese national identity was an advertisement on May 4, 2016, for *Nebular* magazine that said, "May the 4th be with you." As glossed in the previous section, May 4 is known as Youth Day and is dedicated to young intellectuals who initiated a reform movement that began in 1917 and ended in 1921 and was directed toward national independence and rebuilding society and culture. It was inspired by the *New Youth* monthly magazine and defined in particular by a May 4, 1919, demonstration of more than three thousand students in Beijing. The celebration of May 4 by the student-run publication positioned the international students as aligned with this intellectual movement and with leading China into a new global era. The pun on the well-known *Star Wars* phrase "May the force be with you" additionally signaled a shift toward a more playful attitude and Western cultural values. In this fashion, the uptake of the date May 4 echoes the MSUwe54 student group, indicating how these ideologies circulated across an ideoscape (Appadurai 1996).

This ethos was manifested in an article on this same day that included traditional pictures of the Communist regime promoting socialist propaganda. A picture of a confident, smiling Chinese girl dominates the center of the frame. She is wearing a red shirt and scarf as an emblem of the young pioneers and the Communist party. The girl is strong and powerful and is pointing toward factories, electrical grids, and transportation systems in the distance behind students at desks and studying with the use of a microscope. The message is that the Chinese youth will lead the Communist nation toward technological advancement and dominance over the West (which is made more explicit in other images in the article). Yet underneath is text replacing traditional slogans that ironically reveals, "我抽烟, 喝酒, 纹身。但我知道我是一个会背社会主义核心价值观的好女孩" (I smoke, I drink, and I have tattoos. But I know I am a good girl who can recite the "socialist core values"). The appropriation of the narrative is one that shows an increasing gap between the rhetorics of the state and the everyday practices of contemporary youth. The article goes on to plainly state that the youth are rejecting traditional collective values of the state while shifting toward a more individualistic focus. The writer of the article says, "我可以理直气壮地说, 我没有那么在意家国天下, 我只想关心, 我, 和我目所能及的人生活的质量" (I can reasonably say that I do not care that much about the country and the world, I only want to care about myself and the lives of those around me). The article further argues for a shift from the working-class aesthetic (industriousness, discipline, and social good deeds) toward a more free-spirited approach to life embedded in play (see also chapter 6). This theme is showcased in interviews of several young successful Chinese entrepreneurs—characterized as North American leaders—who discuss the role video gaming has had on their philosophies and lives (see also chapter 7). The underlying subtext is that for this post-nineties generation, gaming and play is linked to their identity and personal growth. Yet even as the students were rejecting the traditional sense of the collective based on aestheticism and self-sacrifice, they were also drawing on and reproducing these ideologies as the young generation reconfigured collective values with a twist in a new capitalist system.

SUMMARY

To avoid imposing global frames on the local, Latour (2005) argues whenever anyone speaks of a global system, feature, or structure the scholar should always ask basic questions, such as "In which building? In which bureau? Through which corridor is it accessible?" (183). He contends that inquirers who accept and follow this clue will be surprised at the number of sites and conduits that emerge as soon as those queries are raised. The following analysis is an argument for raising such questions to keep the analysis flat in the tracing of activity in and across a transnational social field. As the case studies have demonstrated, this field is dynamically shaping and shaped by who/what moves, when they move, how far and fast, and to what effect. The reconstruction of the nation-state and the state of higher education is deeply entangled in this process.

Together the case studies of the two focal participants, both the Director and Zi'an, uncover a rich set of underground economies and literacies. Through a complex process of networking, and knotworking, they weave and are woven into wider social and semiotic systems. In this fashion, the students' relationship webs were densely entangled in institutional and cultural networks mediating movements across a transnational social field. Tracing these moments across space and time— coordinated by complex constellations of technologies, ideologies, and cultural practices—has uncovered complicated and messy ways their cultural repertoires and mobile practices were densely intertwined. Part and parcel of the students' grassroots literacies, their relationship webs shaped and were shaped by their social, cultural, and geographic traversals. In this fashion, these mechanisms formed part of a far-flung network refashioning identities, mobilities, and eduscapes.

Central to these politics of mobility is the construction of global geographies of difference. In the case of the Director, he wove and was woven into a complex circuit that led him back to mainland China. Further once back in China, he continued to maintain and extend his links across the nation as well as abroad to the United States, Australia, and Europe. These grassroots webs of activity were both rooted in national forms of identification and also bound up in their reconstruction. Even though he never received his degree or fully mastered English—or perhaps stemming from this situation—he creatively leveraged his transnational positioning while forging connections at the university. He originated from what he described as a working-class family, and the university provided a space where students across different classes could mingle. His networking strategies enabled him to accumulate social capital that was parleyed into a fast-track entrepreneurial career, including a position as a vice president of a for-profit college when he returned to China. Even more broadly his traversals reshaped MSU, as he leveraged his position at the university to construct educational structures in competition with it. Yet in addition to shaping the university landscape he was also shaped by it as part of an asymmetrical and uneven process, as he returned to Beijing with various bits and pieces of his MSU experience complexly rewoven into his identity and practices. Michigan State University has a program called Student Success, which is intended to increase retention (affiliated with the Neighborhood program described in chapter 1) and structure student pathways. In this instance, the Director selected a very different pathway linked to his own brand of student success.

Paralleling the Director's trajectory, Zi'an began his entrepreneurial ventures with the intention of publishing a social media site in English on Facebook modeled after Humans of New York. Though planning to assemble a multicultural editorial staff with the assistance of an American partner, his priorities quickly shifted. Turning more squarely to his home language and a Chinese audience, Zi'an transitioned his efforts toward the publication of a Chinese media site while establishing a dense network of transnational Chinese international students located in California, Boston, New York, Philadelphia, and Illinois. Many of these members in turn traveled back to China or other parts of the world where they remained affiliated with his magazine as the networks continued to expand and shift. However, even as these networks broadened, he integrated bits and pieces of his international experience into his identity and the magazine's design, with stories that wove in topics and themes related to the international student experiences as well as wider Western and marketplace ideologies. In this fashion, both he and the Director were bound up in the production of social spaces and imaginaries. Traversing a transnational landscape, the participants inhabited, performed, reproduced, and reconstructed a shifting set of imagined worlds.

Suggesting the uneven and contradictory nature of this process, the two participants also displayed numerous and sometimes stark differences in their dispositions and social and geographic pathways. Because of the Director's social and working-class roots, he was not averse to serving meals, picking up trash, or cleaning vomit-stained apartments. Uncomfortable around second-generation rich, he established friendship circles comprised those who shared a similar background and his penchant for sales and businesses ventures. Yet it was his connection to a "second-generation rich" student as founder of SCP that ultimately secured him a position back in China. On the other hand, Zi'an, whose mother had worked at a Chinese television studio, was interested in media sales and marketing. He pursued a path based on leveraging communications and social media through the production of high-end and highbrow publications. One of his aims was to enter a communications graduate program at Columbia or New York University, which he preferred because of their reputations and proximity to other members already working on the magazine. Leveraging his social-class affiliations, Zi'an's friendship circles and networks were further intertwined with many second-generation rich students, and his magazine stories often reproduced these social identity types and narratives, even as they set out to critique them. Zi'an seemed to have become aware of this and wanted to change the nature of the stories in future iterations of the magazine. Thus, even as he began to seek more distance from these figures, the trajectory of the Director followed an alternative pathway increasingly entangled with second-generation rich. In this fashion, these telling cases (Yin 2003) foreground the multidirectional construction of a transnational social field, as the actors simultaneously located themselves in relation to near and far-flung spaces. Though Zi'an remained in the States, he was extending his Chinese guanxi networks across the United States and back home to China. As the flip side to this process, the Director relocated to China and then extended his network across its provinces while maintaining ties to the United States. It was through this densely knotted process that places, identities, and cultural practices were complexly rewoven, restructured, and reconfigured.

In sum, the cases illustrate how the participants' relational networks entailed a complex interplay between wider sets of cultural ecologies and moments of everyday mobile practices. This interplay mediated students' social identities and trajectories as they traversed media, modes, languages, spaces, institutions, nations, ideologies, and histories. More broadly, this process of networking, or knotworking, was bound up in the construction of transnational imaginaries and social spaces. This process is linked to the formation of a global eduscape. The next chapter will continue to examine these messy circulations and plural geographies with closer attention to how they mediated everyday academic and classroom practices. Turning more fully to the students' in-school literacy practices, we will explore questions surrounding how their underground economies "sponsor" the development of their academic and disciplinary literacies and identities. The analysis foregrounds how the uptake of English is densely intertwined with this process.

Notes

1. All names have been changed in this section.
2. With permission, I have used Zi'an and Yisi's real names. I use pseudonyms for all other participants.
3. Other terms included "飛葉子" (smoke marijuana), "留學生" (international students), "權力" (power), "網紅" (website star), and "标签" (labels).
4. The magazine was originally titled *Nebula* and later changed to *Nebular* when Zi'an migrated from a personal to professional account on WeChat. Unable to port the name, the altered title uncovers how language was deeply embedded in sociotechnical structures. The modification foregrounds the dynamic and shifting nature of the magazine as it was continually shaping and shaped by an array of actors, symbols, technologies, and objects. For the purpose of consistency, throughout the book I refer to the magazine as *Nebular*.

3
HUMAN RELATION WEBS
IN ACADEMIC LIVES

Whereas the previous chapter looked at the students' relationship webs outside classroom contexts, I, Steve, now turn to look more specifically at how they were densely woven into students' academic trajectories. In making this move, I continue to break down binaries by attending to how the international students' out-of-school activities were deeply intertwined with their in-school literacy practices. To examine the ways this process unfolded in the context of students' academic socialization, I focus on a case study of an international student, Yisi, from the city of Ürümqi in the northwestern province of Xinjiang. She was an aspiring creative fiction writer hoping to publish in Chinese and English, and what emerged over the four years that I followed her literate trajectory was the complex manner in which her relationship webs brokered her literate life and disciplinary socialization. Aligned with the previous case studies (chapter 2), the analysis foregrounds how students' relationship webs were densely knotted into their movement in and across an array of contexts: lecture halls, assignments, instructors, classroom activities, study sessions, genres, languages, class materials (textbooks, assignment sheets, syllabi), presentations, disciplines, and educational technologies. Tracing her movement in and across this higher education landscape, this study offers insights into some of the ways that guanxi networks scaffolded academic identities and activities. Additionally, I selected Yisi because her academic and non-academic literacies were deeply entangled with the social trajectory of another focal actor, Zi'an, and the establishment of the international student publication *Nebular*. Through tracing the manner in which their trajectories intertwined, I illustrate how Yisi's networking, or knotworking, was bound up in remixing academic and extracurricular spaces.

Turning to a fine-grained account of this process, I extend the notion of a literacy sponsor (Brandt 2001) for tracing how a dense web of technologies, cultural frames, and actors mediated her movement across educational imaginaries and geographies. Deborah Brandt adopts the

DOI: 10.7330/9781607327332.c003

term "sponsor" to denote "agents, local or distant, concrete or abstract, who enable, support, teach, model, as well as recruit, regulate, suppress or withhold literacy—and gain advantage by it in some way" (166). This case study locates these practices in wider translingual and globalized spheres of activity. It further situates these practices in material assemblages. This move draws on Jon Wargo and Peter De Costa's (2017) literacy sponsorscape as a term indexing ways that human and non-human actors afford and constrain social literacies and mobilities. It is further aligned with Gail Hawisher et al. (2006), who extend the notion of sponsorship by offering a "more complex, concrete, and global perspective on how such relationships function in an increasingly networked world" (634). More particularly, they study how guanxi relations mediated the transnational trajectories of two female Asian graduate students and their acquisition of English and digital literacies. Broadening Hawisher et al.'s methodological approach, this case study of Yisi's literate trajectory offers a thick description of the material nature of this process and how it was intertwined with rich underground economies of learning. These complex networks, or knotworks, mediated the alignments and positioning of the participants, and the fluid pathways mediating the circulation of actors and objects in motion (e.g., students, textbooks, pedagogies, social media sites, cultural tropes). As a dynamic, co-constitutive, and contested process, this struggle was inextricably linked to the reconfiguration of the higher education landscape.

This chapter extends a wide range of scholarship in writing studies linked to disciplinary socialization (Bartholomae 1986; Casanave 2002; Ivanič 1998; McCarthy 1987; Prior 1998; Roozen 2009; Russell and Yañez 2003; Sternglass 1997; Walvoord and McCarthy 1990; Wardle 2007; Yancey, Robertson, and Taczak 2014; Zamel and Spack 2004) grounded in the notion that learning to write is a process of enculturation in which students learn particular ways of speaking, thinking, and being in the world. While metaphors of travel and border crossing (McCarthy 1987; Yancey, Robertson, and Taczak 2014; Zamel and Spack 2004) have often been taken up in this literature, less attention has been given to these processes from a translingual perspective. Moreover, the majority of studies tend to adopt a relatively bounded approach centered on discourse communities, communities of practice, or activity systems. As Prior (1998) notes, however, such terms are only a partial break from structuralist frameworks. This presupposition is indexed in metaphors such as "going into" and characterizations of academic actors as acquiring fixed sets of disciplinary rules, formats, and conventions. Our mobile literacies framework adopts a more fluid and dynamic orientation that follows the students as they weave and are woven into academic and disciplinary practices as part of a dialogic, contested, and deeply distributed process. Offering a rich account of this pluralized and messy activity, the chapter extends the argument for a "flat" (Latour 2005) approach that localizes the global through tracing situated literacy practices across media, spaces, genres, disciplines, ideologies, histories, modes, people, and technologies. In making this move, the study further links international students' traversals to the construction of wider global eduscapes.

METHODOLOGY

Positioning

I first became acquainted with Yisi after a call soliciting undergraduate students for an intensive study of international students' language and academic socialization. Learning about the project through a friend, Yisi volunteered to participate. She was an avid reader and creative writer majoring in English, and I quickly discovered the complex ways she was moving across her home and second languages in her academic and extracurricular literacy practices. More broadly, what also quickly emerged was the way that wider social webs of activity were intensely intertwined with this process. Charming, graceful, articulate, and insightful, Yisi quickly became a key informant of the first order shaping my understanding of and access to the local community. During one of our extended often biweekly conversations, Yisi explained the importance of establishing good relationships with teachers in China, who hold a strong sway over one's day-to-day life and future. In key respects, Yisi was similarly establishing a relationship with me. In her parents' business dealings, the interested parties often sat down for three-hour meals. In similar fashion, we engaged in extended interactions often lasting three to four hours covering a rich array of topics related to her literacy practices inside and outside the classroom. In this manner, I was enlisted into her network of resources. It was further through this process that I began to enlist her into mine. Through our interactions I became affiliated with other actors in Yisi's social circles. This ultimately led to the subsequent tracing of Zi'an's activity, as I followed students' relationship webs in and across a transnational social field. More broadly, this rich social web allowed a glimpse into how everyday literacy practices—inside and outside the classroom—were bound up in constellations of activities mediating the formation, reproduction, and transformation of the international student community.

Data Collection and Analysis

Through our extended interactions, I constructed a fine-grained account of ways Yisi developed her disciplinary and academic practices. During the 2013–2014 academic year, we had approximately thirty-five meetings typically lasting between two and four hours. The first meeting on September 13, 2013, was audio recorded, and nearly all other subsequent meetings were video recorded. The last face-to-face meeting was on May 2, 2014, though we continued to correspond throughout the summer by e-mail, WeChat, and Skype. Though the primary focus of the analysis is from this period, the case study is also informed by our frequent subsequent meetings, which continued on a regular basis through the 2016–2017 academic year. The initial interviews were semistructured to develop a better sense of her literate history, her daily classroom routines, and her regular reading and writing practices. During these initial conversations, I collected syllabi, assignment sheets, classroom notes (kept in notebooks, iPhone, computer, textbooks). I moreover began to document the types of literate activity she engaged in outside school. In mapping out her writing history, she provided me with her private journal; copies of her high-school writing and short stories; links to texts she had composed for an online literary magazine; and access to various social media sites such as Renren, Weibo, and WeChat.

This process continued over several years; I traced Yisi's writing and literacy practices as they unfolded in the context of her academic and nonacademic activities. In relation to her classroom literacies, data collection included notes, drafts, jottings, worksheets, and artifacts from her Arabic, writing, literature, and social sciences courses. It further included extracurricular texts, such as blogs, fictional stories, and articles for various Chinese media sites. Since many of these texts were in Chinese, I spent extended sessions with bilingual research assistants trying to glimpse wider cultural meanings. Using text-based interviews and intertextual tracing (Prior 2004), many of our meetings were spent discussing her writing processes and rhetorical choices. Towards the end of her first year, we also began to use a screen-capture program to record her writing activity. As part of a routine process, I took written notes during meetings and afterwards reviewed them in conjunction with the recordings. Drawing on a grounded theoretical approach (Charmaz 2014; Glaser and Strauss 1967), I reflexively engaged in open and more focused coding, memos (Emerson, Fretz, and Shaw 1995), and transcription of critical moments and key sections from the recordings. Making numerous passes through the data, I devoted particular attention to what she characterized as significant (an emic perspective) while noting in vivo codes or terms and phrases anchored in her social world. Through this process, one theme that emerged was the way Yisi's relationship webs mediated her literacy and learning. With this process extending to almost all aspects of her literate life (i.e., with broad theoretical reach), I theoretically sampled (Charmaz 2014) and documented these moments to better understand how this process worked at a more fine-grained level. In making this move, I posed questions such as, when do you collaborate? How often do you collaborate? With whom do you collaborate? In what ways do you collaborate? Engaging in a process of constant comparison, I continued this process until I had theoretically saturated the data. Overall, the analysis first shows how her guanxi networks complexly mediated her academic and disciplinary practices. Second, this process became densely knotted into her unofficial literate activities and the production of a complex web of relations mediating her personal and professional trajectory. Finally, these entanglements were connected to a wider set of processes through which the higher education landscape was being rewoven.

RELATIONSHIP WEBS

Mediating Yisi's movement through the university was a philosophy about relationships bound up in the concept of *renji guanxi wang* (人际关系网). As evident from her narrative, this analytic frame is one that she had acquired early on from observing her parents' business practices.

> Usually in China the most important thing is your relationship . . . like you know how to get along with people, and you know which kind of people is useful, they are helpful. Suppose I can do nothing, but I know a friend, so he can help me, he can do these things, I can still finish my work. Or take a company leader who needs to make big decision. Management, if you are good with people, you know how to use these people. You know how to get along with other companies. (Personal communication, October 16, 2013)

By her own admission, this process mediated the ways that she established herself at the university. Traveling from the city of Ürümqi in the northwestern province of Xinjiang, China, first year student Yisi Fan made her way to Shanghai with her mother to shop and then coordinated with other incoming students that she had befriended in online QQ forums, which were moderated by the Director and student group MSUwe54 (see chapter 2). Traveling over as a group on the plane, students stayed together in Detroit for one night before heading to East Lansing. Yisi's story is typical of this population in that she had begun forging friendships before she ever arrived at MSU, a process that accelerated upon her arrival. This process intensified as she moved into

Hubbard Hall with three other Chinese roommates in the East neighborhood and as she oriented to her new surroundings.

This activity continued as she sought to establish relationships that helped her adjust as part of a process involving finding rides to the local Meijer shopping center, setting up her computer, purchasing textbooks, opening a bank account, registering for and deciding on courses, purchasing a family plan with other students for her phone, and performing all the other mundane and routine tasks that were part of being a new international undergraduate student on the MSU campus. These activities were recorded and shared on her WeChat microblog, which served to document as well as reproduce her growing network of resources. The following are some examples from shortly after her arrival at the university.

> September 2, 2013
> 有没有电脑比较好的小伙伴,学校邮箱里只能看到邮件数但是打不开,我需要帮助阿阿啊啊啊啊。在Hubbard。
>
> (Is there anybody who is good with computers. I can see the number of mails in the school email box but can't view any of them. I need help, ahahahah. I'm living in Hubbard.)

> September 17, 2013
> 有木有人去best buy! 或者手里有word这个软件。
>
> (Anybody is going to best buy! Anybody who has word software.)

> September 23, 2013
> 破解版word装不上哇 小伙伴们有擅长电脑的吗 歌姐姐装还好好的 我的就是装不上 不行我就去买正版啦。
>
> (Unlocked word cannot be installed. Is there anybody who is good at computers. It works on Ge Sister's computer. But it doesn't work on mine. If it doesn't work, I'm going to buy the official one.)

These typical entries indexed the myriad of ways that she drew on a network of resources to troubleshoot technical issues: emails, software programs, rides to the local Best Buy. In this fashion, Yisi was entangled in a complex sociotechnical network in which digital technologies became densely intertwined with a wider sponsorscape that helped her to adjust to social and technical structures. She was complexly positioned in material and social spaces mediating her movement across the university.

This process moreover extended into her formal and informal learning, as indexed in an early WeChat entry during her transition to the United States. Having purchased a guitar from a local music store and

Figure 3.1. Seeking a guitar teacher

in search of lessons, she sought someone within the student community who could assist her with instruction (Figure 3.1).

Oct 2, 2013

满地打滚求吉他老师 😈 小伙伴要是有一周能教我一次的就好了。哭。手残星人自己练好恼人。

(Rolling on the floor and asking for a guitar teacher 😈. If anybody can teach me once per week, that will be great. Crying. Clumsy girl practicing on her own is annoying.)

This blog entry characterized Yisi's distaste for learning alone. Within a day, she managed to locate someone through a friend who had provided her with a "name card." This is a way for someone on WeChat to introduce people by sending a referral or contact. The very next day, Yisi posted a message thanking her new guitar teacher. In this fashion, she quickly mobilized her social resources to find sponsors to assist with her learning. This process moreover extended to her academic life.

Signifying her dense and growing web of resources is an entry in which she writes of experiencing a crisis on a day in which everything went wrong at the same time; she thanks eleven different people for their assistance.

September 3, 2013
今天实在太糟糕了,各种巧合不好的事情。谢谢帮我指导电脑和打印的翼飞同学,帮我弄好mail的神烦同学,拔刀相助的kk还有铁老板,还有鼓励我的歌姐姐糖糖,自己忙数学还帮我的师傅,不认识的不收我钱的出租车司机,还有教我读阿拉伯语的很厉害的那个同学,还有kk的小伙伴,还有陪着我的毛线,还有越洋安慰的学长,真的很好。

(Today was so bad, all bad things happened together. Thank Yifei who helped me with the computer and printing, thank Shenfan who helped me with email, thank kk and Tie Laoban who were willing to help me, thank Ge Sister and Tangtang who encouraged me, thank *shifu* [teacher] who helped me even when he was busy with math himself, thank the stranger cab driver who didn't charge me, thank the person who taught me to pronounce Arabic, thank kk's friend, and thank Maoxian who was with me, thank study brother who comforted me from overseas. Really nice.)

On this eventful day, she turned to friends, friends of friends, her old deskmate still overseas in China, and even the cab driver, whom she thanked for not charging her. In addition to the multiple types of people in her translocal network, also telling were the varied forms of assistance: technical support, moral support, and educational support. In relation to her academic learning, significant were references to friends who served as her "teachers." The first was Tangtang, whom she referred to as "*shifu*" (teacher). This person had helped her with her math homework even when he was busy himself. The second person, whose name she had not yet learned, Zi'an, "taught" her correct pronunciation for her Arabic course. The references to key actors within her social web index how she leveraged her guanxi networks to sponsor her academic and disciplinary learning. As this early blog entry suggests, this extended network functioned as a literacy sponsorscape mediating her movements in and across the educational landscape.

LITERACY NARRATIVE

In order to examine this process, I first offer a broad-brush overview of Yisi's background and social trajectory. From the town of Ürümqi in the northwestern province of Xinjaing, Yisi had attended a private school with an American English teacher and had decided to study abroad with encouragement of her parents as a way to avoid a more rigid structure. As a Muslim Hui, her parents spoke Arabic and she had been raised in the Islamic tradition. While a cultural minority in China, her ethnic group was linguistically and culturally similar to the Han. Moreover, as a thoroughly outgoing and winsome personality, she had minimal difficulty seamlessly integrating into the international student community. An avid reader, she had also been engaged in writing creative stories in Chinese and antici-pated to begin writing more in English. This background was explained during our first encounter. Yisi had come to my office—wearing an army-green shirt with a first-class private insignia on her sleeve and a tag on a front pocket that said "reckless," which she had recently purchased from the Meridian shopping mall with some friends—and explained that she had come to the United States to fulfill a "dream." This discourse would repeatedly surface, as evidenced in her online microblog. On November 4, 2013, for instance, she posted a picture (Figure 3.2) of the back of a man sitting alongside a shoreline with a t-shirt that said, "Keep the dream alive." Other examples (February 17, 2014) included a scene from a Japanese anime, *Spirited Away*, with references to not letting go or giving up on one's dreams. Yisi moreover included a link to an article (April 10, 2014) about her grandmother that she had written for a Chinese student publication, *Voice*, in which she reiterated the importance of protecting or preserving one's beliefs and dreams.

February 17
他们说你为什么不能做一直甘心的犀牛呢。可是人只要触碰过一次梦想。就不愿意再放弃。心里装了那么多就不要放弃。希望这一次我能真的真的真的好起来。 🎈 你好,明天。

(They asked why couldn't you just be an easily satisfied rhino. But if a person has touched his *dream* [emphasis added] once, he wouldn't be able to let it go. Don't give up when your heart is already full of dreams. I wish this time I can really get better. 🎈 Hello, tomorrow.)

Such posts were part of a shifting social imaginary (see chapters 2 and 5) densely bound up in Yisi's identity as a writer and her traversals in and across the HEI landscape.

In pursuit of her dreams, Yisi had followed in the footsteps of her favorite author, Geling Yan, who had served in the military during the Sino-Vietnamese war and published highly regarded novels in Chinese and English. The author had been at the cusp of a new wave of interna-tional students (immediately before the 1991 relaxation of laws related to studying abroad) to the United States, where she studied at Columbia University and earned a master's degree in creative writing. Yisi closely identified with the author and was already an accomplished Chinese

Figure 3.2. Keep the dream alive

writer in her own right engaged in publishing and editing stories for her high school student journal and newspaper and seeking to publish her works in popular Chinese magazines.

Rooted in Yisi's dream to write creatively in both Chinese and English was a move to establish a cosmopolitan identity. Far from leaving behind her home culture, she was actively merging her varied lifeworlds. This effort was evident in her identification with her favorite literary magazine *Chutzpah!* 天南. The Chinese 天南 (*Tian Nan*) was from the expression 天南地北 (*tian nan di bei*), which literally means "south of the sky and north of earth." Figuratively, it refers to all walks of life. Titled in both Chinese and English, this experimental journal published stories in multiple languages from subaltern authors around the world. Shaping and shaped by a global imaginary, the genre framed her engagement with a number of extracurricular literacy practices.

Electing to pursue a degree in English as a creative writing major, Yisi was unique among the wider international-student community as one of the 2 percent nationally who had enrolled in the humanities (Institute of International Education 2014). The decision is one that she had not arrived at lightly, and only after consulting with an array of actors in her wider relationship web. The decision is one that she would furthermore struggle with as the semester continued as she enlisted advice from an array of confidants. She reflected that one of the drawbacks of having so many friends was receiving too many opinions. Yisi, however, sought out these varied perspectives in order to find "balance." Continually referring to balance, she was weaving into her decision-making process another key cultural trope within Chinese society linked to maintaining harmony. In this fashion, she was complexly situated in social and material spaces as she wove and was woven into wider institutional and cultural lifeworlds.

Adding to her academic challenges, Yisi moreover decided to study another language, and she chose Arabic as her minor. Though never having gained proficiency in the language, her parents spoke Arabic and had traveled to many Arabic-speaking countries. Beyond reasons related to her religious and ethnic identity as a Chinese Muslim, or *Hui*, moreover, Yisi also made a strategic decision as she imagined that the language would make her marketable in case she ultimately needed to pursue a more practical career. While English was becoming commonplace within China, Arabic speakers were still relatively hard to find. Thus, enrolling in a women's literature and Arabic language course her first semester, Yisi crossed an array of disciplinary, cultural, and linguistic regimes. In the next section, I attend more closely to this process.

TRANSDISCIPLINARY TRAVERSALS

In this section I turn to the ways that Yisi's relationship webs were deeply "knotted" into her everyday academic literacy practices and learning as she traversed her first semester courses: astronomy, Arabic, and women's English literature. The first semester, Yisi registered for an astronomy course as part of her science requirement despite warnings from others on the QQ forums. Enrolled in the course, she found the professor's use of media in his lecture particularly engaging, but at the same time she developed a sense that the amount of work for a course outside her major was overwhelming (she was expected to complete multiple tutorials a week each consisting of fifty questions each). These time-consuming exercises required learning a large number of technical terms, which meant Yisi had to search for the Chinese translations using the online dictionary *Youdau*, which provided discipline-specific

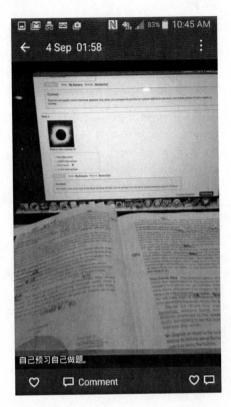

Figure 3.3. Textual ecology for astronomy course

definitions. In an early blog entry (September 4, 2013), she displays a picture of her workspace (Figure 3.3), showing an online tutorial, her textbook, and Chinese translations written on its pages. The comment beneath the blog entry reads, "Preparing for class and doing homework *on my own* [emphasis added]." The reference to learning on her own indexes her disposition toward collaborative learning and foregrounds her sense of isolation. Moreover, the images of the book and computer point to the ways she was emplaced within disciplinary discourses comprised of an ecology of texts and textual practices.

Seeking assistance, she enlisted the help of people in her social network. She sought, for instance, assistance from her roommate, who had taken an astronomy course in high school and was currently enrolled in another section. When doing homework on tutorials, she photographed her homework and sent the pictures to a friend in another dorm for assistance in the evenings. She even received aid from another friend not enrolled in her course, who read through her textbook and helped her organize the material by writing up notes. Ultimately, however, Yisi struggled to stay motivated. Though she sought out collaboration, particularly at the semester's start, these attempts were half-hearted and quickly faded. For instance, she lost her friend's chapter notes, and while she sat with four other Chinese students, she did not study with them or seek assistance in relation to the course content. So despite drawing on her guanxi networks, they were not totalizing or all-encompassing but varied across different domains, with some areas of her literate life more densely knotted than others.

One area that became deeply knotted was her Arabic-language studies. Because she was a Chinese Muslim from the northwestern province of Xinjiang, Arabic was linked to her ethnic identity. Despite her ambition, however, Yisi's challenges in learning the language were amplified due to the fact that her Arabic course was a third language taught in a second (English). For example, on tests, she often understood the Arabic but failed to associate it with the proper English translation. Foregrounding this complex linguistic landscape were her course notes, with Arabic words and phrases, English translations, and Chinese phonetic spellings to aid her pronunciation (see Figure 3.4). Compounding her struggle was her Arabic teacher's style of telling stories about the culture and his large Arabic family, rather than structuring a more focused discussion on the language. While she found this approach interesting and informative, she also became concerned that this style failed to help prepare her for the exams. In this fashion, linguistic, cultural, and disciplinary strands of activity became densely entangled in her everyday academic literate practices.

In response to these problems, she sought someone who could help "carry" (带/dai) her in the course. The term (as discussed in chapter 4) refers to a strong and gifted student identified as a "lord of learning" (学霸/xue ba) who can help weaker learners (学弱/xue ruo). As the only Chinese student in her section, she was elated to one day find another studying Arabic in a study hall. Striking up a conversation, she learned he had lived in Jordan for three years, where he had become proficient in the language. She peppered him with questions about proper Arabic, and he confidently offered to buy her dinner if he was unable to answer them. In this manner, Zi'an and Yisi began to regularly meet over dinner, where they discussed issues related to her course. In Yisi's words, Zi'an became her "teacher," as they regularly also met in the study lounge so Zi'an could assist her with the weekly dictation homework, which required that she listen to online recordings and answer questions about them. Zi'an assisted her with breaking the passage down and creating lists of words for her to remember and pronounce. As the semester progressed and reached a critical juncture before the finals,

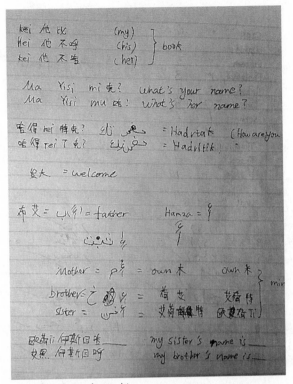

Figure 3.4. Notes for Arabic course

Zi'an also helped her prepare for an interview in a three-hour extended session in which he rehearsed her for the event and video recorded himself pronouncing key questions and passages on her iPad for her review. He even invited her to his teacher's review session for the final. This relationship would become densely interwoven with Yisi's unofficial literacies and the production of the student-run magazine, *Nebular*.

For her third course, Yisi was enrolled in a women's literature course in the English department. The course was in key respects central to Yisi's core identity. As one of the few females from her community to leave the country and study abroad, with her father's friends gossiping about the wisdom of this decision, she felt an additional burden to prove herself. The course specifically focused on Western feminist literature, and students were required to write about issues focused on feminist consciousness. While Yisi had little trouble dealing with high-level concepts, she struggled with English and possessed less experience with writing structured essays, as most of the writing in her high-school courses was based on what she referred to as "freedom style." This term was a gloss for loosely structured thoughts on paper. She further found herself competing with Americans who had grown up with English as their first language and had been socialized into a US educational system. Though contributing to class discussions, Yisi felt out of her element and adrift without anyone to collaborate with or help "carry" her in the class. This lack of support surfaced early after a meeting about her first assignment, which was centered on Kate Chopin's *Awakening* and the question, what is women's literature? Yisi performed poorly on the assignment, and the instructor had called her into her office to suggest that Yisi drop the course. Shocked and surprised, she fretted that her plans to pursue a degree in creative writing were already in jeopardy. Not knowing where else to turn, she enlisted my assistance.

However, when we sat down to review her paper, she realized the file was not downloaded to her computer. It was in fact the technological disruption and her efforts to retrieve her paper that offered insight into a rich sponsorscape mediating her literate activity. I began to uncover her sociotechnical network as I watched Yisi try to contact her roommate, whose computer she had borrowed to write her paper, as she had not yet installed a copy of Microsoft Word on her own laptop. Calling to ask her roommate to send the file, she found her at the social security office, where she was applying for a social security number and card. Yisi then left two voice messages in quick succession on WeChat for her other two roommates, hoping they could return to the room to locate and send the file. With no success on these fronts, she turned to another potential solution: a friend whose printer she had used. She contacted him on QQ chat to see if her file was still on his computer, and he responded affirmatively. Even after he sent the file, however, she experienced technical issues downloading it. She continued to receive assistance as her friend helped her troubleshoot the problem, with communication through a mixture of QQ (instant messaging on the computer) and WeChat (voice and text messaging on her mobile phone). Though she ultimately failed to open the file, the exchanges revealed the complexity of Yisi's network as she mobilized various resources using multiple media and modes. This continual process of weaving and reweaving an instantly accessible relationship web mediated her everyday traversals in and across the university. Collectively, these networks, or knotworks, of technologies, texts, tropes, people, and objects made up a complex sponsorscape.

This assemblage was further distributed across transnational contexts. Meeting with her multiple times to discuss her rewrite, I was enlisted into her network as we gradually reviewed the requirements on the assignment sheet and worked through structuring her ideas for the paper. Working closely together, we tried to define the nature of women's literature and then more specifically attended to how Chopin's story might (or might not) serve as a representative example. Yisi also solicited advice from her former teachers Mark and Tina. The first was an English teacher with whom she kept in contact through long and extended e-mails even after he completed his year of teaching in the northwestern province. Mark was a person from whom she had solicited advice about what school to attend and what to major in and other support about academic and nonacademic issues. Now in Chicago, he read through Yisi's paper with careful attention to her language while making some word changes with accompanying explanations in an e-mail. Yisi had furthermore sought out help from her former IELTS teacher, Tina, who now worked in a bank in Ürümqi. Tina highlighted unclear phrases, changed a few sentences, corrected grammatical issues, and suggested areas where Yisi needed to improve.

Finally, Yisi contacted her former deskmate, James, from Ürümqi, who was now a student in Missouri. In response to her request, he marked up her paper using the comments feature in Microsoft Word and sent an e-mail with his assessment (October 10, 2013).

> Dear Cynthia,
>
> It is obvious that you have improved a lot since I last checked your IELTS essay. I know you were trying wrote good literature article when you devoted yourself into express your feeling accurately. However I found out that if your essay is able to be translated to Chinese directly, that would be a wonderful essay. You have gift in Chinese literature writing instead of English's. You still need to practice more and do your best to transform your thought to English while you are writing English essay. In addition to that, you gotta to know the style of English literature which is totally different from Chinese style. Read more English novels and journals could be good approaches to improve your writing.
>
> Sincerely yours,
> James He

In James's feedback, he adopts a teacherly tone, as he first praises Yisi's "gift" for Chinese writing and her improvement since he last evaluated her IELTS exam and then critiques her English essay as retaining the characteristics of her first language. He then offers unsolicited advice for future improvements by saying she needs to recognize stylistic differences between English and Chinese writing and to practice reading more English literature. In this instance, Yisi recognized that while her deskmate's feedback might not be perfect, it could still be helpful. She sensed James's strength was in grammar, or at least that his level was higher than hers. Reflecting on the tone of the letter, she explained that James often acted like her "teacher" and that she frequently found such people in her life. Her comments echoed her relationship with Zi'an, who assisted her with Arabic. Not taking James's criticism personally, she framed his tone as a product of his history as a struggling student during their high-school years. Moreover, she recognized that his broader comments about her paper did not always fit the assignment requirements. The fact that James changed the phrase "books of this unit" to the "unit of this book" in her text, for example, indicated a misunderstanding of the class as organized around a textbook lesson. Yisi's ability to determine what advice to keep was linked to a skill in recognizing others' assets.

In Deborah Brandt's (2001) terms, these various actors in this scene served as literacy sponsors—distributed across a transnational social field—helping her acquire English and academic literacies. Having received a wide array of feedback, she reflected on what she learned in the process. First, from her deskmate, she noticed the importance of understanding the context of the assignment and reading. Even though his grammar was better, this ability did not necessarily help without wider knowledge of the course content. Second, beyond local grammatical issues, her IELTS teacher as a native Chinese speaker could not understand her points, so she would need to focus on her meaning. Third, Mark helped show her that even with "simple words you can make the sentence really beautiful." Finally, she reflected on my assistance: "I find that the most important help you give me is about ideas, like how to keep asking questions, like how to make me clear what I want to, what I try to write, and how to organize it and how to like highlight like make the points during the essay." Mikhail Bakhtin (1981) writes that one never speaks only with one's own voice, but instead one's words are always double voiced, and in Yisi's text, we can see the complex blending of voices. Her paper was densely intertextual and comprised of various fragments, bits, and pieces. This multitude of voices in the short term helped her survive a new and complex environment, but more broadly, she was learning to assemble these various voices and texts into her everyday academic literacy practices.

When Yisi took the revised essay to her teacher's office, her instructor briefly reviewed it and responded with "perfect work." Yisi felt the paper was still far from perfect (she ultimately received a 3.0 on a 4.0 scale), as she observed a number of lingering issues in her text. The comment, however, indicated that her paper had dramatically improved. Satisfied with her performance, she posted these remarks in her microblog:

October 10, 2013

当老师说,perfect work 的时候,在想,终于终于终于结束了。太难熬了,
这段时间。第一次和native speaker一起写论文,不断地问自己,到底图什么
呀,这么心酸。吃不好,玩不好,睡不好,就惦念着这篇文章。委屈的要命,有
不明白委屈什么。坐在电脑面前发呆,什么也写不出来。可是最后,终于还
是做到了呢。过去所有的得到都是建立在容易的基础上,从来没有像现在
这样笨拙艰难,但是真的很充实充实,并且每一天我都很快乐。

(When the teacher said 'perfect work' I was thinking, it was finally finally
finally over. It is so anguishing, this period of time. It is the first time to write
a paper [in competition] with a 'native speaker,' I asked myself constantly,
what was my purpose, to be this grieved. I didn't eat well, play well, sleep
well, I was thinking about this paper all the time. I was so upset, but I didn't
know why I was upset. Gazing at my computer motionlessly, I didn't produce
anything. But in the end, I finally made it. Everything I gained in the past
was based on that it was easy to get, it was never this clumsy and hard like
this right now, but this is really fulfilling, and everyday I am happy.)

In an interview about the paper, she further noted:

It's a difficult time for me, although I feel happy every day, I feel always
something forced me, I know something I haven't finished it, like there
are something I should conquer with this essay. Like I fight with this essay.
Like I fight with this essay and in the end I think I win. (Personal communication, October 10, 2013)

The comments illustrate Yisi's ongoing struggle as she learned to adapt
to wider institutional, linguistic, and disciplinary structures. This process was richly mediated by a complex literacy sponsorscape distributed
across a transnational social field.

FUEL FOR SNOWY WEATHER

This struggle was one that continued throughout her first academic
year. Central to negotiating these moments were tactical decisions about
how to utilize the resources in her sociotechnical network. She was
acutely aware of whom she could ask, when she could ask, how much
she could ask, and the types of information she could ask for. For the
next paper, for instance, on Sylvia Plath's *The Bell Jar*, she again turned
to Tina, Mark, and me. However, this time she also elected to turn to
her friend Roth, who was still located in Ürümqi. She noted that he was
a "popular boy" whose English was "strong," so she needed to use him
sparingly and carefully. Sending her essay, she received an extensive set
of comments that, unlike her deskmate's, were in many respects much
broader and displayed a sophisticated reading of the paper while con-
textualizing it within the wider assignment. In fact, he had pasted a key

passage from the assignment sheet into his comments while questioning whether she had met the requirements. He further declined to offer feedback on sections for which he lacked a broader knowledge of the class and discipline, as part of a more situated reading. The following remarks appeared as part of his feedback:

> 后面两段有点专业性特征太强了。。。我就不做评论了。但是我看了这个文章的Purpose,我给你粘贴到下面了。我不知道它有没有要求你写现在的这种问题。后面两段注意时态。尼玛大学生半个多学期了还这么多小错误对得起我么你。。。。

> (The last two paragraphs are too professional . . . I won't comment on them. But I saw the purpose of this essay, and I pasted it below. I am not sure if the problem you wrote about is related to the assignment. Pay attention to tense in the last two paragraphs. You have been a college student for more than half a semester and you still make so many mistakes. Is that how you show me respect. . . .) (October 30, 2013)

Yisi noted the differences in his comments from her deskmate's; Roth's were characterized by his broader approach. Through this comparative stance and soliciting feedback from a wide social network of actors, she developed her own attunement to academic literacy practices. She further refined her capacity to seek people who possessed the appropriate semiotic and intellectual resources to assist her.

In yet another essay, which analyzed a poem, Yisi again consulted her IELTS teacher. Generally, when seeking help from this teacher, Yisi strategically knew there was a stronger chance of Tina's being available in the late evening because of the time difference between the United States and China. She also recognized that her former IELTS teacher was no longer formally teaching and was exceptionally busy with a job at a bank. Yisi further recognized that Tina was not obligated to help, as she did not even know Yisi's parents. This assumption indexed a broader framework undergirding the sense of rights and obligations mediating such transactions. Writing a paper on the poem "The Lost Baby" under a tight deadline, Yisi sought Tina's assistance with the interpretation. In a QQ chat, the two discussed its meaning, with Tina offering several links to articles to assist and identifying places Yisi had misinterpreted. In addition, they discussed Yisi's grammar and the best way to learn it, and the conversation concluded with an expression of gratitude: "雪中送炭" (It's like offering fuel in snowy weather). In this fashion, Yisi continually wove and rewove her networks and knotworks as they mediated her academic trajectory and the ways she learned to invent the university.

FINDING A "VOICE"

The following semester, Yisi's in-class and out-of-class social networks became increasingly entangled. As key actors in her network grew busier with other obligations, Yisi enlisted a new actor into her relationship web. Through a high-school friend who was at Purdue University, Yisi had become acquainted with a magazine about Chinese international students living abroad entitled *Voice* 我是 ["Who I am"], which had been started by eight Chinese students on the campus. The magazine was an effort to create a professional publication that bridged Chinese and US cultures. This theme was echoed on one of the covers, which displayed a picture of a Caucasian male with half his face covered by a Beijing opera mask. As part of a transcultural effort, the publication was written in Chinese while also including English. This bilingual format echoed Yisi's favorite literary journal, *Tian Nan*.

Interested in capturing the experiences of Chinese students living abroad, she wrote to the publication in an expression of her appreciation for the magazine. To her surprise, she received an immediate response from one of the magazine's editors, and they soon developed a close relationship. Learning that Yisi was a writer, the editor asked her to submit some samples to the magazine. The editorial team was impressed with her talent and offered her an opportunity to write for the magazine.

More broadly, the group was looking to expand, with plans to distribute the magazine across various campuses, as they recruited photographers, writers, marketers, and editors from other schools to assist. Recognizing Yisi as a potential doorway into the MSU market, they put her in touch with the magazine's president, whom she referred to as "*She Zhang*" (社长). The term is a title that refers to the director or president of an agency, and he and Yisi began detailed discussions as Yisi started to write for the publication. Yisi also began to recruit other writers and friends who could help expand the magazine on the MSU campus, quickly locating a number of people who promptly began making various contributions. Yisi and She Zhang furthermore established plans to distribute five hundred copies across campus for the upcoming fall. Yisi characterized *Voice* as resembling a well-run business more than a student-run organization: "Actually She Zhang treats this magazine like a company and the way he is thinking is totally like a business man." She moreover characterized him as a leader who "kn[ew] how to use different people in different ways." The description paralleled Yisi's own model for interacting with people and the manner in which she recruited others' assistance in other areas, including her academic studies.

Indeed, Yisi discovered that She Zhang had minored in traditional English literature at Purdue. He moreover claimed that his grammar was superior to many native speakers due to his study of Latin. Naturally, Yisi sought his help in English. For instance, Yisi was involved in an undergraduate research project and needed to create a poster presentation for an end-of-year conference. Because it was the first time she had engaged in such an activity and she was anxious about using her English in a professional context, she consulted with She Zhang for feedback, and they developed a list of questions and rehearsed over the phone. She furthermore turned to him for assistance with an end-of-year presentation for a composition course with the theme women in America. Brainstorming together on topics, Yisi ultimately settled on the comparison of two advertisements foregrounding distinct representations of young Chinese women.

The following are the translations:[1]

Advertisement 1

This year I need to get married even though it is just for my grandmother's sake. Every time I meet my grandma she asks me, are you going to get married? [Scene at graduation]. Are you going to get married [Scene in a professional environment]. Are you going to get married? [Scene of sick grandmother]. Are you going to get married? [Scene of women in bridal dress with groom beside grandmother's hospital bed]. I don't have the time for selecting slowly. I need to go to the Lilly Dating Agency. Grandma, I am getting married because love doesn't wait. Text: the Agency is in 60 cities and they are very efficient.

Advertisement 2

There is a Chinese saying that when a girl has a relatively small foot she gets homesick easily and doesn't like to travel around. I think that is bullshit. I had a dream before, it is a dream to go somewhere far away. I have been looking for that place. I believe it exists. [Scene shifts to outdoors and mountains]. I am not worried about my future at all. Because time will make me a better person. The only thing I worry about is I didn't see the world entirely before I died. I'm Molly, freedom to me is even though the road is long it is not longer than my size five foot.

The two advertisements side by side foreground shifts in the social imaginary within a modernizing Chinese society. The first advertisement is targeted at what has been labeled the *leftover woman* (剩女) in Chinese society, an educated female older than twenty-seven and unmarried. The term was popularized through a state-sponsored campaign to pressure women to marry in the interest of preserving social stability. The second advertisement includes a popular writer and model, Molly, who is known for her travels and adventurous life outside China. The ad shows her challenging the notion that a girl should stay close to home while portraying her pursuing her dream of traveling and hiking in Tibet as she lives a spontaneous and free-spirited life. The ad makes use of the terms "dream" and "freedom" as part of a growing discourse centered on individual pursuit, challenging traditional gender stereotypes within the society. The advertisements further point to the complex ways shifting gender roles within Chinese society were being rewoven into her literate identity. In this fashion, Yisi continually wove and was woven into an array of social imaginaries and social spaces. This process mediated the ways she moved in and across a dynamic and densely knotted social field.

Working on a draft of the presentation, she set out to create video subtitles for her English-speaking audience. To perform this task, she sought the assistance of her roommate's boyfriend, who as a computer science major could provide technical support. Once the translations were complete, she worked throughout the night on drafting a script she sent to She Zhang for review. Promptly reading the draft the following day, the leader did not want to simply make corrections. He told her, "Next time you will still be confused and won't have learned." Consequently, he suggested they review the script together on Google Docs in order to work and edit the text simultaneously. Together they combed through the script in a session extending well into the early-morning hours. The session served as an educational space, and Yisi noted the process "took a long time because he tried to be the *teacher* [emphasis added]." As an example of his instructional style, She Zhang put explanations in Chinese after making corrections to the English text. Further sorting through her paper, he attempted to pull out the core ideas from her argument: "I hadn't written too clearly in English, so he tried to figure out what I was saying throughout the whole presentation." Part of an extended interaction by phone and Google Docs chat, the two covered a wide range of issues.

Moving on to the revision of an advertisement analysis, the pair again engaged in a similar process. The following is a transcript from the online chat. Recorded with a screen-capture program, it documented the conversation unfolding in real time (April 28, 2014).

She Zhang: 这句话可以改的更书面一些~

(This sentence could be changed into more formal language)

YISI: 怎么改 [她删除了,然后改成] 我想想哦

(How to revise? [she deletes what she typed] Let me think about this.)

SHE ZHANG: 还是说这是演讲稿

(Or is it a speech?)

YISI: 不是,作文啦

(No, it is an essay.)

SHE ZHANG: 那totally需要书面一些

(Then, it "totally" needs to be more formal.)

YISI: 好的!

(Ok!)

SHE ZHANG: 来 看看这两句的区别

(Come and see the differences between these two sentences.)

YISI: 好

(Ok.)

YISI: 感觉更加工整了。社长你好厉害。要是有一个英语能和你一样强,我睡觉都能乐醒。

(I think the new one is neater. She Zhang, you are awesome. If one day my English could be as good as yours, I will be smiling in my sleep.)

SHE ZHANG: 嘻嘻 学拉丁文吧~~~

(Haha you should learn Latin.)

YISI: 句子更简洁了[她删除了,然后改成] 这句好像。。。越改。。。越奇怪了

(It is more simple and clear [she deletes what she typed]. This sentence seems like, the more I revise, the weirder it is.)

SHE ZHANG: 因为和上面木有衔接。突然冒出来selective display. 一开始总起了,广告日益重要,广告影响三观,然后突然到了selective display.

(Because it is not connected to the sentence above. The expression "selective display" comes from nowhere. The essay starts by making a statement that advertisements are increasingly important because they can affect people's values. Then it suddenly starts to talk about "selective display.")

YISI: 所以要加阐述么。对,可以这么说。

(So I need to explain here? Yes, this is right.)

SHE ZHANG: 亲爱的加点东西吧

(Dear you should add something here.)

YISI: 广告影响着人们的选择,人们的价值观,但是广告为了售卖商品,在大部分情况下,选择了选择性的展示。

(Advertisements can affect people's choice, people's value, but their purpose is to sell products so in most cases advertisements choose to display things selectively.)

YISI: 广告并不是完全诚实的。选择性展示的广告对美国女性产生巨大的影响,其中包括很多负面影响。

(Advertisements are not entirely honest. Selective display has had great influence on American females, including a lot of negative influence.)

YISI: [修改了文中的一句话] 这样呢

(How about this?)

As they worked together on the revision, the exchange covered a range of issues, including organization, genre, tone, and word choice. For example, focusing on the genre and mode, She Zhang clarified differences between creating a presentation and a paper, arguing that the latter was more "formal." In order to illustrate the differences, he composed a sentence for Yisi to compare to the original. In response, Yisi lavishly praised his abilities, saying she could only dream of one day achieving his level of English. However, in the background, Yisi joked with her roommate: "Every time when She Zhang made a revision to my essay I was trying my best to say nice things about him. I was like 'She Zhang you're so awesome.' 'She Zhang I didn't realize that a sentence could be written like this.'" While clearly appreciative of She Zhang's help, Yisi also engaged face work and impression management as she strategically positioned herself in her complex relationship web. It is more broadly through such moves that she developed an academic and literate identity as she gradually socialized into an array of dynamic, contested, and shifting disciplinary practices.

TANGLED HUMAN WEBS AND VOICES

Yisi's extracurricular relationships continued to intertwine with her academic ones. In parallel with her interactions with *Voice*, her other "teacher," Zi'an, had started the online project Humans of East Lansing. As discussed in chapter 2, the project became a platform for an even more ambitious one with the intention of creating a transnational publication on the lives of Chinese study-abroad students.

Directly competing with *Voice,* Yisi and Zi'an decided to create and launch the publication together while imagining it as having a literary bent targeting sophisticated readers. Once again, Yisi imagined *Tian Nan* as a model, indexing how the genre framed her literacy practices as it was translated across contexts. The term "antecedent genre" (Jamieson 1975) is based on the idea that all texts are repurposed from other texts, and in this manner genres travel across contexts as they are repurposed, remediated, and rearticulated in local settings. This was true not only for the textual products but also the processes and practices surrounding the management and production of the publication. Both Zi'an and Yisi recruited friends as core members of the editorial board as they began to develop a business plan in Google Docs. Introduced to the application by She Zhang from *Voice* while collaboratively working on her writing course, Yisi repurposed it to develop a new publication that would compete with his. Suggestive of the ways she wove her various activities together, Yisi articulated that She Zhang and Zi'an shared key characteristics in their ability to form social relations and networks: "Both are intelligent, both know how to get along with people, both know how to make a magazine work, both know how to find different people, they are really similar."

Seeking a broad range of abilities and talents, Yisi and Zi'an recruited friends across the United States and China who could contribute in various capacities to the magazine. One of the people Yisi recruited was an online friend. Never having actually met in person, they became acquainted while producing a digital magazine on a post-bar (forum) dedicated to a Japanese film director. Now they would continue to work at a distance on a new international student magazine. Another of Zi'an's friends, a student by the name of Renee, had attended a Harvard summer business school program and would be starting New York University in the fall as a business major. Even though still in China, Yisi noted that Renee had a distinctly US style, as was evident in the English mixed into the business plan on Google Docs. As this sketch suggests, the production of the magazine involved the reweaving of various languages, actors, and technologies distributed across a transnational social field. Adding an additional dimension to the description of this scene in chapter 2, this account uncovers how multiple layers of histories, people, and practices otherwise invisible were densely knotted into everyday scenes of literacy. As the summer began and Yisi and Zi'an returned to China, the team set up a WeChat group and Skype meetings to plan their first issue, which was targeted for release in the beginning of the following year.

The project, however, was delayed as Zi'an began to expand Humans of East Lansing for a Chinese-speaking audience. He enlisted Yisi as the author for its first feature article, and her widely read interview of the local entrepreneur Baiwei Kong (see chapter 2) established Humans as the leading local Chinese international-student publication in the East Lansing area. It also established Yisi as a writer in the local community as she interviewed other entrepreneurs who began to request her services for their own business ventures. Driven by the desire to expand into larger markets, in February 2015, Zi'an launched a WeChat version of *Nebular* targeting a wider international-student readership, again making Yisi the lead writer for its premier cover story. The piece covered entrepreneur and rapper Zihao Song, who was a student at New York University and founder of various entrepreneurial ventures aimed at China's elite wealthy class. Widely read and well received, the post established *Nebular* as a leading international-student magazine. In a replay of events on a larger stage, the article garnered Yisi national attention.

One of Zihao Song's entrepreneurial ventures was a social media startup, Yeast, that had received $700,000 in venture capital and had an office in a high-end district in Beijing. The company targeted second-generation entrepreneurs with the aim of developing a social networking platform in order to foster innovation. After reading Yisi's story, Song recommended her to his twenty-something partners, who were also international students at Boston University and Sarah Lawrence in New York. Taking gap years to run their company in Beijing, they aggressively recruited her as a writer while offering her a 1 percent share in the company. Working from MSU, Yisi wrote marketing copy and slogans, business-related articles, and speeches. In one of her speeches for the company president, who was speaking at an end-of-year event to members of the Yeast community, she closed by reflecting that Yeast would provide a space to help "年轻人的梦想真正成为传奇" (young people realize their *dreams* [emphasis added]). Writing for the company, Yisi continued to build relationships, including with a manager who subsequently left to found a franchise of coworking spaces in high-rent districts throughout China. Trying to lure her from Yeast, he offered her a position while attempting to persuade her to return for full-time employment in Beijing. Though declining the offer, she accepted a two-week paid summer position from an information-technology company located in Guangzhou, which offered her full-time work upon graduation. In this fashion, Yisi continued to navigate complex social systems as disparate areas of her literate life were increasingly entangled. This process of networking, or knotworking, mediated her movement across a wider transnational social field.

Fluidly orchestrating her complex relationship webs, Yisi often referred to herself as putting on different masks. It was this ability that she had admired in close friends such as She Zhang and Zi'an. Toward the end of her first semester, she noted, "Today I and Zi'an talked about something. Like before he met like some common friends, he changed his face [waves hand over her face]. It is like he always shows a different face to different people. I said, 'Is there a button on your inside like you always control yourself by the button so you can really show the different face and different attitudes to the people?' Maybe I will add this idea to my fictions, something like the Man with 100 Faces." Yisi had a long-gestating idea about writing her own fictional story dramatizing the lives of students abroad. As the story evolved, it became highly imaginative and characterized various actors at MSU as various animals and creatures (e.g., a teacher who had a secret identity as a bird betrayed only by feathers she would leave after class). Grounded in a tradition of Chinese magical realism, the first chapter in her story was titled "Man with 100 Faces" and was about a man who was never able to show his true face without meeting an ill-fated end. As the protagonist in the story explained to a romantic interest, "It's not difficult to attract attention, the difficult thing is hiding yourself among people." The art of changing faces was one Yisi found herself routinely employing as she moved in and across various circles on and off campus.

CONCLUSION

Yisi's relationship webs formed part of a complex literacy sponsorscape that mediated the development of her disciplinary literacies and movement in and across educational imaginaries and geographies. Moreover, these processes were densely intertwined with her extracurricular literacies, as she continually wove and rewove multiple and disparate strands of activity into her literate life. Disrupting disciplinary and national container models, her case makes visible the need to situate literacy and learning beyond single moments, modalities, languages, genres, cultures, spaces, disciplines, and technologies. Because Yisi was entangled in a relational web with the participants in the previous case studies, such as Zi'an and even the Director (whose QQ forum she had joined), her story further illustrates how her relational networks were not only embedded in the interweaving of her academic and professional lifeworlds but also in the construction of broader transnational social fields.

It was this process that shaped a wider sociotechnical system, or spon-sorscape, mediating who moved, when they moved, how they moved, and to what effect. In the next chapter, we complicate the analysis by illustrating how these cultural practices not only afforded but also con-strained learning, literacy, and mobilities.

Notes

1.   These translations were completed by a research assistant.

4

LEARNING LORDS AND SCUMBAGS
Hidden Literacies and Learning Economies

I overheard Xiao Hong and Xiao Li chatting as they waited for our regular lab-hour meeting to begin. As I looked over, I saw both women's
gazes were directed at Gao, who sat across the aisle from the women
and was busy fussing with pages of worksheets scribbled with handwrit-
ten graphs, notes, and numbers. As I approached and chatted with him
briefly, I learned that he was reviewing his notes from an introductory
economics class, for which an exam was impending. Xiao Hong and
Xiao Li, two of the more talkative women in my classroom, obviously
noticed the same. As I walked back to the podium, I heard Xiao Li whis-
pering, "高肯定是个学霸,咱俩可得抱上他的大腿" (Gao has to be a "lord
of learning." We have to grab his thigh). Xiao Hong responded, "你确定
啊?我怎么觉得他看起来不像" (Are you sure? He doesn't look like one to
me). Gao, having overheard the exchange, turned around and smiled,
nodding knowingly as if to say, "I heard you." The women, both flus-
tered, giggled and chuckled. As I moved to the podium, the classroom
fell quiet. For the next minute or so, I found myself thinking about this
conversation. The Chinese these students speak is definitely not the
language I grew up speaking and still use. What is a "lord of learning"?
What does one do to "grab a thigh"? The meanings and social effects of
these strange terms evade me. Also, what triggered the brief exchange
among the students? What kind of social identities and relations were
enacted? (Fieldnotes, Oct. 18, 2013)

The above is a conversation I, Xiqiao, overheard in my bridge writing
course, Preparation for College Writing (PCW), comprised primarily of
Chinese international students. Though I myself am a Chinese speaker
who grew up in the northwest Gansu province and later moved to the
United States to receive my graduate degree in writing studies, I was
unfamiliar with the terms used by my post-nineties-generation students.
What was a "lord of learning" and what did it mean to "grab a thigh"?
As I gradually uncovered during my semester-long study involving

DOI: 10.7330/9781607327332.c004

thirty-six Chinese students, this demographic shared a rich set of hidden literacy practices and learning networks. In this chapter, I wish to take a closer look at the cultural logics underlying this underground literacy network and how it was intertwined with the construction of disciplinary and academic literacies. Whereas the previous chapter foregrounded how guanxi sponsored a student's academic development, in this chapter I complicate the analysis by uncovering how this cultural practice also constrained and restricted this process. Core to this focus is attention to networking and knotworking, or the complex tying and untying of people, texts, tools, actors, and objects. Bound up in a vast underground economy of literacies and learning, these practices shaped and were shaped by the plural geographies and messy circulations remaking the world grant university.

The study took place in the broader context of a PCW course and the online digital spaces where much of student learning happens. As a teacher/researcher in the study, my interests stemmed from some similarities between the students and myself, which provided me with distinct insights into their literacies. As an immigrant who came to the United States from China in my early twenties and is now a writing researcher, my proficiency in Mandarin and involvement in the local Chinese community helped me develop rapport with the students, which made it possible to explore their informal literacies. However, students often saw me as a cultural outsider due to my limited knowledge of digital technologies and Internet dialects central to their literacy practices. These differences served as rich points for interrogating the ways students leverage a translocal dispersal of discourses, narratives, and multilingual resources. To study these issues, I drew on classroom observations, field notes, and interviews with forty-five students enrolled in the two sections of a spring 2013 writing course. Using constant comparative methods, I sought to build a grounded theory of the students' transnational experiences, literacy practices, and identities. Thirty-six of the students were from China, while the rest were individual students from Saudi Arabia, Vietnam, and the United States. As articulated previously, this demographic portrait resembles the broader makeup of the student population enrolled in PCW. The focal students in this study were two student-identified experts, Yan and Lee, who were both nineteen years old at the time of the study and had just begun their freshmen year at the university. I selected them because of their central roles in students' grassroots literacies and guanxi networks.

I chose Yan because she was unwittingly identified by her peers as the expert in the classroom despite her sustained resistance to such an identity. Yan was from the commercial center of Shanghai, and she was persuaded by her parents to study finance despite her passion for early-childhood education. Like most of her peers, she was convinced that her parents would not finance her education if she chose a major they did not approve. In this fashion, she was entangled in wider economic and cultural regimes of filial piety. Her approach to the writing course was very much like her general approach to education at the university—adhering to the norm without caring too much about what she studied as long as she received decent grades. She paid attention; she took notes assiduously; she was careful with her assignments; and she worked for a good grade. At the beginning of the semester, I did not see Yan as an expert in the class. She started the semester sitting in a row in the far back; I could tell her attention during class was sporadic. She did not go out of her way to make new friends; in fact, she often intentionally distanced herself from other Chinese students. However, my observation was soon disrupted by the realization that Chinese students had quickly identified Yan as *the* expert in the class. The short time after the conclusion of each class was a precious small window in which students approached each other and me for clarifications on course-related issues. Yan was often the center of this bustling activity. One day after class, I noticed several students coalescing around Yan with their heads bent over their cell phones. Another one wielded her phone in the distance, yelling "我来了,加我,加我!" (I am coming! Add me! Add me!). As I approached, the congregants quietly dispersed. I later learned thirteen of the seventeen Chinese students in the class approached Yan within the first month of the semester, asking to befriend her on WeChat. When I asked her why her peers all came to her for help, she seemed genuinely puzzled and suggested that she did not go out of her way to do a good job in the course. In this fashion, Yan was at the center of a complex and overlapping network that spread across digital and face-to-face spaces.

Lee was a first-year student with a strong reputation in student circles for his god-like study skills. As articulated in chapter 1, approximately 60 percent of international students in incoming classes sought degrees in business and were enrolled in different sections of an introductory microeconomics course. This demographic overlap between the bridge writing and the economics classes led to the formation of informal peer groups that were sustained across courses and beyond, which created ample opportunities for relationship building. In a way, this demographic overlap illustrates the intricate ways in which the university functioned as a complex network, or part of a mobility system, mediating student trajectories. As I engaged students in conversations about academic expertise in and across disciplines, Lee's name quickly surfaced as a common point of reference. Lee, though not a student in my writing course, was widely known among the participants because of his exceptional performance in introductory economics. With half-baked gossip and lore circulating about this mythic figure in student social circles, Lee became known as a "god of learning," an Internet phrase used by students to describe someone who achieves highly in academic testing without seeming to make much effort. Entangled in a web of social relationships, to some, he was a dear friend who offered generous help for altruistic reasons; to others, membership in a highly exclusive inner circle Lee maintained was a desirable but unachievable privilege; to most, however, Lee was simply referred to as a mysterious god who seemed to achieve high scores with little effort. Through several private WeChat study groups and private tutorials he offered to his peers, Lee extended his academic expertise to help many peers succeed at the university. Signifying the significance of these study groups to the local community, multiple interview participants insisted that I "ha[d] to talk to Lee." With their assistance, I connected to him—a student volunteered to introduce me to Lee, and another helped me create a WeChat account. Although Lee accepted my friendship request and responded positively to my proposal to discuss his experiences, he also expressed the wish to remain anonymous. I later learned he was concerned that others might perceive his WeChat activities as "against university rules." Therefore, I never met Lee in person, and interviews with him took place through WeChat.

As we discuss across all chapters, our complex positioning in the study, simultaneously teachers, researchers, and confidants, indexes how international students were institutionally located as they strategically engaged in underground literacies that challenged and subverted higher education structures. In the course of three months, I was able to interview Lee on multiple occasions to discuss his first-year experiences, especially his activities on WeChat. With the permission of students participating in his WeChat study groups, I was also able to collect chatting records that documented several private tutorial sessions he offered.

This chapter details the complex ways in which Yan and Lee were entangled in complex relationship webs that afforded and constrained both their own and their peers' identities, literacies, and learning. I further provide a fine-grained account of how students' guanxi practices were deeply intertwined with an imagined world (Appadurai 1996) of conducting business in China. In this fashion, multiple and competing strands of activity became densely entangled in the reconstruction of the social and geographic landscape.

REMIXING DISCOURSES OF "GOOD STUDENTS"

Circulating across a transnational social field are informal educational theories of academic achievement, expertise, and identities. Woven together by Chinese international students to formulate a hybrid discourse, these theories shape and are shaped by social identities and trajectories as students traverse the HEI landscape. Most notably among these translocal discourses are (a) a Western discourse of "geek culture" as embodied and propagated by popular television shows like *The Big Bang Theory*, (b) a Chinese discourse of academic achievement embodied in students' prior schooling experiences, and (c) ambivalent celebration and critique of Chinese educational culture as satirized in a popular Internet meme. Students mobilize these discourses as they continually enlist and are enlisted into a stabilized-for-now social matrix.

Western Geek Culture

Students draw on popular US television programs as the basis of a "tool kit" they use to identify and recognize types of youth. Many students mentioned that shows like *Gossip Girl* served as their guide into teen fashion and US social scenes; many students found their career aspirations from criminal dramas like *CSI* and hospital dramas like *House*. Of particular relevance here is the popularity of *The Big Bang Theory*, in which the geekiness of four physicists is contrasted with Penny's (a waitress) social skills and commonsensical approach to life's problems. The show's comic effects arise from an exaggerated portrayal of exceptionally intelligent young scientists and their eccentricities, including their unattractive physical appearances, their failure to grasp many routine aspects of daily life, their odd, eccentric, and often wildly inappropriate behaviors, and their ultimate failures in initiating and maintaining romantic relationships. However, these exaggerations often go uncritiqued by the show's viewers in China, who watch them in part for entertainment and in part to learn about US culture and the English language. In our interviews, many students drew on the experiences of watching the show to discuss why and how they recognized certain students as "geniuses" or "lords of learning." When I asked a group of students to identify the "lord" of the class, one male student was nominated, while others explained,

XIAO HONG: 他看起来就是学霸啊,你看他的发型,都是朝天的。我一看到他就想到谢耳朵。

(He looks like a lord to me. Look at his hair, all his hair is pointing upwards. He reminds me so much of Sheldon [a character in *The Big Bang Theory*].)

XIAO LI: 对啊对啊,不都说美国人里的学霸都是那种很邋遢的,穿着破破烂烂的衣服,你看路上那头发也不梳的, 那种一定是学霸。

(Yes, yes. Isn't it true that American "lords of learning" are the ones that are poorly groomed and unkempt. Those who walk on campus without having combed their hair are typically lords of learning.)

XIAO QIANG: 你别看他上课老是很瞌睡的,但是人就是有一种气场,武林高手一样的。一睁眼眼神凌厉地跟刀一样。而且你不觉得人说话和我们学渣都不在一个频道吗?

(Even though he always looks sleepy during class, he has an aura with him, just like a Kung Fu Master. The second he opens his eyes, he is sharp like a knife. Don't you feel like, when he speaks he is not on the same channel with the rest of us scumbags?)

(Focus group interview, December 13, 2013)

In these commentaries, the discourse of *good student* starts with a clause about physical appearance. A male student's unkempt hairstyle is often interpreted as the side effect of an absolute commitment to learning. Similar comments have been made about female students' appearances. For example, the absence of makeup and expensive accessories on a female student is often interpreted as signs of someone's commitment to school work. In many ways, Yan certainly fit this stereotypical view. Slightly overweight in her own opinion, Yan was not very confident about her appearance. Unlike many of her peers, Yan was not very comfortable with taking and posting selfies on social networking sites because she was concerned about others' perceptions of her. She kept her straight hair tied up into a ponytail most of the time and wore comfortable sweaters and jeans. She once jokingly said that those who dressed up to attend a class did not behave like "normal students." On a related note, other students observed,

JING: 每次去BCC 上经济都觉得, 都感觉学校风气太差了。你看看那些大冷天穿着黑丝,短裙,拎着个小包包,连支铅笔都装不下,别说课本了。她们根本不是来上课的好吗。

(Every time I attend my economics class in BCC (Business Building), I feel the school spirit has been damaged (by certain international students). Look at those who wear black pantyhose and mini-skirts to class. They carry such tiny handbags that won't even hold pencils, let alone textbooks.

They are not here to study at all!)

LI: 是啊,我上次遇到一个女生平时上课从来没见过,那天打着呵欠说,上课要起来好早,洗澡要半小时,梳头要半小时,化妆要半小时,好辛苦哦。我真是给她跪了,她是来上课还是来走秀啊。

(That's right. I met a girl the other day, who never showed up for class. She was yawning and saying that she had to get up too early for the class; she needs half an hour for a shower, half an hour for her hair, and another half hour for makeup. What a lot of work [sarcastically]. I kneel before her [a popular Internet phrase to express sarcasm towards bizarre behaviors that are hard to believe]. Is she coming to learn or to walk in a fashion show?)

XIQIAO: 那学霸不可能美美的吗?

(Can't lords also be beautiful?)

JING: 学霸都还是很朴素的好吧,主要学习太用功,哪里有那么多时间化妆和花心思买包包上。

(Lords usually take a plain and simple approach. [It is] mainly because they are hardworking. Where would they find the time and energy to wear makeup and to shop for luxury bags?)

(Focus group interview, December 16, 2013)

Indeed, Yan also stressed the importance of looking and acting like a "student," not someone who is getting ready for a fashion show. In addition, both Yan and Lee were very explicit about the fact that their families barely managed to gather the funds to send them abroad for college. The message was clear—they did not have the financial means for luxury items as did some students on campus. Embedded in these discourses are intricate ways in which students weave a transnationally distributed web of meanings into a translocal understanding of what it means to be a good student. To "feel" like an expert, one pulls off a socially situated identity (Gee 2005, 22) through embodied performance, including ways of acting (e.g., doing the right thing, being socially awkward), thinking, and valuing (e.g., good grades and being attractive are competing enterprises that exist in conflict with each other). Students draw from the hybridized discourse as a toolkit made up of these values and attitudes, together with words (e.g., *lords* and *scumbags*), imageries (e.g., Sheldon, bird's-nest hairstyle), and objects (e.g., luxury handbags and black pantyhose). This toolkit is dynamic, emergent, contested, and continually being reconstituted as students weave and are woven into complex semiotic systems.

THE CHINESE EDUCATIONAL SYSTEM

Another discourse that gets woven into students' identities-in-the-making is linked to a hypercompetitive educational culture that emphasizes rote memorization, standardized tests, and ranking. Students label and identify each other based on evidence gathered from observing others' behaviors in and after classes. To many, the fact that Yan often furiously took notes by hand was read as a marker of her devotion to school. During our focus-group interview, Jing and Ya expressed their surprise that I did not see Yan as the "best student" in the class.

> JING: 她明显就是啊。一看就是那种好学生,老师在上面说,她就下边不停地在记笔记。那起码说明人家听得懂老师在说什么啊。
>
> (It is so obvious that she is [a good student]. She looks the part. As the professor keeps talking *from above*, she keeps taking notes *from below*. This [note taking] at least means she understands what the professor [you] is talking about.)

> YA: 我第一次去找她借笔记简直被惊到了。真的好多而且好整齐的。像我们这种学渣,最多就最后老师的作业ppt照张照片,也不一定会去看。可是人家是在用手记笔记啊。哪里还有人那么认真的?
>
> (I was shocked when I saw her notes for the first time. [She had] so many notes, all written in neat handwriting and well organized. The most we "scumbags" do is to snap a picture of the teacher's last PowerPoint slide with homework assignment on it. Sometimes I don't even review it afterwards. But she takes her notes by hand. Where do you find students as conscientious as that nowadays?)
>
> (Focus group interview, December 16, 2013)

These commentaries drive home the idea that students' theories were indexical of a traditional, teacher-centered educational culture in China that operates around a direct transmission model of learning and instruction. For example, Jing used two spatial prepositions to mark the geographic feature of a typical Chinese classroom, with the teacher situated in the front the classroom, standing behind a podium and lecturing to the students from "above." Students, often seated in rows of connected seats in a large classroom of forty to seventy, constitute the silent mass that receives information from "below." Such socially constructed spatial terms also take on metaphorical meaning, pointing to the centralized, authoritative role teachers play in classrooms. Most students are "lazy" in comparison to Yan because they are satisfied with a picture of a professor's PowerPoint, knowing they might never return to it. The fact that Yan's exhaustive notetaking is seen as model behavior is telling of a mindset students have internalized—effective learning entails recording and reviewing lecture notes, which embodies the transmission of knowledge from the teacher to the students. More importantly, Yan's ability to take extensive notes is not only indicative of a careful attitude toward learning but also a superior capacity with English, which allows her to have a fuller mastery of course materials and tasks.

The strategic ways students identify experts is further accompanied by several attempts to gauge a student's mastery of course-related materials. Many mentioned that they started approaching Yan about insignificant questions just to get a sense of her as a "person." The fact that she was willing and able to provide help that "points one to the right direction" became a piece of gossip that was spread in existing friend circles. Though such processes, guanxi relations mediated the complex flow of discourses. Yue, for example, said she encouraged her friend to befriend Yan soon after she received Yan's good-faith help. Last but not least, the intensity with which students approached Yan in succession was followed by a small episode in class, when I commented on the strength of a draft Yan had just submitted. I did not realize the effect of the public commendation until it was brought to my attention during an interview.

> XIAO MING: 我都根本搞不清楚project two 是干嘛的。结果老师上课不是表扬了她的文章吗?老师肯定不会表扬学习差的吧。
>
> (I didn't even understand what project two was all about. The teacher [you] praised her draft in class. A teacher will surely not praise a student who does poorly.)
>
> XIQIAO: 那你有去问她要文章来看看吗?
>
> (Did you ask her for the draft of her essay?)
>
> XIAO MING: 没有,但是我就加了她微信,在微信上有什么不懂的就问她。
>
> (No, but I added her on WeChat. Whenever I had questions, I would ask her.)
>
> XING: 对对,我也是那时候加的她。老师上课有问题,都是她回答。老师肯定也喜欢这样积极的人。
>
> (Yep, that was when I added her. Whenever the teacher had a question, Yan was the one to answer it. A teacher surely likes a student as active [as Yan]).
>
> (Focus group interview, December 16, 2013)

This public recognition, what I perceived as a routine pedagogical move to further illustrate my expectations for an assignment, was interpreted by many not only as my recognition of Yan's ability but also as my personal preference for her as a student. What is really interesting here is that students did not consult Yan or her work in order to revise their own essays. What matters more was that they now had a weighted indicator of Yan's status as an expert in the class. Several students drew on their experiences with teachers in Chinese schools to argue that a teacher would only favor a student who does good work and tests well and that a teacher's preference and recognition are instrumental in determining a student's overall experience with schooling.

As these commentaries make clear, students draw on previous experiences with Chinese educational culture to rationalize their identification of experts. In an educational culture still largely organized around teacher authority and driven by rigorous standardized testing, expertise is dependent upon assiduous note-taking, undivided attention during lectures, and thorough absorption of information. In these scenarios, literacy practices, such as note-taking, and pedagogical ones, such as teacher commendation, become discursive artifacts embodying values and beliefs about what makes one a successful student. As these discourses get reenacted in the context of a US classroom, they bring into convergence two cultures and systems, often creating tensions and sometimes offering resolutions. Entangled in how students learn to invent the university, their educational histories and discourses are rewoven into new contexts.

A Learning Quadric

Indexical of student status is a rich set of labels students use to locate themselves within an underground educational learning economy. Of particular interest in this mix of translocal discourse is an Internet meme (Figure 4.1) that satirizes a dominant social discourse of academic achievement in contemporary Chinese society. Satires and parodies are particularly suited for unmasking social languages (Bakhtin 1981), as they serve to invert, amplify, and reaccent meanings and underlying power structures. An artifact with no obvious origin, the graph first became popular on Weibo (a Chinese microblog platform) and quickly went viral. This quadratic, arranged on two scales, has been used as a way of categorizing learners based on two capacities. On the vertical scale, those who score poorly are mapped into the lower half, while those who score well are mapped onto the top. The horizontal scale, from left to right, represents an incremental increase of levels of effort. The intersection of these two scales, therefore, creates a mapping scheme that separates learners according to different intellectual capacities and levels of effort. The lower-left corner, for example, is designated for 学渣

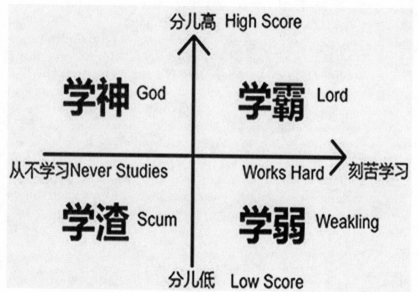

Figure 4.1. Internet meme satirizing academic achievement

(scumbag of learning)—those who spend little time studying and score poorly. The upper-right corner represents 学霸 (lord of learning), referring to those who are always studying and score well. The lower-right corner refers to 学弱 (weakling of learning), those who spend much time studying but score poorly; the upper-left corner refers to 学神 (god of learning), those who seem to never study but score exceptionally well.

In a culture that heavily emphasizes grades as the sole factor in determining the social standing of a student, lord and god are social positions students aspire to but often find hard to achieve. As the majority of my students humbly admit, they are scumbags who perform inadequately but aspire for higher levels of achievement and efficiency.

At the time of the study, these phrases had become a part of students' everyday lingo through mass distribution on social networking sites. The meme became a contagious pattern of cultural information that was quickly and widely passed through digital media, directly generating and shaping the mindsets and significant forms of behavior and actions of college students (Knobel and Lankshear 2007). Through multiple remixes, the meme triggered a whirlwind of social conversations that point to the particular mindsets, power, and processes associated with academic expertise. Some commentators argue that such phrases have become new testing-based "class labels" that may harm the "equal, harmonious, and friendly" relationships among students (Xian 2014);

others see the popularity of these phrases as the result of students using humor to release tension inherent in an intensely competitive "examination-oriented educational system" (Lin 2014) or to celebrate "lord of learning" as exuding positive energy (Yu 2014); others have cautioned that unreflective celebration of "lords" may create conditions for educational inequality by encouraging schools to devote limited educational resources to a small number of students who test well and validate parents' unhealthy impulse to put children in more after-class tutoring classes and add homework (Chen 2014). The array of stances toward these terms signals ways they are bound up in a dynamic and contested field, as they are continually taken up, resisted, and transformed.

In close relationship to the meme is another Internet phrase, "抱大腿 (*grab a thigh*)." Yisi was described in chapter 3 as taking up this meme, and students commonly used the phrase to describe how a "scumbag" strategically initiated friendship with a "lord" in order to receive help. The origin of this popular Internet term is a matter of controversy. Some argue *World of Warcraft* players invented the term to describe how players team up in strategic ways to move ahead in the queue to enter a game session. For others, the term was used to express fans' disappointment in LeBron James's decision to leave the Cleveland Cavaliers for the Miami Heat of the National Basketball Association in 2007. Following Michael Jordan's criticism of Lebron's decision to play with, not against, strong players, Chinese fans raised scathing commentary on his lack of sportsmanship, describing his decision as an act of "grabbing a thigh." In these scenarios, a "thigh" refers to an unwarranted advantage one does not deserve if judged solely on one's merit, be it the position in a queue, an opportunity to win the championship, or other social goods, such as fame. "Grabbing a thigh" describes the ingratiating acts taken by someone in order to be under the shelter of someone powerful, with the goal of achieving success, upward social mobility, and benefits otherwise unachievable. The phrase has also been used to criticize various forms of social injustice, ranging from a starlet scoring a role in major production to someone in the office courting a favor from a superior through flattery. Entangled in discourses of social and class struggle in modern China, the phrase indexes an underground mobility system used to navigate regimes of practice.

The term has been adapted by students to satirize a common practice—low-achieving students seek the help of good students to better their academic standing. As manifested in many student-initiated activities, the prevalent invocation of this practice among Chinese students

constructs a dynamic scene of collaborative learning that has both positive and negative implications. For example, it is typical for students to
create and maintain course-themed, digitally mediated study groups
on WeChat and QQ. On these online platforms, students may discuss
challenging concepts, prepare for quizzes and exams, and offer and
receive help on homework. It might unfold in private tutorial sessions
organized by students during which a lord unpacks course materials in
accessible language to scumbags. Collaboration can also transgress into
the realm of cheating, as students illegally acquire and trade answers to
exam questions across sections and semesters.

Enacting these literacy practices situates students in a transnational
circuit in which they are exposed to narratives, social expectations, cultural values, and educational experiences not confined to a single social
system. As I have observed above, the learning space is infiltrated by
"wider, real, imagined worlds of conflicting identity formations, creative
cultural hybridities . . . and extensive microcosms of everyday life at
multiple geographical scales" (Soja 2004, x). The formulation of a dual
frame of reference is a process filled with uncertainties and crises during which discourses and practices embedded in home and host societies are mobilized and reconfigured. It is this orchestration of activity
that mediates ways students invent disciplinary and academic identities
as they traverse a global eduscape. In what follows, I unpack how these
processes were deeply embedded in Yan's mobile literacies and disciplinary learning.

IDENTITY AS SITES OF NEGOTIATION

Yan's case critically illustrates that these social-identity types were not
monolithic or totalizing but were instead deeply contested as students
aligned and positioned themselves in relation to wider cultural tropes
in varied ways. Indeed, despite her familiarity with the discourses that
have informed her peers' theorization of academic experts and the literacy practices revolving around them, Yan resisted them by intentionally distancing herself from her Chinese peers in subtle ways that would
not be interpreted as rude. A focus on these tensions illustrate wider
ideologies and belief systems underlying these key conceptual and cultural tropes. Yan was the only Chinese student who made a point to get
to know the few domestic students enrolled in the course. She sought
friendship from Anna, a domestic student, after she was placed at the
same table with Anna during a peer-review workshop. In addition to sitting close to Anna and trying to engage her in conversations, Yan also

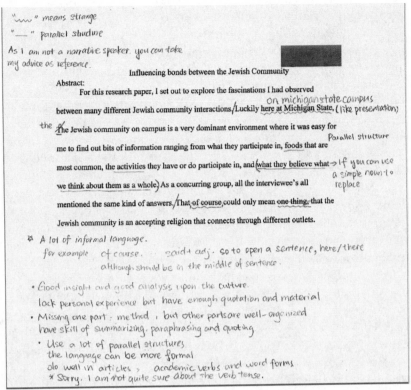

Figure 4.2. Peer review

asked me to keep assigning her to the same peer-review group. When I asked her about this active agenda, she shrugged, "I don't necessarily see how Chinese students can help me when it comes to writing. We don't see each other's problems." Even as she maneuvered to navigate these cultural and linguistic boundaries, her collaboration with Anna during the peer-review exercise (Figure 4.2) did not seem productive or rewarding.

In this peer review, Yan carefully noted issues she observed in Anna's essay, ranging from analytical depth and organization to local arrangement concerns. Even though she did not feel confident about her grasp of English grammar, she thought her review would be of value. Yan felt demoralized when she discovered Anna brushed off her comments as irrelevant. None of her recommendations for global and local changes were reflected in Anna's revision. In the meantime, she revised her own essay based on Anna's feedback, which focused on surface concerns and grammatical errors. After this encounter,

Yan seemed to retreat from her bold endeavors and began to befriend Chinese students. Although such social adventures might have helped Yan develop adaptive skills important in the process of immigrant uprooting and resettlement, they often came with significant social and emotional cost (Suárez-Orozco and Suárez-Orozco 2001, 191). Yan was concerned that her efforts to socialize with US students might be read as "trying too hard" or being unfaithful to her cultural and ethnic roots. In a transnational context, where one's sense of self is constantly crafted and recrafted in reactions to how the self is mirrored in the social milieu, framed by both the dominant society and the transnational social field, it is especially challenging to achieve a transcultural identity in which one creatively fuses aspects of two or more cultures rather than having to choose one (192). In this fashion, Yan was entangled in contradictory and disjunctive threads of a densely knotted social system. Ensnared in these messy circulations and plural geographies, she was unable to fully take part in domestic student life yet also found herself on the periphery of Chinese student circles.

Yan slowly returned to the circle of Chinese friends after feeling rejected by Anna. However, Yan never truly felt comfortable with the expert identity almost imposed on her by her peers. To her, being bombarded with questions was not only annoying but confounding. What was really puzzling was that her classmates seemed to have no grasp of what was happening in the classroom. Instead of reading a project description I distributed in class and online, students resorted to Yan to provide explanations in a language they understood. These explanations ranged from basic questions about due dates, length requirements, or submission guidelines to more complex issues with assignment completion, as revealed in the following WeChat conversation.

2013/10/07 22:20

XING: Is this Yan?

YAN: uh huh

XING: Can you tell me what our homework is, in words [Chinese] . . .

YAN: consent and question list

XING: Can I take a look at your template... I will just take a look, I won't copy it.

YAN: .. [to get the template] log onto angel.
Click open the last ppt in agenda [folder].

XING: . . . ok . . .

XING: Just upload those two and we are done?

YAN: Ye[s]

YAN: [Ye]s

2013/10/7 23:22

XING: . . . are you there?

YAN: ?

XING: .

XING: I still want to take a look at your homework . . . is that ok . . .

2013/10/8 0:08

YAN: My roommate is asleep; I have turned off
my laptop.

XING: okay then. Is yours exactly the same with
the template?

YAN: You just fill in the blanks.

YAN: I made some slight changes.

YAN: It is roughly the same.

YAN: Work hard~

XING: . . .

XING: How long did it take you?

YAN: 20 minutes, including printing.

XING: . . . alright, I'll get to work!

When I asked Yan to explain what happened
in this short exchange, her face twisted with
mild annoyance. Xing initiated this exchange
as his first attempt to actually "talk" to Yan on
WeChat. Yan explained she sensed Xing's hesitation in his use of ellipses at the beginning and

end of sentences, as if he knew that he was making an inappropriate request. By using an extended ellipsis " . . .," which in Chinese writing indicates omission or pauses that puncture speech, Xing, as Yan argues, "肯定有点不好意思 (must have felt slightly embarrassed)" and was "求帮助求同情啊" (begging for help and sympathy). Xing's embarrassment was probably rooted in his lack of preparation, given the fact that I had verbally explained the assignment and posted detailed instructions on the course website. Indeed, Xing asked questions that could be easily answered if he read and understood the instructions. When I asked Xing and other students, however, I was slightly surprised to discover the extent to which they struggled with the procedures, practices, and processes I considered normal. To most of these students, English is still a matter of "心痛又头痛" (heartaches and headaches). Xing, for example, says,

> 我每次都还是想认真看看你给我们发的那种一张纸一张纸,可是每次看不到两行就觉得头痛,还不如直接问同学。

(I knew I should read the "one-page thingies" [one-page project descriptions I created] you gave us, but I always got a headache a couple of lines into it. It is much easier to just ask a classmate.) (Personal communication, December 14, 2013)

Headache, as used here and in general, describes a state of frustration. While cognizant of the fact that they need to improve their English, students struggle with the reality of having to spend twice the time to read half as much text written in English. Similar concerns are prevalent in trying to follow class discussions. One student described this concern:

> 不知道为什么我听英文就很容易走神,一般刚上课还能听明白老师在讲什么,可是到后头经常是忽然就发现自己走神10来分钟了,再想听就再也跟不上了。

(I don't know why, but my mind easily wanders off when I hear someone speaking English. I could usually follow the teacher at the beginning of the class, but as the class progresses, I often caught myself in the middle of a daydream. I could never catch the flow of the conversation.) (Personal communication, December 17, 2013)

Against the backdrop of these struggles, it is not hard to understand why Yan's ability to comprehend and grasp English is a valuable asset. Students like Xing saw her as an agent who could translate and broker course activities in ways that bridged their own and the teacher's expectations. In the first exchange, Xing seemed interested in clarifying the nature and expectations of the assignment. When Yan pushed back on his request to "look at" her homework, Xing left the conversation. Xing returned almost an hour later to again request to "take a look," with a stronger sense of hesitation on his part. As Yan gently refused again, Xing inquired about the amount of time Yan took to complete her work. Yan mentioned,

其实每次有作业要due之前就很多人问，半夜才开始做,微信群上就每个半夜最活跃. 我也觉得很烦的。很简单的作业吗,怎么总是要看我怎么做的。可是也不好伤了人的面子吧,总是要给人家台阶下的。

(It is often the night before a due date that many people start asking questions. They don't start until midnight. The [class] WeChat group was always most active at midnight. I found that so annoying. Some assignments are so easy. I don't get why people always want to see mine. However, I can't make him lose his "face." You have to "give [him] a ladder.") (Personal communication, November 14, 2013)

Negotiating these relationships was a complex process, as the academic and cultural systems became densely intertwined. To Yan, these exchanges could be annoying if only for the fact that most people asked the same questions, questions that "lack[ed] substance" (没营养的问题). As a matter of fact, it was out of a concern for her own time that she created the class WeChat group. An important cultural assumption arises here from Yan's comment: the notion that one should not reject others' requests in a blunt fashion because such acts might lead to the loss of "face" for the other party. Scholars have offered various definitions of face (面子), such as self-image and social standing (Cheng 1986); "respect, pride, and dignity . . . as the consequence of [one's] social achievement (Leung and Chan 2003); or "image and status within a social structure" (Cardon and Scott 2003). Both Xing and Yan were aware of the fact that his request breached ethical boundaries—asking to copy others' answers (as seen in Xing's hesitation and Yan's refusal to comply with this request). However, Yan did not make her disapproval of Xing's transgression explicit. Rather, she phrased her indirect rejection in ways that preserved Xing's dignity and spared him any shame that might result from disapproval. According to Qi Xiaoying (2011), an individual in China is often socially obligated to give, maintain, and save the face of another in order to make sure the person is able to perform a role and maintain a position in their social circumstances and location (12). "Giving someone a ladder" is a cultural practice of saving and giving face. That is, Yan created an excuse or pretext to avoid the embarrassment encoded by the awkward position. When internalized at a social level, practices such as these are means of enforcing control in interactions with the goal of ultimately promoting conformity and creating social harmony (14). In multiple scenarios like this one, Yan involuntarily and reluctantly took on the roles of translator, mediator, and bridge, probably out of an internalized appreciation of her role in a social network of translocal students and a felt sense of social obligation toward harmony and conformity.

Another way *face* (see also chapter 3) plays a role in the dynamic learning scene lies in the fact that most students chose to approach Yan in private chats with questions about the course, even after she had created a group chat that included fourteen of the seventeen Chinese students in the class. In the public space of the group chat, exchanges revolved around low-stakes inquiries, such as due dates and homework check, announcements for social events, generic greetings for special occasions, advertising messages for student-owned businesses, and resource building (e.g., information for class registration, finding restaurants, etc.). Students often approached Yan individually through private chat when they had genuine concerns about an assignment.

Ming was one of the "regular" inquirers on Yan's contact list. Ming's exchanges with Yan were often a mix of voice and text messages, often sent out while she was on the run between places on campus. The following exchange is illustrative of a broader pattern of students' exchanges with Yan in which Ming does not engage Yan in substantive *discussions* around complex issues of writing but rather works to acquire information from Yan. When I asked Ming why she approached Yan in private, she explained,

> 有的问题是我自己听不懂,或者上课没去,我觉得别人应该都懂吧?要是贴群里别人还说这谁这么渣。

> ([I had] some questions because I did not understand [the teacher's instructions] or because I was absent. Others would not have a problem, I assume? People are going to wonder "Who is that scumbag?" if I posted these questions in the group.) (Personal communication, December 17, 2013)

Although Ming did not reference face explicitly in this comment, the underlying shame of her incompetence was present. Ming also assumed others' knowledge and the possibility of being judged as too much of a "scumbag," used here to describe how a strong façade one builds up easily crumbles in the face of the smallest challenges. As David Yau-fai Ho (1976) argues, face, in Chinese society, is to be protected from being lost because of the "demoralizing repercussions" of losing one's social standings (871). The loss of face is often the result of a public demonstration of inadequate performance. A student's decision to approach Yan privately, in this line of thinking, is an attempt to avoid potential public performance that might show that student in less than flattering light. Given the nature of these inquiries, much is at stake with regards to failure, shame, and inadequate performance, as the following episode illustrates:

YAN: you start with title, and then abstract, introduction, method, findings, conclusion, reference.

YAN: you can leave out the reference section for now.

YAN: to be honest, I don't know the specifics. I just followed the format. I don't even think this is a research paper.

MING: how long does it have to be?

YAN: I followed guidelines she gave us on Tuesday, but I don't know how to write it, because my paper is more and more like a narrative. It doesn't look like a research paper. Let's wait and see what happens. I am going to revise with feedback from others and the teacher. Let's wait and see.

10/17/2013 0:50

MING: Yan, what is an abstract?

YAN: It's a summary of the entire essay.

MING: How is a conclusion different from an abstract?

YAN: conclusion is just a summary. An abstract is like mini essay. You put everything in there.

10/17/2013 0:58

MING: You know I didn't go to class Tuesday. I am confused. What do we do next? How do we write the introduction? What about the middle part? I have no idea what is going on.

MING: I can't find the ppt from Tuesday. What is the format? I am completely lost right now. What is Method?

YAN: Method is basically what you did to do the research.

YAN: I am not sure about that though. I wrote it based on my guesses.

MING: Are we using the format found in the reading?

YAN: 12 point font, double spaced, three pages. Abstract is not included in the three pages. You need to put it on a separate page.

MING: I don't think I did the right thing, but I am going to turn it in anyways. Is there anything else we should watch out for?

YAN: I give up. I am printing it out.

Ming asked for clarification on several issues concerning an assignment. In this assignment, the class discussed various genres of disciplinary writing, and students were asked to write a short social-scientific research report on a cultural issue of their choice. In the class preceding this exchange, I drew on a sample essay to discuss various writerly moves a social-scientific researcher might take and explored the rhetorical exigencies behind such decisions. I also shared a PowerPoint that included a brief description of the forms and functions of each section. Ming's absence from that meeting seemed to have motivated her inquiry. In this exchange, Yan responded to each of Ming's clarifying questions, explaining the forms (reflected in Ming's concern with format) and functions of each section. Several layers of translation were involved in this effort. Chinese and English terms referring to genres of writing often mirror each other, as Yan drew on concepts developed in her Chinese writing to explain the English counterparts. For example, she used 总结 (summary) to mirror *conclusion*, and she used 小作文 (mini essay) and 缩写 (abridgement) to explain *abstract*. In equally important ways, Yan drew on her understanding of a research paper, as informed both by her previous experiences writing research papers and by reading the sample essay, to not only comprehend but also interrogate the assignment. To her, this type of writing did not seem like a "research paper." In addition, she translated my explanations from English to Chinese to help guide Ming in the right direction. For one thing, her explanation of the function of methods section is almost a direct translation from mine during class.

Common to such efforts to make sense of new academic concepts is a stance of ambiguity and uncertainty. As Yan made clear on several occasions during this short exchange, she was not "sure" whether she was doing the right thing, and her draft was based on "guesses" and awaited further revision in anticipation of peer and teacher feedback. However, Ming did not participate in the construction of emergent understanding because she seemed to take Yan's words as a guiding principle for her own writing. To Yan, however, this lack of reciprocity was frustrating. In her own words,

我其实更希望是有人跟你讨论一下作业。我很希望有时候也有人跟我说我想得不对。那样起码我也能有提高。

(I wish someone came to me to discuss an assignment. I wish someone would tell me I was wrong. That way, I would at least have a chance to improve.) (Personal communication, December 27, 2013)

But the students never did challenge her. Indeed, of a small number of substantive exchanges in which students did want to discuss an assignment, only one instance involved the active input and critical perspective of another student. In all other cases, information flew in one direction and was interrupted by frequent protests from Yan, suggesting her uncertainty about the teacher's expectations. Even though others looked at her as an expert, Yan often felt inadequate and unfulfilled in that role. In the end, she argued that being the "expert" did not help her grow as a writer. Aside from the fact that she felt liked and respected by many students, Yan felt she wasted much time offering time-consuming and tedious explanations to her peers. In this fashion, students were complexly positioned in this social network, as the collective mitigated against the development of literacies and academic identities. While guanxi exchanges are often used to accumulate social capital, in this instance Yan elected not to leverage her own position within this social field. The next case serves as a contrastive example.

THE MAKING OF AN EXPERT

In contrast to Yan's passive stance in extending help to her classmates, Lee actively built a network of resources and relationships to allow others and himself to succeed at the university. This process allowed him to develop his disciplinary literacies. Moreover, this process spun off into nonacademic contexts as he accumulated social and material capital. Although he recognized that his mediocre TOEFL score stopped him from joining a more prestigious university, Lee did not see his lack of a stronger facility in English as detrimental to his academic success. Negotiating an English-language regime inscribed into university life, his genuine interest in economics gave rise to a proactive approach to learning, which was marked by his active efforts to marshal diverse, multilingual resources. Lee maintained a repertoire of recreational and academic reading experiences, including best-selling books that popularize financial theories (e.g., 货币战争/ *War of Currencies*)," translated versions of textbook and scholarly work (e.g., *Principles of Economics*), and business sections in mainstream news outlets (e.g., CNN Money and Yahoo Finance). While Lee relied primarily on Chinese, he was willing to tackle English texts to get a better grasp of challenging academic content.

> 有些概念用英语讲出来就是比较难懂。就算我百度它,也就是找到一个中文的术语,你再百度又来一堆术语。最后你就是对着一圈互相解释彼此的术语互相,你还是不明白。学科里不管中文还是英文都一样。

> (There are certain concepts that are hard to understand when they are delivered in English. Even if I Baidu it [Chinese equivalent of google search engine], I just get a Chinese jargon. Oftentimes, I would end up with an expanding web of jargons that seem to go in circles, as they seem to explain each other. You still don't get it. But [the struggle] is the same [when learning academic content] in Chinese or English.) (Personal communication, November 4, 2013)

A multilingual approach allowed Lee to capitalize on the affordances of all available languages in his effort to grapple with challenging disciplinary modes of thinking and reasoning. In addition to translating jargon, Lee constantly consulted Chinese resources. When studying aggregate demand, Lee was not able to fully grasp the idea despite much effort. After hours searching online for cases and definitions, he finally discovered a video lecture by a Chinese scholar.

> 看完那个讲座之后我真的有豁然开朗的感觉。我也不明白为什么,美国教授也讲了很多,但是我就是不懂得。他说的所有的词我都知道,但是我就是跟不上他的思路。我觉得着可能是因为美式中式思维还是不同。

> (After watching the video, I had an epiphany. For reasons I still don't understand, I couldn't understand it when an American professor tried to explain it to me. I know all the words he used, but I couldn't follow his reasoning. I think that has something to do with the different ways of thinking between Chinese and Americans.) (Personal communication, November 4, 2013)

This anecdote illustrates the manifold challenges international students face. Learning in the discipline is complex and involves layers of translation, inquiry, and articulation. Beyond language barriers, students learn to decode disciplinary jargon, modes of inquiry, and genres. Weaving together different social and linguistic resources, Lee developed a repository of strategies, resources, and tools that boded well for his success. Furthermore, Lee often extended a helping hand to his fellow students, who took a less proactive approach to similar struggles. In comparison to Yan, Lee welcomed these exchanges. In the following, Lee shared an example of how he helped fellow students make sense of

---

Aggregate Demand and Supply
Classical Version

- Relationship between demand for goods and price level
- $Y^d = MV/P$
- Aggregate supply is simply Y^s as determined by productivity and the labor market
- Velocity is stable of, at least, predictable
- **$Y^d = MV/P = Y^s$**

Figure 4.3. PowerPoint slide on aggregate demand

course materials. The conversation revolves around a PowerPoint slide (Figure 4.3) presented in class.

XX ~ 19:35:58 这个呢

(What about this slide?)

Lee 19:36:22 他这里说的是古典二分法

(Here he is talking about the classical dichotomy.)

Lee 19:38:55 分割名义的和实际的 即货币理论和经济理论。假设 V 是稳定或者可预测的,你可以看作常量。。同样YS 也是常量。

([It is used to] separate nominal and real [values], in other words, principles of currency and economics. Let's assume that V is stable or predictable, you can consider it a constant variable. By the same token, YS is a constant variable.)

Lee 19:39:32 简化得 Y demand=M/P 即 对于货币的需求只和通货有关

(When you simplify that, you get Y demand=M/P, that is the demand for currency is only related to currency.)

Lee 19:39:48 通货一定 价格水平越大 demand 越少

(When the currency is stable, the higher the price, the lower the demand.)

Lee 19:40:54 =。-如果通货变多 那么新的平衡中 实际GDP还是不变的 就像之后那个图 通货变多的后果就是价格水平提高 没别的影响.

([emoticon indicating confusion] If currency increases, the actual GDP doesn't change in the new balance. It's just like what the graph shows, the increase of currency results in higher price, nothing else.)

XX 商科 ~ 19:41:36 大神,我发现你的最近解释越来越专业的,专业到我都看不懂.

(*God*, I think your explanation has become more and more professional. It's so professional that I don't get it.)

LEE 19:42:30 其实 原因是 我的能力已经不足以把文言文翻译成白话文了哈哈.

(It's actually because my ability is falling short and I am not able to translate classical Chinese into colloquial Chinese.)

XX 商科 ~ 19:42:57 能看懂文言文不愧是大神23333.

(You are the *God* because you can understand classical Chinese [laughs].

In this exchange, Lee helped a fellow student bridge the official and unofficial worlds of learning. He unpacked routes and modes of reasoning by providing a detailed explanation of the underlying principles encoded in an equation, which he accomplished through translating jargon across disciplines and languages (e.g., his translation of currency into 通货 in the context of the formula and 货币 in the context of folk financial theory). However, this exchange was not completely successful. The fellow student politely complained that the explanation did not make the content more accessible. Jokingly equating his explanation of economic principles with translating classical Chinese, Lee articulated a keen awareness of his role as a translator that brokered the everyday lifeworlds of the students and academic disciplines.

Lee's expanding, self-designed "arsenal" of learning resources emerged in response to a range of problems and exigencies present in a networked, collaborative learning community. Orchestrating a complex network or knotwork of actors, in the course of a single semester, Lee managed seven tutorial groups that varied in levels of exclusivity and intensity of exchanges. These groups, maintained through WeChat's group-chat function, ranged from discussion groups consisting of several hundred students to a small, private group serving seven close class-friends (课友). *Class-friend* was a term students coined to describe a category of social relationship driven by academic interests, particularly in trading information and seeking help with course-related questions. Lee was at the center of an expansive network of class-friends and worked to offer lecture notes, quiz answers, and tutorials. However, his intentions were not only altruistic. He appreciated such experiences for presenting opportunities to identify unrecognized problems and consolidate his understanding.

In contrast to Yan's frustration over fellow students' inquiries, Lee was proud of the fact that he could "treat" dozens of students a night before a major exam. He did not feel "bombarded" by questions or burdened by repeating explanations. Instead, he celebrated the fact that he often stumbled upon new problems through such exchanges. Making concepts accessible to others also allowed him to clarify, consolidate, and articulate his own understanding. In Lee's words, these tutorials served as rehearsals for impending exams.

> 每次还是会有自己不明白或者没关注到的知识点。要是我讲解了别人还不明白,那肯定是因为我自己的理解还不到位。我自己明白了,才能让别人明白。我给你举个例子吧。期末开始前我自己也没有复习ppt。好几个人来问我问题,我帮她们梳理ppt的过程中其实等于是自己把材料复习了好多遍。

> (There are bound to be concepts that I was not very clear about or didn't pay attention to. If my explanation doesn't clarify the concepts, it is probably because my understanding was limited. I should be able to make myself understood when I know what I am talking about. Let me give you an example. I didn't review the course ppt before the final exam, but quite a few people came for help. I "combed through" the course ppt with them. In some ways, doing those things allowed me to review the material multiple times.) (Personal communication, December 6, 2013)

Seeing the value of these tutorials, Lee incorporated them into the complexly organized repository of skills and relationships that was critical to his success. Although these tutorials were extremely time consuming and tedious, they acquired great "market value" that could be traded for social and economic benefits. Many self-identified low achievers commented they were more than willing to maintain a mutually beneficial relationship with students like Lee. Many noted they often reciprocated by offering Lee dinner invitations, car rides, small presents, and compliments. From their perspectives, experts were entitled to these tokens of appreciation. Jean, a self-identified low achiever, argued that he had much to offer to experts.

> 您想啊。所谓学霸是什么人?他们把所有的时间都用来学习了。玩的事情他们不会啊。像我这样的就不一样了,我可知道去哪玩。我们可以带他们玩啊,把他们带进我的朋友圈。他们也是人不是。他们也需要朋友,妹子嘛。

> (Think of it this way. The so-called experts have spent all their time studying. They know little to nothing about having fun. People like me, on the other hand, know where to go [for fun]. We can take them out, show them around, introduce them to my circle of friends. They are human after all. They also need friends, girls, and such.) (Personal communication, December 14, 2013)

Lee confirmed this observation, suggesting that his expert status lent to an expanding network of relationships and resources that helped him counter the myriad challenges international students faced, such as getting a ride to the social-security office or finding a vehicle to practice driving. A kind smile from a class-friend was as heartwarming as the numerous dinner invitations he received. The social prestige also showed through a massive female following that stirred up jealousy toward Lee. Several students half-jokingly mentioned that Lee's all-girl entourage made his presence on campus very noticeable. Popularity among the female students was a powerful label of social prestige, as many students suggested one's capability of getting dates largely rested on family wealth, which showed through expensive accessories and luxury cars.

Although Lee maintained a critical distance toward perceived advantages, he appreciated the potential of an expanding social network in benefiting him.

> 帮助课友会在现在,或者将来给我带来帮助。我的做法会有很多现在看不到的益处。譬如,就跟好多中国学生会说的,人脉。人脉有什么用?给你举个简单的例子。寒假的时候我需要用车,我呆在这里,可是我自己并没买车。我在朋友圈发了一个消息,马上就有好几个人自愿借车给我用。对我来说,这就是人脉的作用。譬如现在我两辆车轮流开,一辆宝马和一辆捷豹。借车给我的都是大一新生,他们寒假要么回国要么出去玩了。不过我也不是随便什么人的车都愿意用,和我熟的我才借。

(Helping my class-friends will help me now and in the future. There are so many potential benefits to my approach. For example, I get to build Renmai [a network of social relationship], as many Chinese students would say. Let me give you a very simple example. I need a car because I am staying here for the winter break, but I don't have a car yet. I sent out a message in my friendship circle [on WeChat], and several people volunteered to lend me their cars. To me, that's one way how Renmai works. Now I drive a BMW and a Jaguar in turn. The guys who lent me their cars were both freshmen students. They went on vacations or went back to China during the break. I wouldn't just borrow anyone's car, only good friends of mine.) (Personal communication, December 14, 2013)

This anecdote, along with other narratives of treating an expert to a hot-pot party or an expensive spa, points to ways in which the students strategically position themselves in relation to each other in the production and performance of identities. Various forms of social goods changed hands in this transnational community, including expertise in content areas, popularity, favors, material goods, and prestige. Part of a complex semiotic system, Lee accumulated social and material capital.

This conception of social positioning is informed by a cultural understanding of the nature of transaction and relationship. Here arises the significance of *renmai* (人脉). A combination of *person* (人) and *arteries* (脉), the term describes an intricate network of social relationships one inherits and maintains to advance one's career and social standing. Renmai is tied with various affiliations one inherits, such as family connections (relatives) and regional identities (people born and raised in the same geographical region). Renmai can be acquired through chance encounters and professional affiliations, such as colleagues, class-friends, and clients. Many students emphasized the potential of building renmai as a benefit of attending a US university with a sizable Chinese population. Jun, a student from Shanghai, suggested that his mother warned him never to offend anyone because they might come from prosperous families and might become potential clients. Considered from this perspective, the exchange of favors through learning activities is a process of formulating renmai. In this context, academic expertise becomes a commodity of great market value. In this fashion, these wider cultural ecologies served as a complex social system mediating social trajectories inside and outside the classroom, as these two areas became densely blended or knotted together.

Mediating the construction of these networks, students repositioned themselves in light of transnational experiences, which often lead to heightened awareness of one's identity as a member of a national collective. Although Lee was concerned about his relative academic standing among Chinese students, for whom career resources are scant, he was more concerned with the relatively low social standing of the Chinese community,

> 很多人都问过我,帮别的同学就不怕他们的成绩比自己还高嘛。其实的确有这样的事情发生。不过我想了挺多的,最后我的结论有两点。一我们是在美国,中国学生更应该互相帮助。我更希望更多的优秀的中国学生能进入商学院。只有这样我们才能和美国人竞争啊。大家都优秀了,我才能更优秀。在这方面我是有点理想主义。我们是少数,甚至是弱势群体。我们得要抱团才行。

(Many have asked me if I was concerned students I helped might surpass me. Indeed, this has happened, but I have thought carefully about it. There are two points in my conclusion. First, we are in America—all the more reason that Chinese students should help each other. I'd love to see more high-achieving Chinese students in Business school so that we can compete against the Americans. Second, I am a firm believer that I will be able to improve myself by helping others. I'll be more successful if everybody else [Chinese] does well. I am idealistic in that way. We are the minority here, or I would even go so far to say we are a socially vulnerable group. We should really stick together to succeed.) (Personal communication, December 14, 2013)

Lee's thinking was heavily influenced by his affiliation and identification with the geopolitical circumstances of China as a rising economic power that often competes against the United States on the global stage. *Socially vulnerable group* (社会弱势群体) is a phrase commonly used by Chinese mainstream media to portray migrant workers who move to metropolitan areas for better-paying jobs. In making this comparison, Lee brings to the foreground his self-identification as a migrant who finds his position on the periphery or at the bottom of the social strata. Engendered by this identification was a heightened awareness of his own cultural and ethnic identity in relation to the host country as well as the recognition of Chinese students working together to compete against US students. Arising from such thinking was a dynamic underground world of academic learning, which both afforded and *restricted* social and geographic movement across the HEI landscape. The students' tightly knit social networks helped them navigate the Western educational system yet enabled the population to maintain a distance from it.

INDEXING THE SOCIAL WORLD OF COMMERCE

In many ways, Lee's practices were indexical of the imagined world of commerce in contemporary Chinese society. Most students come from affluent families that have made their fortune during China's economic boom in the past two decades. Through the lens of their family businesses, some students have had a rare glimpse into the realities of contemporary commerce. A good number of students mentioned that their upbringing included practices of acculturation into the world of commerce, such as attending business dinners, working as interns in family businesses, receiving seed money for business ideas, and participating in business decision making (see the case of Yisi in chapter 3). Xiang, a twenty-one-year-old student from Sichuan province, quit high school to help in the family business at the age of fifteen. His work involved formulating and maintaining relationships (关系/guanxi) with the weaving of one-to-one relationships manifested in the notion of "我用你,你用我" (I use you; you use me). He shared the following anecdote:

> 我们公司由此要投标一个政府项目。投三次三次都没中。我们就想请招标局的领导吃饭。你知道啦,他就是个典型的政府官员。吃一次,不行。两次还是不行。我后来想着我得找个新的切入点。正好要过节了,我就打电话说请他和家人吃顿饭。他带了夫人和小孩。当时我就和他儿子聊天,问他喜欢做什么啊。后来我发现他喜欢打游戏。更重要的是,他学习很差啊。我学习蛮好,正好可以帮他补习。不过补习不是重点。最重要的是沟通,和他交朋友。他正在叛逆期,老是和父母打架。我的机会来了。有一次他和他爸吵架给跑了,我马上出动把他找回来,还给他们劝好了。项目我们就拿到了。

(We were once bidding for a government project. We submitted the bid three times but didn't get the project. I then invited the director from the bureau that takes bidding to dinner. You know he is like a typical governmental official. One dinner, no deal. Two dinners, still no deal. I figured we needed to find a different entry point. It just so happened a holiday was coming up, and I called to invite his family to a dinner party. He brought his wife and teenage son. I started to ask his son what he liked to do and discovered that he liked video games. More importantly, he was doing poorly at school. I then volunteered to tutor him. I was good at the kind of (academic) things he was working on. But tutoring itself is beside the point. What really matters was communication and becoming his friend. He was at that rebellious age, where he fought with his parents all the time. That was my opportunity. There was one time when he fought with his dad and ran away. I found him, brought him back, and helped him reconcile with his dad. We got the government project.) (Personal communication, December 16, 2013)

In this instance, getting acquainted with a stakeholder's son was a strategic business move. The notion of guanxi conflates personal relationships with business decisions. The formulation of a personal relationships might drive the consolidation of a business opportunity, while the breaking of a personal relationship might lead to the dismantling of a business transaction. Xiang's use of tutorials to forge relationships was strikingly similar to Lee's approach. Indeed, Lee's thinking echoed this understanding, as he commented on how significant guanxi was in performing a multitude of social practices in Chinese society, from finding a good doctor in a local hospital to getting a business license from the taxation authority. Lee even attributed his parents' struggling business to their failure to establish good relationships with officials in local government agencies.

有没有好的关系网差别太大了。你要是够机灵有个强大的关系网,那你就爬得快。不然你要是事事按规章办,那你缴了税以后就不要想挣钱了。就剩一点钱还得跟上安全,卫生啊这些规定。这样缚手缚脚的。如果你按照规章去申请营业执照,他们就叫你等啰。这里一个章,那里一个章子,每个章子都要等几个月。等你好不容易开业了,别人早都占了先机。或者说你要投标一个五百万的生意,别人要是有关系很容易吹到一千万。照规则办不赔本就不错了。

(Whether or not you have a solid network of relationships makes a big difference. If you are smart enough to build strong relationships, you will rise on the social ladder much faster. Instead, if you follow the rules as set by the government, you can barely make any money after paying all the taxes. You will spend what is left keeping up with the regulations for safety and sanitation. Your hands will be tied. If you follow the standard procedure for applying for a business license, they will have you wait. You need to get a stamp here, another stamp there. They have you wait months for each stamp. When you finally get your business open, others would have already taken the market. Or if you win a bid for a contract that is worth five million, with connections others can easily blow it up into ten million. You will not break even if you follow the rules.) (Personal communication, December 14, 2013)

Lee and others observed relationship-building practices as critical to the success of family businesses. Furthermore, they were often recruited into such activities. For one thing, Lee was charged with selecting and purchasing "appropriate" gifts in the United States to help maintain business relationships. To that end, Lee made frequent trips to Chicago to shop for luxury handbags, cosmetic products, and jewelry items.

From these accounts, we see how the imagined world of commerce is dialectically connected to students' performance of identities as college students, future businesspeople, and delegates of family businesses. This idea of using relationships to practice commerce was taken up to reorganize and reconfigure students' literacy learning. The understanding that one's ability to maintain a social network rests upon and congeals around persons of power, expertise, and connection played an important role in how students identified and positioned each other in the context of academic learning. In this fashion, educational and business networks were densely entangled.

In this dynamic, the value of academic expertise was contested. Xiang's academic expertise in high-school math opened the door into the personal life and professional endorsement of an important business associate. On other occasions, academic expertise was dismissed as irrelevant to business practices. Although Lee hoped to pursue a degree in accounting, he was dubious that training received from a US university could translate into skills that could benefit the family business. In Lee's words, one must be very "flexible" to be employable. As a matter of fact, accountants who receive Western training are often considered too "stiff" for a flexible market economy that holds rules and regulations in contempt. Systematic training in the disciplinary field and the professional ethics the university hopes to cultivate in students might conflict with employers' expectations for their staff—to bend the laws and find loopholes if necessary. This awareness was reflected in Lee's daily practice. He saw the tutorial groups as a way to develop his "book smarts" and "street smarts." From students who sought his help, he acquired opportunities to see and experience the world from their perspectives. After all, he said, "their families probably do better than mine does. And there has to be reason for that." Through these exchanges he was navigating two historically and socially situated but complexly intertwined regimes of mobility (Schiller and Salazar 2013).

CONCLUSION

This chapter complicates the analysis of the students' underground economies and networks and the ways they both afford and constrain disciplinary learning and identities, as relationship webs in and out of class become complexly entangled. Lending layers of support to the previous case studies, literacy is a commodity exchanged for social capital. Yet this chapter also renders visible the highly contingent and contested nature of this process. While cases such as Lee's demonstrate how literacy serves as a form of capital that enables students to accumulate other forms of social and material resources, in other cases literacy fails to hold or loses its value. Furthermore, while students such as Lee capitalize on their positions as lords of learning within the higher education system, others such as Yan resist these labels. In this manner, the students are entangled in densely knotted networks or knotworks as they continually weave and are rewoven into socially embedded systems. These densely knotted threads of activity mediate the positions of the actors as they traverse geographical, social, and virtual landscapes. Furthermore, this process mediates wider geographies of difference, as some international students achieve social and class mobility while others are left out of this process.

Contrary to what previous research has often characterized as the expanding potential of students' hidden literacies, namely how digital practices serve as dynamic representational spaces for youths to express multiple identities and multiple loyalties and to reflect on the different social and cultural contexts of their lives, these cases point to another side of such cultural practices, how they can afford and limit the possibilities for students' identities and mobilities. In this regard, the lord-scumbag meme circulates in the translocal space as a historically developed social imaginary, which orients students to interpret their experiences with schooling and position themselves according to a particular perspective about expertise and success in schools. This notion is indexical of an imagined world with its own ideological and social values and expected behaviors for students. The meme, as a semiotic structure, is inscribed with the values and expectations students have internalized through years of experiences with schooling. Upon invocation, it orients students toward *the* way to interpret experiences according to ideological values sanctioned by the community. Another lifeworld (of the geeks), as embodied by popular television shows such as *The Big Bang Theory*, brings another configuration of social, cultural, and ideological meanings into the social context where students function. The convergence of multiple social worlds compels reconciliation, reconfiguration, and remix. When people appropriate genres and semiotic structures, they also inherit these ideologies and make them anew. As these dialectic processes get enacted, social spaces shape and are shaped by material structures (Leander and Sheehy 2004) as the world grant university is reinvented. In the next section of the book, we extend the analysis to the ways this process is linked to near and distant spaces in a summer school in Guangzhou, China.

5

STUDY ABROAD AT HOME

I, Xiaoye, had rice cake and soy milk for breakfast before heading to Kaohsiung International Airport. The flight to Hong Kong was brief, airborne for about an hour. After deplaning and clearing customs, I waited for a city bus in the steaming hot transportation area outside Hong Kong International Airport. After a forty-five-minute ride to Sheungshui metro station, I took a light-rail train to Luohu, a checkpoint on the border between Hong Kong and Mainland China. When I walked across the border into the train station of Shenzhen, a border city, the time was past noon. I purchased a speed-train ticket for Guangzhou. The train was set to leave in ten minutes, so I wasn't able to sit down for lunch before boarding. The train was packed but comfortable, with large seats and mild air conditioning. It was exciting to watch the train speeding up rapidly to about 150 miles per hour. The China high-speed rail network, constituting more than 60 percent of the total high-speed rail routes in the world, was the Chinese strategy to solve issues of mass transportation, energy consumption, and air pollution. The one-hour-and-fifteen-minute travel time was enough for me to review my course syllabi for Sinoway International Education (SIE) summer school. The train pulled into Guangzhou East Station on time.

It was June 30, 2013, a day when SIE faculty would arrive at Sun Yat-sen University (SYSU) in Guangzhou, a metropolis in South China. A Hong Kong-registered for-profit organization, SIE provides US-style college summer programs in China. With courses taught by Western professors, it promises students will be able to transfer credits back to their North American institutions. It houses its programs in prestigious Chinese universities, including SYSU that year. Established in the 1920s, Sun Yat-sen University was named after the founder of the Republic of China. Sun and his cohort overthrew the Imperial Qing government in 1910 and forged a new nation on the ruins of feudalism and colonialism. The SIE program would start the following day. Like me, the SIE faculty and students had traveled from different parts of the

DOI: 10.7330/9781607327332.c005

world to SIE campuses in four cities—Beijing, Shanghai, Nangjing, and Guangzhou. Most of the students studied in North America and had returned home for the summer. On their way, they had crossed borders, not only national but also institutional and linguistic. On that day, I went through border controls of three polities and shuttled between scripts (English, pinying, traditional Chinese, and simplified Chinese) and between dialects and accents (English, Mandarin, Cantonese, Hakka, and Hokkien). The students' and faculty's mobilities composed the SIE enterprise, an immobile spatial fix that would produce geographic and social mobilities.

The mobilities of the SIE faculty and students were produced, facilitated, and constrained by institutions, discourses, technologies, and languages. Their mobilities epitomize the types of movements that occur in transnational higher education these days. In this chapter, as we have done thus far, I will chart the mechanisms that structure Chinese international students' mobility, focusing on their movements at home. Using SIE as a focal point, I will show that Chinese higher education's marketization and Chinese universities' internationalization drive have helped cultivate a transnational education marketplace. Key players (governments, universities, administrators, teachers, and students) must negotiate the values, assumptions, and practices of different national education systems that participate in the marketplace. While transnational higher education typically refers to "study programs where learners are located in a country other than the one in which the awarding institutions are based" (Wilkins 2016, 3), the SIE summer school embodies a burgeoning alternative in which both the awarding institution and students are located in the same country. This alternative features multidirectional mobilities of programs, peoples, credentials, and resources in the global eduscape.

To trace the assemblage of actants and networks in the global eduscape, in this chapter, I focus on several disruptions I encountered while teaching in the summer school. As diverse as academic papers, government policy documents, wall posters, trailer trucks, and administrators, these actants ushered me into the local interactions unfolding on the SYSU campus, and, through associations they wove, global interactions. As Bruno Latour (2005) suggests, "What has been designated by the term 'local interaction' is the assemblage of all the other local interactions distributed elsewhere in time and space, which have been brought to bear on the scene through the relays of various non-human actors" (194). One local-global interaction takes place in scholarly papers and policy documents.

STUDY ABROAD IN TRANSNATIONAL HIGHER EDUCATION

As we demonstrate through Michigan State University, Chinese international students have become important financial contributors to US higher education. Both Michigan State and the Lansing community view the influx of international students as adding economic vibrancy to the otherwise economically depressed rust-belt town. At the same time, however, the university has worked with an age-long logic in US higher education in terms of foreign students. That is, US universities import problems and export expertise, knowledge, and solutions to other nations (Donahue 2009). As part of the state apparatus, Michigan State established an infrastructure to accommodate, monitor, and discipline international students. Lansing newspapers portrayed Chinese international students as often driving luxurious cars recklessly and sometimes getting into fist fights with each other.

While one would assume that the strong presence of international students marks US universities' internationalization efforts, the universities and mainstream media have favored students' outward movements, promoting study-abroad programs as the chief form of internationalization. In various initiatives to promote study abroad, US universities have portrayed this experience in a positive light. The mainstream perspective of such programs is deeply grounded in a nation-state framework. Universities are commissioned with the task of educating national citizens for an increasingly interconnected world. To understand this world, study abroad has meant sending students to study outside the United States. Within a few weeks or a year, students return with credits that can be used toward their graduation requirements. Along with the logic of study abroad came US universities' interest in establishing offshore campuses. Profit driven, these campuses help extend a US education, providing US students opportunities to study abroad in a familiar academic structure.

In both institutional initiatives and scholarly discourse, study abroad has been celebrated for its advantages over study at home (Clarke et al. 2009; Williams 2005). First, proponents claim students will increase their global awareness and intercultural competence, which are critical for functioning in this interconnected world. Students may understand and appreciate different values and lifestyles as a result of their exposure to religions, languages, and lifestyles outside their nation. Second, a globally focused education can promote international peace and enhance national security in the long run. Third, study abroad can enhance academic learning. Students can improve their learning of foreign languages as they interact with native speakers, and they can take courses that may not be offered in their home institutions. Fourth, study abroad may be conducive to personal and professional growth. Confronting and overcoming the challenges of living in a foreign country may build confidence and critical-thinking skills. However, these are study-abroad myths, as research has shown that students returning from sojourns do not always reap these benefits (Kinginger 2008). And some of those benefits, such as global, international, and intercultural competencies, may be achieved through on-campus programs at home (Soria and Troisi 2014). These study-abroad myths have prevented universities from tapping resources at home, including the potential for developing domestic students' global, international, and intercultural competences through interacting with international students.

Study abroad is also increasingly valued in Chinese higher education, however, with distinct assumptions and approaches. Chinese authorities have been proactive in importing expertise, human resources, and capital as part of their efforts to internationalize higher education. A key form of this approach is the joint-degree programs the Ministry of Education (MOE) has promoted in a series of its stipulations since the 1990s. This move resembles a strategy in the nation's economic reforms initiated in the late 1970s. Concerned about economic sovereignty, China required that foreign businesses enter the country in a joint-venture model, taking up no more than half the total share. They were allowed to operate solely on their own only decades later. In a similar fashion, only one out of twenty-four (4 percent) transnational educational institutions had an independent legal-person status in China in 2003. By 2015, the number climbed to eight out of sixty-four (12.5 percent). In the same year, Chinese universities ran over a thousand joint-degree programs with overseas universities (He 2016; Ministry of Education 2015a; 2015b). With a curriculum developed by both institutions, Chinese students typically do two years of course work in China and then complete the rest of their studies overseas. Upon graduation, they receive a degree issued by both universities. Formerly viewed as a complement to Chinese higher education, the joint programs are now viewed as an integral part (He 2016).

In its efforts to marshal foreign expertise and resources to strengthen its higher education, the Chinese government is also vigilant about practices that would undermine its "educational sovereignty" (Ministry of Education 2006). In a series of directives, the Ministry of Education (2003; 2006; 2007; 2009) warned against certain practices in running joint programs, warnings that came to define what "educational sovereignty" meant. In a directive, for example, the Ministry of Education

(2006) identified several issues plaguing these joint programs. First, some programs focused on financial profiteering rather than the public good (公益性). Second, some programs violated Chinese laws. The ministry warned that these programs must enhance their "political sensitivity" and guard "national security, social stability, and normal educational orders" (par. 3). This warning aligns with several notices issued by the ministry in recent years urging Chinese universities to censor instructional materials from the West. Third, foreign educational resources had not been channeled to disciplines and regions traditionally weak in higher education. The Ministry of Education (2007) criticized some joint programs for offering preparatory classes with the sole purpose of recruiting Chinese students for foreign universities.

Serving as another actant in the global network of scholarly writings, this sketch of US and Chinese universities' approaches to study abroad underscores an important difference in their values and assumptions related to transnational higher education. US universities view study abroad primarily as an opportunity for their students to broaden their linguistic and intercultural competences. Typically, they encourage almost every student to study overseas if the student has the resources. By contrast, Chinese universities see study abroad as an opportunity to amend weaknesses in its higher education system. Weaknesses are understood more on disciplinary, institutional, and geographic terms than in terms of individual students' intellectual and transcultural development. Therefore, Chinese universities typically do not encourage every student to study abroad even if a student has the resources. Chinese scholars and policymakers on internationalization hardly mention the opportunity to bolster students' linguistic or intercultural competences. These distinct values as well as the institutions that operate with them produce and structure the mobilities of students in both nations. To better understand how these values and institutions structure students' cross-national mobilities, next I examine the SIE summer school, which is at the nexus of these values and institutions.

As part of the mobile and connective approach this book undertakes, I studied administrators, faculty, and students inside and outside SIE, online and offline. I informed my colleagues and students at the beginning of the semester that I would conduct research on the SIE Guangzhou campus, focusing on Chinese students' literacy practices. As a faculty member, I had access to both the faculty and administration. I interacted with colleagues at weekly faculty meetings and lunches and on sightseeing trips. I took field notes and audio recorded all faculty meetings and my interviews with the administrators. After class, I spent time with my students almost every day, tracking and tracing "unexpected trajectories" both "within and across multiple sites of activity" (Marcus 1998, 80). We often ate in local restaurants and went to bars some evenings. I followed them into subway trains, movie theaters, and Internet cafes. I took notes on the sounds, sights, smells, and feelings in those sites. I also entered their virtual worlds by befriending them on Facebook, Weibo, and WeChat. In addition to field notes, I audio and video recorded my classes and audio recorded student interactions outside the classroom. At the end of each day, I quickly reviewed the recordings and took notes on student and faculty conversations that were revealing about the students' literacy practices. In addition to these recordings, I roamed the campus and collected artifacts SIE faculty and students interacted with (see details of data collection and analysis in appendix I).

Because I was simultaneously teacher and researcher, the study was ethically challenging. Following the protocol of qualitative research, students were instructed by a third party at the beginning of the semester that participation in the study or not would not affect their grades and that their consent would not be revealed to me until the end of the semester. Although both the students and administrators graciously granted me consent to include them in the study, they were not fully aware of the consequences of my study, and neither was I in the beginning of the study. As the research unfolded, I constantly had to make decisions on whether I was fair in representing SIE and the participants. Some of my representation would turn out to be negative, or "bad news," for them. Although I shared my writing with some key informants during the study, they did not always fully comprehend the negative side of my representation. Thomas Newkirk (1996) emphasizes that a researcher has the responsibility to intervene when perceiving issues or problems with the subjects. During the study, issues constantly arose with my students. However, as a teacher, sometimes I did not perceive them right away, thus missing the opportunity to intervene. Or, as illustrated in chapter 7, I saw issues but was not certain whether I should intervene at that moment. Sometimes, as illustrated in chapter 6, I was able to capitalize on their issues as teaching moments. Research and writing thus became a process of nonstop self-questioning and positioning.

In the rest of the chapter, I map out the infrastructure of the transnational education market by focusing on disruptions and the key actants therein. These human and non-human actants mediated the formation of the academic culture in this translocal space, where Chinese and US educational practices meet, collide, and reconcile with each other. SIE must negotiate the values and practices of both systems to carve a space of its own. In the next two chapters, I assess some of the study-abroad myths prevalent in US higher education by focusing on my middle-class students' literacy practices and subject positions constructed inside and outside the classroom.

CONTENDING DISCOURSES IN THE CHINESE EDUCATION MARKETPLACE

To map out the sociopolitical relations the summer school was entangled in, I first conduct linguistic landscaping on the SYSU campus, followed by cultural landscaping around the university. Public signage provides important information about the social space, including the social structure and practices, the summer school occupies. Jan Blommaert (2013) explains the affordances of an ethnographic method for linguistic landscaping as follows:

> By looking at public signs, therefore, we can perform *a reconstruction of the communicative patterns for which such signs were manufactured.* Communicative patterns are, in turn, social patterns and an ethnographic study of situated signs can thus lead us towards insights into the social structure in which they fit. Signs lead us to practices, and practices lead us to people: individuals and groups who live in a given area in a particular configuration, with a particular degree of regulation and order, and with different forms of social and cultural organization in relation to each other. (50; emphasis in original).

Signs are "aggregate of discourses," or néxuses of social interactions (Scollon and Scollon 2003). In their nexus analysis, Scollon and Scollon (2004) suggest that we consider the place in which signs appear, the life experiences people bring with them to the social interaction, and the "interaction order" emerging from the interplay between people and place. Signs are crucial actants of the social. According to Actant-Network Theory, interacting with other actants, signs can translate and mediate the global and the local, the macro and the micro. Both the associations out of which signs are made and the social ties they have renewed must be examined (Latour 2005). When looking at public signs on the SYSU campus, therefore, we must consider the meaning of the location where a sign is placed, life experiences, motives, feelings of the sign creator and audience, and the ways people come to the sign. In sum, examining the signs on the SYSU campus opens a window to the social and institutional structures as well as to discourses that produced, facilitated, and constrained the operation of the summer school.

Along with public signage, I also read streets, buildings, and people as cultural texts. Nedra Reynolds (2007) suggests that "places, whether textual, material, or imaginary, are constructed and reproduced not simply by boundaries but also by practices, structure of feelings, and sedimented features of habitus" (2). Raymond Williams (1977) defines structures of feeling as "meanings and values as they are actually lived and felt" and "specifically affective elements of consciousness and relationships" (132). In other words, a place is constructed and reproduced by people living there. It embodies the meanings, values, stories, and social relations lived and felt by its residents, and it is shaped by their social behaviors and habits. Walking around the university, I took in what I could see, hear, and feel. I paid particular attention to the buildings and spaces SIE administrators, teachers, and students occupied. The spatial arrangements indexed social and institutional relations. The spatial practices, including the SIE community's experience with these buildings and spaces, came to shape the community's identity.

Before joining the welcome dinner for the SIE faculty, I went to the building where I would teach the following day. Having taught on the SIE Shanghai campus two year before, I was curious about the Guangzhou campus. As I walked along Garden East Road, students strolled in and out of residence halls amidst the high-pitched sounds of cicadas. On both sides of the road, photocopy shops, cell-phone stores, grocery stores, a cafeteria, and bulletin boards lined up. The bulletin boards were filled with advertisements for housing, summer jobs, and used appliances. In large posters targeting students living in the residence halls, preparatory schools promised top scores in GRE, SAT, GMAT, TOEFL, and Chinese graduate-school entrance exams. Market forces had ostensibly joined the educational order, which is an important feature of Chinese higher education these days (Yang 2008).

These bulletin boards staged multiple discourses in Chinese higher education, contending with or supporting one another. Take one of these boards as an example (see Figure 5.1). On the top is a multilingual billboard erected by the SYSU administration. Its size, position, and high visibility unequivocally index authority. To the left, in traditional Chinese script, it says 毕业季 (time of graduation). To the right, against an English poster saying "I ♥ SYSU," two students wearing commencement gowns smile at the camera, one thumbing up and the other gesturing a V sign. A caricature of Sun Yat-sen stands by, smiling too. Clearly, the billboard depicts joy, pride, and optimism among seniors soon to graduate. The board constructs an official statement: with a degree from this prestigious university, students can anticipate success in their

Figure 5.1. A bulletin board standing on East Garden Road on the SYSU main campus

future careers. The administration marks its credibility with a university seal and traditional Chinese script in a large font. The students voice their feelings through the English poster and the Sun Yat-sen caricature. With Sun's image placed in the center, the audience is reminded of the nationalist nature of the university. At the same time, however, Sun's Western-style clothing, rather than the Chinese style named after him, reminds the audience familiar with Sun's life that he embodies both Eastern and Western education. Sun was born in China but was later educated in the United States. He received training in Western medicine and was inspired by Western democracy, which provided a foundation for his political vision. For several generations, like Sun, many SYSU faculty members received their education overseas. The education SYSU promotes is transnational by nature.

The transnational nature of Chinese higher education is affirmed by the advertisements posted underneath the billboard. Ads are laid on top of others like a palimpsest. The most eye-catching ones feature prep schools vying for students. Framed under the university billboard, the prep schools construct an unofficial discourse, suggesting their parasitic relationship with the university. Taking up most of the bulletin-board space, Jiazhuo School presents two pairs of posters for visual emphasis.

Jiazhuo means "excellence." One poster declares, "嘉卓, 全明星海归顾问团队, 留学品牌" (Jiazhuo, all-star consulting team made up of overseas returnees, famous brand in study abroad). The statement is anchored by a lineup of neatly dressed professionals placed underneath it. The other poster stakes a claim in a couplet style with seven Chinese characters in each line: "摆脱"鸡肋"大课堂, 专注1对1特训" (breaking away from the "chicken ribs" of large classes, focusing on one-to-one training). Literally meaning "chicken ribs," 鸡肋 (*ji lei*) refers to things of little interest or value. The expression originally came from a general's comment on war strategies in the Three Kingdoms period (220 CE–280 CE): "Chicken ribs do not have much meat to eat but it would be a waste to throw them away" (夫鸡肋,弃之如可惜,食之无所得). With historical meanings and forms (underscored by the quotation marks), "chicken ribs" is used here to poke fun at Chinese universities and some prep schools that offer large-class-size lessons. Implicitly, the expression references the three kingdoms fighting for power, which is fitting for the ongoing wrangling among the higher education modes in China (traditional public universities versus private prep schools). Underneath the claims in large fonts, one of the supporting details mixes Chinese and English scripts: "十年托福/雅思/GRE/SAT/AP培训经验" (ten years of training experience in TOEFL, IELTS, GRE, SAT and AP). The statement insinuates that clients will have a good chance of scoring high in those international exams. While TOEFL, SAT, and AP exams are typically required for entering US universities, the IELTS test is required by universities in Commonwealth nations. If the poster design is striking, it is equally striking to note a fist fight among the prep schools. In the top left corner, traces of a poster for another school are discernible. Someone tore away most of it but left the school's name intact: 易藤国际教育 (Easy Test Institute). The competitiveness in the transnational education market is thus laid bare. The schools fight not only verbally in their persuasive posters but also physically.

The prep-school posters index a major challenge to Chinese higher education. Before the global financial meltdown in 2008, most high-school graduates took Chinese-university entrance exams and ended up entering or failing to enter a university. During the financial crisis, Anglophone nations with developed economies heightened measures to recruit Chinese students to make up the budget shortfalls of their universities. These students came from emergent middle-class families, families that could afford exorbitantly high tuitions and fees. Implicitly, these posters remind SYSU students of higher education alternatives. They can participate in the joint-degree programs SYSU established with a foreign university; they can transfer to overseas universities; or they can go overseas for graduate studies. Study abroad stands as a viable means to a bright future, undermining the appeal of Chinese higher education.

The promises of Chinese higher education are undercut by other advertisements on the bulletin board. With what they sell often viewed as illegitimate and condemned by Chinese authorities, the ads come in small posters, some dotted in the margins and hardly noticeable. They offer further insights into the higher education marketplace. For example, underneath the prep-school posters are a pair of small ones, repeating probably for visual emphasis. Under the heading "论文发表" (Publishing Academic Papers), the ad claims,

您正在为发文章担忧吗? 您正在为毕业、就业机会、评奖学金、评职称、保研所需 的论文发表发愁吗?本中心代理百余种覆盖文、理、商、科技、教育等不同学科、不同等级(CSSCI、北大核心、中文核心、国家级、省级)期刊,全部正刊, 不受 中介公司价格控制,全国最低价!服务承诺:发表不成功, 全额退款!版面有限, 早发早安排早排版!合法正刊,全部上中国知网和万方数据库, 价格低、出刊快,上网快。

(Are you worried about publishing papers? Are you worried about the publications required for graduation, jobs, scholarships, promotions, or graduate school entrance? Our center represents over one hundred journals in the humanities, sciences, business, technology, and education across different levels, such as CSSCI, the Peking University Core Journal Index, the Core Chinese Language Journal Index, national level, and provincial level. All publications will appear in officially registered journals. Free of price controls by any agencies, we offer the lowest pricing in the nation! Our promise: Shall we fail to publish your work, we will fully refund you. The number of pages in an issue is limited. The earlier we slate your article, the sooner the page layouts will be set. Appearing in officially registered journals, all articles will enter the China National Knowledge Infrastructure and Wanfang Data. Low price, speedy publication, and quick online availability.)

Like the prep-school posters, this one advertises a service. It has painted a dreadful picture of academic life: one will be required to publish at multiple junctures—graduation, job search, scholarship awards, promotion, and graduate-school entrance—and publishing papers could be a headache. The poster obviously targets a broad clientele on campus: students, faculty, and staff. Positioned underneath the university billboard, the poster reminds the audience that graduating from this prestigious university does not guarantee a rosy career path. The poster also shows that publishing papers, an academic's lifeline, is no different from other businesses. It can be outsourced for a fee. Knowledge is a business; it can be sold and bought, and it can be faked. The academic black market is so prevalent in China that, as a *Science* investigation reveals, it has become a transnational operation. Some Chinese scientists pay brokers an exorbitant fee to place their papers in Science Citation Index (SCI) journals (Hvistendahl 2013). The poster demystifies academia as a sacred palace of knowledge, as universities are commonly portrayed in mainstream Chinese discourse. Like the prep-school posters, the "Publishing Academic Papers" posters subvert the university's authority, chipping away at the integrity, pride, and optimism the university wants its graduates to take away.

SIE is also in the knowledge business. Established in 2009 by Hao Liu, a returning Chinese international student from Wabash College, SIE offers credit-bearing courses to Chinese students studying at North American universities. Importing the North American educational model, it offers general education requirement courses as well as entry-level courses in certain popular majors. Through word of mouth and social media, it recruits students who return to China for summer vacation. As a key feature of its business model, SIE sells prestige. It hires professors from well-ranked North American and European universities. Working with renowned Chinese universities, such as Sun Yat-sen University, SIE offers summer sessions on their campuses and issues academic transcripts bearing these universities' seals. SIE grew exponentially during the first three years, attracting 234 students in 2010, more than 1,000 in 2011, and over 2,000 in 2012. It also expanded from one campus in 2010 to four in 2012. SIE credits were accepted by more than 240 North American universities. In 2013, SIE planned to operate on eight campuses, including two in Vietnam. Its business model attracted copycats, giving rise to a dozen summer schools in China in 2012 (McMurtrie and Farrer 2013; SIE 2013).

The momentum, however, was stalled by North American and Chinese educational establishments. In fall 2012, as a flood of Chinese international students requested that North American universities accept credits gained at SIE and other summer schools, some universities became suspicious. They sent queries to the China Academic Degrees and Graduate Education Development Center (CDGDC) asking it to verify these summer programs. They would only accept credits from an institution accredited by the Chinese Ministry of Education. CDGDC operates under the joint leadership of the Ministry of Education and the Academic Degrees Committee of the State Council. Among its various administrative functions, it provides accreditation, authentication, and consulting services for degree and related materials. The center's response confirmed the North American universities' suspicion: SIE was not accredited. Therefore, many North American universities rejected credit-transfer requests made by students who attended these summer schools that year.

These summer schools remained a mystery to North American universities until the publication of a *Chronicle of Higher Education* article titled "Chinese Summer Schools Sell Quick Credits" in January 2013 (see also chapter 2). According to the report, inspired by the success of SIE, a dozen summer schools had popped up in China. Interviewing program organizers, teachers, and students, the reporters tried to fathom this new scene in the Chinese higher education landscape. They summed up their findings: "These entrepreneurs have taken an American product—the Western college course—and created a shorter, cheaper version to sell to their peers. In doing so, they have tapped into the seemingly insatiable demand for Western education by China's growing middle class" (McMurtrie and Farrer 2013). The reporters described the summer schools as business operations and pointed out the "insatiable" Chinese middle-class desire for North American-style education. However, their tone was critical. They viewed "Western college courses" as original, authentic, and authoritative products and their replicas in China as counterfeits. Further, the reporters claimed that "the programs vary in quality, oversight, and structure." The CDGDC response and the *Chronicle* report caused great damage to the summer schools. SIE enrollment plummeted by half in 2013, and only five campuses were actually open, all inside China.

Amidst these setbacks, SIE launched a series of public-relations measures. First, it sent student representatives as well as SIE professors to meet North American university registrars to explain how it ran its programs. Second, on January 30, 2013, Melissa Butler, the dean of SIE and a retired political science professor at Wabash College, wrote to the *Chronicle* defending SIE (Butler 2013). Titling her letter "Chinese Summer Program's Credits Are Not for Sale," she first pointed out that the *Chronicle* article title was "a bit too facile." Then she argued, "Offering students the opportunity to earn summer credits is hardly the same thing as 'selling quick credits.' The Chinese summer programs are condensed, but they are comparable in length to American summer programs. Furthermore, each SIE summer course is the equivalent of a semester-long course with 39 hours of classroom instruction, as well as out-of-class work." Third, SIE elevated oversight in its academic programs by installing an academic director on each campus in 2012 and appointing Butler as the dean to oversee all campuses in 2013. The academic directors are veteran teachers at SIE and full professors from North America. Finally, SIE worked with the CDGDC to initiate a review-and-approval process for its programs. It adjusted its program structure and operation hoping to obtain the center's verification.

Working with the CDGDC, however, was a challenge, exposing tensions between the modes of educational sovereignty sponsored by the Ministry of Education and SIE's business model. The ministry encouraged Chinese universities to develop joint-degree programs with foreign universities; it emphasized public good rather than financial profits as the purpose of these programs. The SIE model obviously deviated from these principles. It was not truly a foreign educational entity. While it was registered in Hong Kong, its headquarters was based in Beijing. Furthermore, profit making was its sole purpose. In an e-mail addressed to the SIE faculty in March 2013, Hao Liu, the CEO, emphasized the conflicts among Chinese higher education modes.

> When students from last year's program tried to obtain CDGDC verification, their credits were rejected because CDGDC stated that our program "was not a part of China's National Education System." Our business model is a new one—Chinese students earning summer school credits for transfer to America through coursework done in China taught at Chinese universities by American faculty according to American university standards. CDGDC is based on a system for Chinese local students to earn their degrees after four years of studying in Chinese universities, and wasn't really set up to deal with this sort of request.

The CDGDC was established for higher education conducted within a nation-state. It could not verify SIE's credits partly because the school represented a burgeoning form of transnational education different from the joint-degree programs commonly found in China. In these joint-degree programs, the students are typical Chinese university students who receive an academic degree issued by the Ministry of Education. At SIE, however, the students and teachers came from outside China and the credits were used for fulfilling degree requirements outside China. To further complicate SIE's approval process, as Chinese higher education scholars have pointed out, the Ministry of Education had never published specific selection criteria for the establishment of transnational education institutions and programs (He 2016; Sun 2004). The vagueness in how the ministry actually put its policies into practice made SIE's struggle for accreditation unpredictable. SIE was forced to work with the CDGDC guidelines, although, as Hao Liu suggested in his e-mail, "working with the Chinese government agencies is almost always slow and time-consuming."

After some wrangling, SIE received accreditation in late 2013. Once gaining this status, it leveraged CDGDC as a new selling point. On its website, for instance, SIE claims it is the first American-style summer school to receive CDGCD verification. Further, in a gray box on the top of the index page, a location anyone visiting the website would not miss, it highlights CDGDC's relation to a host of national powers sanctioning transnational education.

> At present, CDGDC, as an administrative department directly under the Ministry of Education and operating under the joint leadership of the Ministry of Education (MoE) and the Academic Degrees Committee of the State Council (ADSCS), is the only authority to verify the domestic higher education certificates and transcripts. It is also recognized by mainstream American education verification institutions, colleges and universities, especially for WES (World Education Services) and ECE (Educational Credential Evaluators), which take CDGDC Verification as a prerequisite for the issuance of final verification report. (SIE 2015)

The statement highlights a network of institutions that authorize and legitimize transnational higher education. The network involves institutions in both nations. They represent various institutional powers: the government (the Chinese Ministry of Education, the Chinese Academic Degrees Committee of the State Council, and the CDGDC), business (social media sites such as Renren and verification services such as the Educational Credential Evaluators and the World Education Service), and the university. By leveraging this network of powers, SIE substantiates Melissa Butler's argument made to its clients (both Chinese students and North American universities) that "[its] credits are not for sale."

The way SIE works with the Chinese higher education system is to integrate its summer sessions into the international education programs already in operation in partner universities. International higher education can take multiple forms in a Chinese university. Under the Ministry of Education directives, a university can run joint-degree programs with educational entities from outside China for both domestic and foreign students. It can also offer degree or training programs geared toward foreign students. SIE operates in a mixture of these forms. At SYSU, for example, SIE joined hands with the Office for International Students' Affairs, which promoted SIE summer sessions as North American students' study-abroad programs. On the office's website, SIE students were portrayed as foreign students.

中山大学SIE国际暑期学校于7月2日正式开学。来自美国,加拿大12名知名大学的知名教授和来自国外40多所知名大学127名学生欢聚在中山大学,开始他们的国际暑校之旅,......中山大学 SIE国际暑校采用 美国大学标准学术体系,各国学生在中 山大学SIE国际暑校学习后,可以把所修得课程学分转回自己所在国的大学。······课程主要面向来自北美以及其他地区的大学生。

(SYSU-SIE International Summer School officially started on July 2. 12 famed professors from well-known US and Canadian universities and 127 students from over 40 famous foreign universities joined together at SYSU to start their international summer school journey. . . . The summer school adopts the academic standards of American university system. After studying at the summer school, students of different countries can transfer credits to their home institutions. . . . The courses are designed for students from North America and other regions.) (SYSU Office for International Students' Affairs 2012)

By foreignizing its students, SIE joined SYSU's international education efforts. Like foreign students, as shown on their transcripts, Chinese students receive credits from this officially credited university instead of from SIE. The head of the SYSU Office of International Students' Affairs presided over the welcome dinner for the SIE faculty. She stated that her office was pleased to work with SIE because the latter helped promote international education at SYSU, underscoring the value of their collaboration. However, the unspoken truth, as revealed to me by one of the SIE administrators later, was that the SYSU office received a handsome dividend: half the tuition SIE collected.

STRATEGIES OF LOCATIONS

The wrangling of national and transnational modes of education also played out in the material world. The physical and institutional locations these modes occupied shaped their strategies of operation. One day soon after the summer session started, as I walked down Garden East Road, a few container trailers slowly pulled into the student-residence-hall compounds. I was surprised by the presence of these trailers, which are more commonly seen on highways and in seaports. After the trucks stopped, porters flooded the compounds. Not knowing what was happening, I queried a student who was standing by. She told me these trailers transported the belongings of students coming from the SYSU Zhuhai campus. Chinese universities underwent rapid expansion beginning in the late 1990s as part of the marketization of higher education. Students were charged about 5,000 RMB (about 800 US) a year for tuition and fees rather than attending school for free as before. They were not assigned jobs upon graduation but had to find employment in the marketplace. These moves were made to help sustain the rapidly growing Chinese economy. Within less than two decades, the number of university students quadrupled, turning higher education as a privilege for a few into a commodity affordable to many. As SYSU expanded, it annexed a medical university and opened two new campuses, one of them located in Zhuhai. Every year, hundreds of undergraduates on the Zhuhai campus moved to the main campus to complete their junior and senior years. Helping the students move across campuses, the container trailers "mapped out" the new geographies of Chinese higher education.

Despite these increased mobilities and changes, Chinese higher education has retained key socialist elements. The university provides its members with care and protection. With heavy government subsidies and bank loans, it charges students relatively low tuition and fees. Almost all students graduate within four years, during which the university provides subsidized food and lodging. As living off campus is more expensive, most students choose to live on campus and eat in the university canteens. After living in a guarded compound on Zhuhai campus for two years, the SYSU students moved into another one on the main campus. Like their students, a majority of the faculty and staff are offered campus housing. The university also runs kindergarten, elementary, and middle schools for the faculty's and staff's children. With concrete walls and guards, the university marks its boundaries, trying to ensure that its members are protected physically and socially. Huang Youqin (2006) suggests that the widespread gating practice in urban China resulted from both the collectivist culture and tight political control. As a result of providing a socialist safety net, many universities are burdened by heavy debts these days.

Representing a new mode of education, SIE inhabits the margins of the university. Instead of teaching in a building designated for general instructional purposes, we taught in one designated for the School of Continuing Education. The building is located in the southeastern edge of the main campus. The majority of SIE students live off campus—at home or in hotels nearby. A good number of them stay in brand-name hotels such as the Marriot and the Hilton. SIE faculty is assigned to live off campus, immediately outside the university walls. Our building, also guarded, was a commercial high rise overlooking the campus. It sits on Binjiang East Road, a business street along Pearl River. Next to the building and intersecting with the bustling street is a quiet alley with a fishy smell, filled largely by food venders. Sometimes I walked through the alley to Shangdu Road to take the subway. Near the subway station, there were signs everywhere competing for attention, inflecting diverse discourses in Chinese society. For instance, on a wall along Shangdu

Figure 5.2. A "Chinese dream" wall poster on Shangdu Road

Road, the local government made a giant poster to promote the "Chinese dream," a slogan put forward by the Communist Party in 2012 (see more on the Chinese dream in chapters 3 and 6). In the middle of the poster, in the style of four-character expressions familiar to ordinary citizens, are the words "国家富强、民族振兴、人民幸福" (The country becomes rich and strong; the nation develops vigorously; people live a happy life). To the right, the expression "中国梦" (Chinese dream) aligns with two authoritative national symbols: the Great Wall and an ornament column erected in front of the imperial palace, the Forbidden City in Beijing (see Figure 5.2). This official discourse is responded to by a palm-sized poster stapled to the trunk of a tree facing the wall poster. It advertises a clandestine service: selling certificates, including academic degrees, college diplomas, English proficiency certificates, marriage licenses, divorce certificates, and premises permits (see Figure 5.3). The juxtaposition of these posters suggests that this certification business, despite its illegitimacy in the eyes of the government, is one pathway to the Chinese dream. This poster reminded me that, also in the certification business, SIE embodies another pathway, a pathway to middle-class dreams. Living off campus, one would encounter discourses of different social scales like these.

In the middle of the semester, I interviewed two SIE administrators on how SYSU shared resources with SIE. Andy and Sean codirected the

Figure 5.3. An advertisement on Shangdu Road for certification service

SYSU campus.[1] Andy used to work at the Ministry of Education overseas studies service center in Guangzhou. He gave up this position, claiming he believed in the promise of the new educational mode. Sean had graduated from Franklin and Marshall College a few years before and planned to return to the United States for graduate studies. Taking place in SIE's teaching building, the interview reveals the complex ways SIE negotiated a spatial relationship with SYSU.

XIAOYE: 你们在留学生那边挂靠的话,那为什么不用留学生那边的一些教学楼,或者宿舍,或者说外教的一些房子?你看像在上海的话,它是逸夫楼,当时让我们住。

(Since you work with the foreign student office, why don't you use its teaching building, or its dormitories, or the rooms for foreign teachers? Look, [on the SIE campus] in Shanghai, they let us stay in Yifu Building.)

ANDY: 我知道,是这样子的,因为我们这边不一样。因为去年有很多教授强烈建议 一定要有厨房,所以像那次没有。去年有,有几个教授,有一个教授,他说他有个孩子说有哮喘,他不能吃外面的东西,只能自己煮。这次我们就全找了外面的,校内的有,但它是什么都不包了。

(I know. It's because we are different here. Because last year many professors strongly recommended that a kitchen be provided, but it wasn't last time. A few professors, one professor, he said his child had asthma. He couldn't eat outside, so they cooked at home. We searched for rooms off campus this time. There are rooms on campus but they don't have kitchens.)

SEAN: 现在也有学生也住校内,可是条件就不够,不如那么好了。

(Some students also live on campus, but the living condition isn't that great.)

XIAOYE: 不如外面的好一些。

(Not as good as that off campus.)

ANDY: 还有另外一个就是,假如说,留学生楼我们也有空了位置,但是,不可能。留学生,你也知道,国内条件, 住宿条件相差好远……

(There is another reason. For example, there are spare rooms in the foreign students building. But it's impossible to use them. Foreign students, you know, the living condition in China lags behind that overseas.)

SEAN: 这个就跟美国就差好远。

(It lags far behind that in the US.)

XIAOYE: 对,对,对。

(Right, right, right.)

ANDY: 去年很多学生一过来,然后家长就说,"这地方我孩子不住,我要去住五星级的"。

(Soon after some students arrived last year, their parents said, "my child won't stay here. I want to stay in a five-star hotel.")

XIAOYE: 噢,住外面。为什么选这个教室呢?

(Oh, they wanted to stay off campus. Why did you choose these classrooms then?)

ANDY: 这个地方比较特别的是,因为这里是本部,本部现在很少教室了,全部是行政用的办公楼。(XIAOYE: 或者是研究生的一些教室。) 对,对,对。所以,因为仅有的几栋公共教学楼,他们六月29,30号一直还是上课,有些是七月的十号才放假,我们用不了那些楼。

(This place is special in that this is the main campus. There are few classrooms left, and most of the buildings are for administrative functions. (XIAOYE: or classrooms for graduate students) yes, yes, yes. So, the few buildings used for general teaching purposes, they were being used by the SYSU students on June 29 and 30. Some won't end their semester until July 10th. We could not use those buildings.) (July 24, 2013)

The interview centered on my concern that while both SYSU and SIE advertised the summer school as the former's international education program, SIE did not occupy the space SYSU had designated for such programs. Like other Chinese universities, SYSU allocated space for its international education programs: guest houses for foreign teachers and residence buildings for foreign students. Like its treatment of domestic students and teachers, the university guarded these spaces under its parental wings. SIE decided not to use these spaces for an array of reasons—the faculty's desire for family-friendly apartments, the poor living conditions in student residence halls, and scheduling conflicts for using buildings designated for general instructional purposes. Andy also emphasized spatial choice as an identity marker for the middle-class students. Living off campus, off the guarded spaces, SIE found its own place physically and institutionally.

The School of Continuing Education building was the only SYSU space SIE occupied, symbolizing the relationship between traditional and new modes of higher education. With a modernist design, the building manifests authority and rigidity inside and outside. It has only one entrance, and it is always guarded. The classrooms are equipped with modern technologies, but the desks and chairs are lined up and nailed to the floor, a design that reinforces a traditional classroom power structure. The SIE administrative office is located on the third floor, adjacent to the faculty office. Both offices are makeshift, originally audio-visual classrooms. So every desk is fenced with glass and equipped with earphones. The administrative office, in Latour's (2005) term "a center of calculation" (178), is occupied by the two administrators, teaching assistants, and welfare assistants. The administrative intentions and orders are delivered, all except e-mails and phone calls, by the assistants to the faculty office or the classrooms. The School of Continuing Education provides short-term training courses and correspondence courses to nontraditional students. Its space seems fitting for SIE's educational model—providing short-term courses to nontraditional Chinese university students. SIE students are nontraditional because they are deterritorialized.

SIE faculty are deterritorialized too. Their academic lives span national borders. Among my colleagues, three had career trajectories like mine. I completed my undergraduate studies in China before heading to the United States for PhD studies. Upon receiving my doctoral degree, I was hired for a tenure-track position by a US university. Stranded between cultures, I have focused on cross-cultural communication in my teaching and research. With family ties in China as well as being involved in research related to China, I have often traveled back to my homeland. I hold both a Chinese passport and a US green card, which allow me to cross national borders with ease. Like me, my three colleagues chose to teach at SIE because they could then both conduct research and visit families in China. The rest of the faculty came to SIE largely because they wanted to see China. One professor was born in Taiwan and grew up in the United States. A faculty couple, now teaching in Quebec, Canada, grew up in France and had taught in France and the United States. Two of the remaining three teachers, all Americans, had taught in other countries before.

Conducting North American-style education outside the United States posed logistical challenges. Issues of teaching materials and record keeping, as well as quality assurance and pedagogical adaption (see You and You 2013; You 2016), were raised at faculty meetings in Guangzhou, as well as in Shanghai two years before. In terms of the teaching materials, the professors wanted to adopt textbooks they used at home. In the first few years, SIE asked that students purchase textbooks in the United States and bring them to the summer school. However, most of the students ignored the request, believing they would be able to purchase them in China. Once in China, they had difficulty locating these texts. To solve the problem, SIE stipulated in 2013 that the faculty adopt e-books. The e-book policy seems to have solved a thorny issue in conducting transnational higher education, as many of the SIE administrators thought it would.

The issue of textbooks was revisited during Dean Butler's visit to the Guangzhou campus. At the end of the first week, the faculty gathered to meet with the dean in the administrative office. The following faculty discussion underscores once again the material consequences of the sovereign boundaries in conducting transnational education. The faculty shared with each other the challenges brought on by the e-book policy and the solutions the SIE community had improvised.

> BUTLER: We had a person in Beijing test Kindle and test CourseSmart and it worked. And Saturday before our meeting in Beijing, I got an email from one of my students, say "we can't get access to CourseSmart in China." Oh, it turned out that the person who tested it in Beijing had tested it on a server that was routed through Taiwan and did not encounter the same problem. I don't know how you handled the situation here.
>
> SMITH: Kindle.
>
> BUTLER: In Shanghai students have found the Kindle site blocked. It was not blocked like by the Chinese side, but was blocked by, restricted commerce, something like that. It's copyright basically that's being protected. Nobody here had problems?
>
> MORRISON: The students are pretty ingenious. They had figured out ways to get copies of the book. As long as one of them had the book, by the end of the week they all got it.

SMITH: One problem with Kindles, the best books that I've read, they are not available in Kindles. I am stuck with books that I probably won't use.

BUTLER: CourseSmart has a wider selection. But again, the only way, next time we will fix some of these. CourseSmart, you can sign into it from China if you have a preexisting account. If you didn't have a preexisting account, you cannot sign into it. You can't buy a book from China unless you do it behind VPN. So we ended up doing the same. TAs are going to sit in the TAs' office, and several TAs have VPNs. "Come in, give me your credit card, and buy the book." Then you can download it from Kindle or from CourseSmart. (July 5, 2013)

The discussion underscores a central challenge in implementing the e-book policy: the inaccessibility of e-books on Kindle and CourseSmart sites in China. Although the Internet has enabled ideas and cultural products to travel across national borders instantly, various institutions are monitoring and regulating such mobility. They continue to work within or for the sovereign borders, guarding the national borders virtually. Copyright laws, often nation based, for example, could lead to restricted commerce on the Internet. At the same time, the SIE community found ways to evade the controls of these institutions. The students accessed websites through VPNs and shared texts among themselves. They developed local strategies to resist and subvert these boundary-setting practices. As revealed in the next two chapters, grasping the rules of an institution and playing them as a game was a distinct strategy among the middle-class students. Broadly called *shanzhai* (山寨) practice, the strategy not only enabled them to navigate various institutions but also often coordinated their literacy practices inside the classroom.

Sound recordkeeping was another logistical challenge. At the first faculty meeting, the academic director of the Guangzhou campus advised that we keep track of the students' grades for each assignment. At the end the semester, instead of handing in just the final grades, we needed to turn in an excel file showing the grade for each assignment. In case a student filed a complaint about a final grade after the program ended, the administration would be able to respond to it. In his French accent, the academic director couched his directive in the discourse of professionalism and prestige: "[This practice] will make the program a little more professional. . . . Students won't complain because they know SIE has all the paperwork" (July 4, 2013). The SIE administration was keenly aware of professionalism and prestige in conducting transnational higher education, for which it was once challenged by *The Chronicle of Higher Education* article.

CONCLUSION

Transnational education entails mobilities across borders. Administrators, faculty, and students travel across physical spaces, but administrative, pedagogical, and literacy regimes engage in such travel as well. As revealed in this chapter, for example, inhabiting a translocal space, SIE had to make administrative decisions that are hardly local. It could not operate as an independent educational entity due to its lack of government accreditation and had to team up with multiple bodies through its credit-bearing courses. Even after receiving accreditation, it had to maintain affinity with North American universities and their value systems. It continued to recruit Western professors to teach its courses and emphasized their compatibility with courses offered in North America. The professors could not fully import their pedagogical practices from home. As I have reported elsewhere (You and You 2013), they had to modify their teaching based on local educational tradition and sociopolitical concerns. We get a glimpse of their adaption in their negotiation of old and new technologies to get their students textbooks.

What has produced and structured mobility in transnational education includes policies, laws, administrative programs, discourses, material conditions, and technologies. In the United States, there has been a long tradition of an open-door policy that encourages college students to study abroad. It is commonly held that study abroad will benefit them in their multilingual and intercultural competencies. North American universities tend to run study-abroad programs themselves or in alliance with one another or to establish branch campuses overseas. In contrast, the Chinese government has promoted transnational education largely for importing expertise, human resources, and capital to support weak academic disciplines. It prefers joint-degree programs as the chief form of transnational education. At the same time, it guards against certain practices that may infringe its "educational sovereignty." SIE had to negotiate these policies and administrative programs to carve a space of its own. In addition to policies and programs, the mechanism that structures mobility has a material dimension. In the case of SIE, faculty and students are supported by modern transportation, which makes their travel possible. SYSU provides a physical space for teaching but not a living space that meets the expectations of SIE faculty and students. While SYSU is able to provide reliable Internet access, nation-based copyright laws create obstacles for the access of certain instructional materials.

As revealed in this chapter, what counts as legitimate education is a central issue in transnational education, an issue fully controlled by national authorities. For both North American and Chinese universities, legitimacy means study-abroad programs must have received government accreditation. Accreditation ensures the value of the course work in these programs, which becomes fluid capital that is transferable and mobile. At the program level, as shown in SIE's arguments, the length of the study program as reflected in the credit hours, the qualifications of the teaching staff, and the types of academic support are all critical constituents of quality assurance. Quality assurance guarantees the exchange value of the course work and hence the legitimacy of transnational education.

Facilitated by institutions, policies, discourses and technologies, SIE students are able to travel across national and institutional borders. But will these mobilities lead to enhanced intercultural competence or the ability to move between cultures discursively and imaginatively in an ethical fashion, as celebrated in the United States for promoting study-abroad programs? Cultivating intercultural competence, or a transcultural citizenship, is also an ideal in literacy and communication studies (Guerra 2008, 2015; Sobré-Denton and Bardhan 2013; You 2016). My own teaching at SIE provides a window into the students' mobility or immobility in the cultural domain. Their literacy practices reveal their sensibilities as students and citizens, their ways of constructing academic and social identities as they engage the discourses of a wide spectrum—sociopolitical, economic, and cultural. Now, we turn to their literacy practices and identity construction in the next two chapters.

Note

1. All names used in this and the next two chapters are, with the participants' permission, either pseudonyms or English names adopted by the participants.

6

ASSEMBLING THE COSMOPOLITAN

One of the study-abroad myths is that students will develop global, international, and intercultural competencies. These competencies include knowledge about several dimensions of global and international cultures; appreciation of cultural, racial, and ethnic diversity; understanding of the complexities of issues in a global context; and comfort in working with people from other cultures (Burnett and Huisman 2010; Greenholtz 2000; Hammer, Bennett, and Wiseman 2003; Kimmel and Volet 2012; Lee et al. 2012; Soria and Troisi 2014). Related to literacy practices, study abroad promises to offer students opportunities to communicate across linguistic and cultural borders. At Michigan State, Chinese international students developed strategies in their socialization into the university. Their linguistic and cultural adaptability evidenced their growing intercultural competencies. However, cultural isolationism or immobility was also one of their strategies to cope with the menacing challenges in studying abroad. As illustrated in the case of Yan in chapter 4, a god of learning recognized by her peers, Chinese students sometimes fell back on their Chinese cultural and linguistic enclave to seek comfort and help. Upon returning home, would they continue to swing between being open and being closed to other cultures and other peoples? Openness to the linguistic and cultural Other in cross-cultural interactions may be termed *cosmopolitanism*. As Robert Holton (2009) explains, "Cosmopolitanism involves inter-cultural openness on a transnational stage. . . . Openness may be combined in practice with elements of cultural or institutional closure, but the more closed the less cosmopolitan. . . . Trans-national openness . . . does entail some kind of mobility whether of the imagination, or through activities that engage with the wider world" (117).

To seek answers to whether Chinese students move transculturally when they study abroad at home, in this chapter, I focus on my own students. This decision came from the recognition that the students and I did not live in two separate worlds. Together we constituted the mobile

DOI: 10.7330/9781607327332.c006

field site and the SIE subculture. What I did at SIE as a teacher and a researcher influenced the students, and they influenced me. Further, as both parties interacted in the subculture, "conceiving the field as a fluidic, active, complicated and messy terrain that is encountered in surprising and uncertain ways would be a more accurate portrayal that is sympathetic to the mobilizing process of the research itself" (Adey 2010, 146).

However, tracing my students' cultural mobilities or immobilities is not the exclusive end of the study. As Newkirk (1996) suggests, a researcher has the responsibility to intervene when issues and problems arise with the subjects. With my own cosmopolitan disposition, I wanted to see my students move across the boundaries of nation, class, gender, and sexual orientations, to be open to and tolerant of difference. In actant-network theory, Latour (2005) urges social scientists not only to study associations but also to assemble them for the common good of the humanity.

> This is where politics again enters the scene if we care to define it as the intuition that associations are not enough, that they should also be composed in order to design one common world. . . . We look for ways to register the novelty of associations and explore how to assemble them in a satisfactory form. . . . [We] have to establish connections with the others that cannot possibly be held in the nature/society collectors. (259–62)

In the classroom, I need strategies to capitalize on my study of associations and mobilities to assemble them for "one common world." To present observations of my students' transcultural mobilities and my pedagogical intervention, I must first lay bare what I did in the classroom as well as my own ideologies.

CULTIVATING COSMOPOLITANISM IN COMMUNICATION EDUCATION

My teaching at SIE emphasized a cosmopolitan orientation to communication education, integrating Western models with local traditions and concerns. I taught English Writing and Public Speaking on the SYSU campus, two general education courses commonly required by North American universities. In keeping with how I usually handle first-year writing in the United States, the writing course consisted of a research project, an assignment that aims to socialize students into academic discourse. Students chose a topic of personal interest and wrote a series of papers that would eventually lead to an argumentative essay. These papers included a research proposal, an interview essay, a literature review, and finally an argumentative essay. In the public-speaking class, which will be the focus of this chapter, the students first were introduced to the five canons of rhetoric (invention, arrangement, style, memory, and delivery). To promote civic engagement, they were to deliver a series of speeches on a topic of public interest, a topic they chose in the beginning of the semester. These speeches included a problem speech, a policy speech, and finally a motivational speech. In both classes, the students were encouraged to identify a topic of their own interest and to explore it through reading, writing, interviews, and class discussions. By focusing on one single topic for the semester, the students would be able to explore pertinent discourses in depths. Further, as I have suggested elsewhere (You 2016), through continuous conversation with others, the students might develop understanding of and empathy with them.

These two courses carried values central to communication education in the United States, including personal voice, authorial expertise, and democratic deliberation. The writing course focused on fostering students' authorial expertise. By building their knowledge on certain topics, students can develop confidence and the skills to participate in public debates. Ilona Leki (1991–1992) describes a similar sequenced assignment approach; the students "are not asked to wait until their skills and knowledge base develop piece by piece before addressing important issues. Rather, they are allowed a voice in public debates on important issues and learn that they can contribute to those debates" (23). Similarly, the public-speaking course focused on cultivating students' skills for participating in public deliberation. The textbook, *The Art of the Speaker* (Johnstone and McCullough 2008), is used for the same course at Penn State University. In the beginning of the text, the authors stress the centrality of speaking well in a democracy: "The main emphasis is on how public speaking can be used in community life to address important social issues and problems. The ability to speak well in public and to argue forcefully for one's beliefs is at the heart of democratic citizenship" (v). The emphasis on cultivating personal voice and participating in public deliberation as a citizen is central to North American higher education tradition.

In addition to importing North American models, I integrated elements of a cosmopolitan pedagogy in the public-speaking class. Sobré-Denton and Bardhan (2013) view a cosmopolitan pedagogy for intercultural communication as "an embodied, socially conscious and egalitarian form of education" (165). This pedagogy includes several principles, which I consciously adopted in my teaching: learning is dialogic and takes a ground-up rather than a top-down approach; the cosmopolitan pedagogy teaches the value of valuing humanity and social justice at local and global levels through multiple learning styles, such as experiential learning, dialogue, and reflection; it gives alternative voices a central position and to "translate voice and culture" (165); it emphasizes engagement with the cultural Other as well as critical self-reflexivity; it stresses multiple perspective taking to inculcate the value of empathy; it focuses on the interconnectedness of the local and global and encourages the use of imagination to link the two; it commends an ethical obligation to the Other both at home and at a global level; it constructs an egalitarian educational space where all have the same rights to and responsibility for knowledge.

While the notions of cosmopolitanism and intercultural competence typically focus on intercultural and international openness at a transnational level, they also promote respect and empathy for the Other within the nation, which in the present study is China. Indeed, China is not culturally monolithic or static. Rapid economic development has caused change in social relations, people's politico-economic outlook, and lifestyle. Cultural Others have emerged due to difference in political views, economic status, class affiliation, sexual orientation, and lifestyle. Often, cultural Others, particularly the socially underprivileged, are treated unfairly in Chinese society. As a result of China's joining global capitalism four decades ago, privatization of small and medium-sized state-owned enterprises in the late 1990s led to a large number of layoffs. At the same time, young people in the farming population left their villages and became migrant workers in the city. They do not enjoy the same benefits as the city residents. As reported in the news, they are paid much less and are often late; they are not covered by the government healthcare system; their children cannot enroll in schools designated for city kids. Therefore, when my public-speaking class debated domestic issues, they all had to confront social injustice. As the privileged, they were forced to examine their positioning in relation to the Other. Through debates, they had the chance to hear other perspectives and sometimes shifted their positions as well as their identification with the Other.

I harmonized foreign pedagogical models by couching them in local rhetorical traditions. I exposed my public-speaking class to the Chinese tradition of political rhetoric, emphasizing the long history of the Chinese literati's fight for social justice. On the first day of class, for instance, I reviewed the world history of public speaking by drawing the students' attention to certain aspects of the Chinese tradition: political debaters traveled between rivaling states to promote their political visions in the Spring and Autumn (771 BC–476 BC) and the

Warring States (475 BC–221BC) periods; in the late nineteenth and early twentieth centuries, intellectual debates exposed the Chinese public to Western political philosophy and to imagining a political structure other than the two-millennium-long feudal system; college students were always active participants in those intellectual debates (You 2010).

Working for social justice in transnational education requires both cultural sensitivity and caution. In the history of English-language teaching in China, while writing has been a college course for a long time, public speaking was seldom offered in Communist China. Over the last two decades, English speech contests were widely conducted on university campuses. However, students' topics and arguments had to conform to the Communist Party ideologies and government policies. Skilled debaters were selected to participate in national television contests (Lucas 2013). Therefore, when encouraging my SIE students to write or speak about social issues critically, I was nervous, not sure whether the classroom deliberation would migrate outside the classroom and incur intervention from SYSU authorities. I was also concerned that with the firewall set up by the government, my students would not have access to certain critical information on the Internet. This concern was shared by foreign universities that established campuses in China (Fischer 2015). Soon, I discovered my students were able to subvert the government censorship by using their home institution's virtual private network (VPN).

In their speeches and class discussions, my students engaged the Communist Party ideologies and government policies, which promote a particular version of cosmopolitanism. Aligned with the slogan "constructing socialism with Chinese characteristics," this version emphasizes national strength and harmony as the foundation for world peace and justice. Central to this version are two concepts introduced by the Communist Party over the last decade—a harmonious socialist society (社会主义和谐社会) and the Chinese dream (中国梦). By arguing for building a harmonious society, the party appeals to the Confucian vision for human relationships. It emphasizes democratic and legal principles in government, equality and justice, a convivial and orderly life, and harmonious coexistence between humans and the natural world. The proposal for a harmonious society has been generally viewed as the party's response to growing socioeconomic disparity, and the ensuing tensions and conflicts, in Chinese society. The notion of a Chinese dream was first articulated by the party leader Xi Jinping in 2012. He called for concerted efforts to realize the rejuvenation of the Chinese nation. While Western critics tend to read the Chinese dream as a nationalist campaign to resolve internal contradictions (Kuhn, *New York Times,* June 4, 2013; Wasserstrom 2014), some Chinese commenters view it as a way to imagine the relationship between China and the rest of the world (Chen 2013). Central to the Chinese dream is the party's emphasis on collaboration with other nations to pursue peaceful development, to promote and guard diverse cultures in the world, and to build a just, democratic, and harmonious world order. One actualization of the dream takes place through the government-sponsored One Belt and One Road initiative, an initiative that focuses on investing in infrastructure projects in emerging-market countries in Europe, Asia, and Africa, with a total of $900 billion in investments by the end of 2016. *Fortune* magazine describes the initiative as the way "China spreads the wealth around " and as at least twelve times the size of the Marshall Plan, which rebuilt Western Europe from rubble after WWII (Cendrowski 2016). In short, the realization of the Chinese dream is anchored in the peace and prosperity of the world. The dream positions the party as the legitimate leader of the nation, who, by following Confucian teachings and by managing the family and the state well, will bring peace and prosperity to the world. If the party stands for a version of cosmopolitanism, the question for me became, will my upper-middle-class students accept this version?

Thus, my public-speaking class constituted a translocal cultural space. On one hand, the central pedagogical framework was imported—the textbook, the assignments, and the cosmopolitan pedagogy. On the other hand, both the audiences and the issues addressed by my students were local. My students debated current Chinese social issues critically and in great depth. If this class had been taught in the United States, these issues would hardly have been addressed. Even if they were discussed, they might not be dealt with in great depth or in nuanced ways because US students lack the cultural knowledge, if not interest. The Chinese Communist Party's version of cosmopolitanism is derived from both the international Communist movement and the Confucian tradition. However, addressing Chinese social issues, my students often deviated from the Communist Party ideologies and government policies. In the end, their ideological, epistemological, and aesthetic deviations helped construct their identities.

In the rest of this chapter, I focus on how my middle-class students mobilized their intercultural competence to address issues of social injustice. To identify evidence of such competence, I marked in the data moments in which my students revealed knowledge about global and international cultures; showed appreciation for cultural, racial, ethnic, and gender difference; and contextualized issues in a global context. My data consisted of classroom video and audio recordings, students' speech drafts and notes, and my research notes. My observation reveals that the students consciously drew on their knowledge of international cultures, particularly of the United States, to make arguments on Chinese social issues. Further, the growth of their intercultural competence paralleled and sometimes facilitated their construction of positions and identities in a shifting Chinese society. To understand their construction of positions and identities, I follow one term, *diaosi*, an evocative contemporary street-slang term for losers ("China's Losers" 2014), which surfaced multiple times in my SIE classes. Used by a large Chinese population for identity work, the term indexes socioeconomic disparity in a shifting Chinese society and often refers to the lower class. After first noting its use among my students, I evoked the term strategically in my teaching to prompt my students to explore Chinese social issues and to construct positions and identities. While constructing their identities, as this chapter will reveal, my students moved between being open and being closed to the cultural Other.

DIAOSI AS AN IDENTITY STRATEGY

Most of the SIE students came from upper-middle-class families. Owing to the CDGDC verification obstacle, the SYSU campus enrollment dropped by half in 2013, down to about 60 students from 127 the previous year. Among them, three took the writing and nine took the public-speaking course. All my students attended private US universities: Clark, Lehigh, Rochester, Syracuse, Miami, and Pepperdine. SIE students' transnational mobility is closely linked to social-class reproduction in China. A study published in 2014 revealed that Chinese families sending their children for high school or college overseas were middle-class families. In those families, at least one parent held an advanced degree, occupied a high-ranking position, and earned a high salary (EIC Education 2014). Sending their children to well-ranked US universities, the parents paid at least 40,000 US dollars a year for tuition, more than forty times what was charged by a Chinese university. With urban household incomes nationally averaging less than 10,000 US dollars a year (National Bureau of Statistics 2014), most Chinese families cannot afford a North American education. Upon returning to China, those with credentials from North American universities, particularly from prestigious ones, earn significantly more than do Chinese university graduates (Wang and Miao 2014). Chinese international students' academic success leads to social success (cf. Waters 2006 on Hong Kong students studying in Canada and returning to work in Hong Kong). My SIE courses, thus, focused on teaching upper-middle-class students how to exercise their citizenry rights and duties through speaking and writing.

While the enrollment number disappointed the SIE administration, it reaped multiple benefits for the faculty, one of them being that we taught smaller classes and formed a close-knit community with students. Probably due to their shared education and class background, my students often hung out together, forming an affective collective. They had lunch together, went to bars and movies in the evening, and played video games in Internet cafes. A distinct community practice among my public-speaking students, as I soon discovered, was having lunch together after my class. As part of this community, and also due to my interests in their literacy practices, I joined them for lunch regularly. We usually walked out of the SYSU campus and sampled restaurants near the East Gate area, a bustling business district. Along Xingang East Road were sporting-goods stores, clothing stores, Internet cafes, and restaurants serving different cuisines—Cantonese, Hunan, Sichuan, Shannxi, Japanese, and Korean.

At one of those lunches, my students demonstrated to me the ways they constructed class identities and a guangxi network. Our group, about ten people, sat down in a Sichuan restaurant in the second week of class. Most of the dishes were priced around 20 RMB, or about three US dollars, an affordable price for white-collar professionals in the city. Eating inexpensive lunches was the first identity marker I noticed for my upper-middle-class students. As we were flipping through the menu, an important "actant" mediating the construction of the students' guangxi network (Latour 2005), Juliette typed on a large Huawei phone. When I asked her about the phone, Danny showed us his Xiaomi phone, another Chinese brand. These smartphones indexed unique class identities, as the students immediately explained to me. These home brands were originally imitators (山寨/shanzhai) of foreign brands like iPhone and Samsung. Designed for the domestic market, they appealed to the majority who could not afford foreign brands. Now these two Chinese brands have transcended their imitator status, not only seizing a large share of the Chinese market but also selling well overseas. The students viewed these phones as identity markers for *diaosi* (屌丝, literally pubic hair), a self-deprecating term popularly used by the rising Chinese middle class, although by definition it refers to the working class. Using phones affordable to the diaosi was a sign of my students not wanting to show off their wealth. It was both a way to identify and to disidentify with the diaosi, a way to mark class distinction.

The first time I heard someone using the term diaosi in conversation, I asked my students what exactly it meant. Mixing Mandarin and Cantonese, they explained it to me as an urban legend.

DANNY: 屌丝都用这种东西。教授,知道屌丝吗?

(Diaosi all use this stuff [phone]. Professor, do you know about diaosi?)

XIAOYE: 不知道。

(I have no idea.)

DANNY: 屌丝用英文来说就是 . . . dick 加 nerd。

(Diaosi in English means . . . dick plus nerd.)

XIAOYE: 丝是什么意思?是fans的意思吗?

(What does si mean? Does it mean fans?)

EVERYONE: 不是! (No!)

DANNY: 这个故事很长,让我来说,因为我见证了屌丝这个词。那个因为,因为,你们知道百度贴吧有一个最大的吧吗?

(This is a long story. Let me tell you because I witnessed the rise of the word "diaosi." It was because, because, do you know the largest bar in Baidu Post Bar?)

EVERYONE: 李毅吧。 (Li Yi Bar.)

DANNY: 李毅我们管他叫李毅大帝,大帝王嘛,因为他有一次说我的护球像亨利。

(Li Yi, we call him Li Yi the Great, the Great King, because once he said, "I guard the soccer ball like [Thierry] Henry.")

CHRIS: 不是,不是,亨利的护球像我。

(No, no. Henry guards the ball like me.)

DANNY: 我们都是大帝的粉丝,叫帝丝。帝丝都特别屌,屌就是很牛逼的意思。所以说叫屌丝。但是在帝吧里发帖的那些人都是一些奇奇怪怪的人,工作的底层的那些人。

(We are all fans of the Great King, called disi. And disi are especially diao, diao meaning niubi. So we are called diaosi. But those who post on the Li Yi Bar are of all kinds, like lower-working class.) (July 9, 2013)

Danny's minilecture, echoed by other students, indicates that despite being members of the upper middle class, my students identified themselves with the diaosi culture, either seriously or playfully. They performed their identification through eating inexpensive lunches, buying domestic-brand smartphones, and watching soccer games. Danny's lecture also reveals that the diaosi culture is intimately connected to the Internet culture. He mentions Baidu Post Bar. It is a platform provided by Baidu, the largest search-engine provider based in China. Baidu created different virtual spaces, or bars, based on frequently used search terms, for like-minded people to congregate. Li Yi is a former striker on the Chinese national soccer team. His fans created the Li Yi Bar on Baidu to talk about soccer and other matters of interest. Both 屌 (*diao*) and 牛逼 (*niubi*) refer to the male sex organ in regional Chinese dialects. When they are used as adjectives referring to the attributes of an individual, they mean "strong and proud": a person is strong in certain areas; thus they show pride or even arrogance. 丝 (*si*) refers to thin hair or hair-like objects, like angel hair. Thus, 屌丝 (*diao-si*) literally means "male pubic hairs," and, according to Danny, refers metaphorically to the lower working class.

However, since being popularized by the Li Yi Bar in year 2012, diaosi has meant more than lower working class. As Danny explained, it has also been adopted by individuals like him who are not working class to signify their strength and pride. Using survey responses from people in fifty cities in China, a study found that being a diaosi means being a single man between the ages of twenty-one and twenty-five, or a single woman between the ages of twenty-six and thirty, who has little money to their name. Different from China's impoverished population, generally speaking, diaosi are gainfully employed and making ends meet but struggling to establish themselves socially and economically (FlorCruz 2014). According to Baidu Encyclopedia (2013), it has become a term of self-deprecation among the middle class, a humble way of viewing one's ability, condition, and dreams measured against the unreachable standards glorified in mainstream Chinese society. On simple terms, these standards include such personal attributes as being tall, rich, and handsome for men (*gao fu shuai*/高富帅) and having light skin color and being rich and pretty for women (*bai fu mei*/白富美). These attributes (see also chapter 2) have been metonymically used to refer to those who are in possession of them. Virtually anyone who is not content amidst China's rapid socioeconomic transformation, with its unreachable expectations and unrealizable inspirations, could call themselves diaosi. "Figuratively it is a declaration of powerlessness in an economy where it is getting harder for the regular guys" ("China's Losers" 2014, 39). Diaosi are said to carry unique characteristics in their growth, personality, life habits, romance, work, health, and career paths, characteristics different from those found in people who are tall, rich, and handsome. One of their habits, as explained by Danny, is using domestic-brand smartphones with an Android operating system because they cannot afford foreign brands. The Baidu Encyclopedia concludes that "diaosi culture is another emergent Web subculture, signifying that Chinese people have gained more perspectives and rights in interpreting their own lives. . . . As a culture, diaosi undermines traditional authorities through self-deprecation and opposes holiness through self-degradation."

Adopting the expression diaosi for self-deprecation shows the ambivalence of the Chinese middle class. On one hand, they aspire to join the upper class but cannot. In sexual intercourse, as Danny explained to me later, pubic hairs are kept outside the vagina and thus cannot enjoy orgasm as the penis does. Symbolized by the tall, rich, handsome man or the light-skinned, rich, beautiful woman, high-class life is unreachable to them. On the other hand, calling themselves diaosi, the middle class shows alignment, sometimes playfully, with the lower working class, a class traditionally celebrated in Communist China. It can be viewed as a political move the middle class makes for masking their wealth, for self-protection. Using domestic smartphones and calling themselves diaosi suggests that this identity strategy was adopted by my students to deal with the shifting relations in Chinese society.

This identity strategy, however, was critiqued by Siwen, a student in my writing class, in one of her Weibo posts. Literally meaning "mini-blog," Weibo allows users to post messages, pictures, and video clips like Facebook does. Siwen defended a recently released movie called 小时代 (*Tiny Times*), a movie that depicts high-class lifestyles. The story focuses on four young women who work in Shanghai's fashion industry and struggle with work, love, and friendship. While the movie became an instant hit among Chinese youths, it was severely criticized by commentators for depicting unrealistic high-class scenes. More broadly, their criticisms were linked to the high-class, consumer-based, Western lifestyle the movie promotes. Their criticisms were constructed based on a particular frame, a "figured" world in socialist cinema (Gee 2005). Influenced by Soviet socialist realism, films produced in Communist China, particularly in the Maoist period (1949–1976), tended to promote party ideologies and goals and to portray the lives of ordinary people living under the party in a positive way. The lower working class tends to be the hero and the rich the villain (Wang 2014). While commercialized films dominate the Chinese cinema market these days, socialist realism continues to be valued by the Chinese movie industry. By depicting the relationships between individuals and their social environment truthfully, realist films reveal the complex contradictions and conflicts in society (Chinese Film Association Theoretical

Commentary Committee 2008). According to a movie commentator, nowadays realist films should seek to cultivate humanism with a modern and liberal consciousness. They should focus on the living conditions of ordinary people, giving them genuine and profound humanist care (Rao 2007). Thus, valuing realism in film production aligns with the Communist tradition in seeking social justice. Focusing on the living conditions of ordinary people means to give voice to them, often members of the working class who struggle with social changes in the economic-reform era.

Siwen fundamentally disagreed with this ideological stand. She criticized the commentators for following socialist aesthetics and being afraid of embracing class divisions.

现在的影评人脑子都进屎了@周黎明为首。说什么小时代炫富不写实,如果是这样那钢铁侠也在炫富了,人家一套装备多贵?设备多先进?欧美大片的那些跑车呢?小时代其他的我也不懂也不评论,我只给hold住姐赞一个但是我懂客观性。中国电影事业在进步,非要大农村屌丝逆袭中国的电影就他妈写实了

(Led by Zhou Liming, movie commentators these days had shit in their brains. They said Tiny Times wants to show off wealth and reflects no reality. Following this logic, Iron Man also shows off wealth—how much does a prop cost? How advanced is the equipment? How about the race cars in Euro-American big hits? I don't understand other aspects of the movie, so I have no comments. I only want to give Sister hold zhu a 👍. But I understand objectivity. Chinese movie industry is making progress, but do we call Chinese movies realistic only when they portray diaosi from countryside fighting back) (July 7, 2013)

屌丝逆袭 (*diaosi fighting back*) is a key term in Siwen's critique. 逆袭 (*nixi*), originally from Japanese, means fighting back or launching counterattacks. Often used in online games, it refers to extraordinary counterattacks, which often lead to unexpected success. Siwen suggests that many commentators would rather watch success stories of ordinary people or of lower-working-class people struggling toward social progress for a better life than stories set in a high-class context. In making this comment, she expands the meaning of diaosi from a typically unmarried and socioeconomically unestablished urban worker to include the rural poor. She praises the Chinese movie industry for breaking away from the shackles of socialist realism in depicting the real. Indirectly, she wants the middle and upper classes to celebrate their identity bravely. In doing so, she argues for a new aesthetic as well as for an epistemic frame. More profoundly, Siwen distances herself from the use of the term diaosi and moves toward a willingness to acknowledge a separation or division of the classes. In other words, her rejection of the term is, in a sense, a rejection of a classless system, a rejection of the Communist ideal. She wants to be guilt free about having wealth and status.

The two scenarios in which my students used the term diaosi demonstrate that diaosi culture has percolated through their lives. My public-speaking class seemed to have adopted this term to gloss over their ways of thinking and behaving as members of the upper middle class. Once, in class, Danny joked that he was not tall and not rich, but that he was handsome, which I read as trying to contrive a comic instance of diaosi launching counterattacks. Using humor, Danny seemed to fight back against the absolute, glorified standards unreachable for the middle and lower classes. However, this is just another use of the identity strategy: Danny appropriated the diaosi discourse to construct his upper-middle-class identity. He came from a wealthy family that was able to pay for his education at Lehigh University. He was dating a female Chinese student at Syracuse University. Both are prestigious and expensive US schools. While Siwen rejected the term diaosi, her comment squarely underscores the place this term occupies in the Chinese mentality as a trope. She evoked it to distance her from the working class and to highlight her upper-middle-class identity.

SHIFTING CLASS RELATIONS IN CHINESE CINEMA

To explore how my students related to the Communist Party version of cosmopolitanism, the use of the diaosi identity strategy can be further traced in the classroom. In discussing social issues, my students had to take positions in relation to those of the party or of the government. While diaosi culture was part of their identity makeup, the articulation of their positions also helped construct their identity. Therefore, in my teaching, I purposefully drew their attention to the tensions in Chinese class relations and encouraged them to consider how diaosi culture had mediated their ways of being and thinking about the self and the shifting Chinese society. Following Latour's (2005) admonition, this was my strategy to assemble associations in my class. As Siwen's post reveals, the movie industry is one of the institutions engaged in the production of new identities within modern-day China. Therefore, some class discussions centered on Chinese cinema, particularly the production and consumption of *Tiny Times*. I took notes on moments in which my students discussed Chinese social classes and revealed their positioning on this topic. For each moment, I closely looked at the linguistic and cultural resources my students deployed.

Siwen's Weibo post caught my attention because a student in my public-speaking class was also critical of *Tiny Times*. For his three speeches (problem, policy, and inspirational), Michael wanted to address the Chinese movie industry. In his view, it was problematic that poorly rated movies had box-office success while well-rated movies did not. As he stated on one of his PowerPoint slides when delivering his problem speech, "Good movies bankrupt, bad movies died hard." In the same presentation, he compared four recently released Chinese movies regarding their Douban (豆瓣) and IMDb ratings and their box-office numbers. Douban is a China-based movie-rating website. Michael presented *Tiny Times* as an example of those "bad movies," or poorly rated movies. In the question-and-answer session, I asked him why, despite being poorly rated, the movie was a box-office hit. Michael offered his perspective, using the diaosi identity strategy to show his alignment with working-class interests. Like other film critics, he emphasized socialist realism as the proper way for representing life in cinema and for educating the youth.

> All the works by Guo Jingming had his target audiences, which are usually teenagers under sixteen years old. They do not have proper moral values. For example, Guo Jingming, he likes to put everything luxurious, like enjoy high-class life. But that is not true. In Xiaoshidai [*Tiny Times*], he introduced eight people and they all had rich families. The movie shows how hard they work and how hard their lives are. But that is not the fact. And it is important for us to understand that our life is not that easy. We are not born with money, in our, in our mouth. And we should, we gonna have a harder life than theirs. So they are, they are conveying a wrong idea to us. So for many, for many scholars, teenagers without, without an established moral standard will be largely affected by the values adopted by Guo Jingming. That's why Xiaoshidai is morally defective and not very popular among scholars. Well, teenagers loved it because it tells beautiful stories. But stories are actually stories. They have no relationships to reality. So that is why it was popular, it sucked, and it's earning money. (July 18, 2013).

Michael disagrees with the playwright and film director Guo Jingming in his approach to youth literature and cinema. Guo created youth idols by displaying his own luxurious lifestyle in his blogs as well as that of the handsome and beautiful protagonists in his novels and films. In the movie *Tiny Times*, Guo depicts high-class scenes the majority of Chinese youths would dream of. However, influenced by socialist realism, Michael wants to see scenes that show the hard lives of ordinary Chinese. He believes that portraying working-class characters struggling for the betterment of their lives would teach young audiences "proper moral values." He does not count individuals with upper-class backgrounds working hard and living hard lives as reality. Michael seems to align himself with the Communist Party in terms of film aesthetics.

Michael's identity work can be further understood by considering the rhetorical resources he deployed. First, he appropriated expressions from the English-speaking world to mark his transnational, middle-class identity. He used "die hard" in his speech title, which was the title of a Hollywood movie series. Michael also said, "We are not born with money, in our, in our mouth." Probably he intended to say, "We are not born with a silver spoon in our mouth." Second, he adopted inductive reasoning to explain why movie critics and scholars did not favor *Tiny Times*. Arguably, this is a down-to-earth reasoning style found among people regardless of their education background. Michael starts with the playwright's intention to reach young audiences, moves into the moral values portrayed by the movie, and arrives at the conclusion that scholars do not favor these values. While Siwen emphasizes the legitimacy of high-class lifestyles in the movie, Michael criticizes it for failing to reflect ordinary people's lives and thus harming youths with its "morally defective" values. Like Danny, while not a true diaosi himself, Michael served as a spokesperson for diaosi, defining and interpreting Chinese society from a working-class or middle-class perspective. Siwen and Michael were divided in their epistemology, in their views on what is true life in China and how to represent it.

The students' competing views of the movie and in how to position themselves in relation to the working class encouraged me to juxtapose their views in the classroom. I saw this as an opportunity to cultivate transliteracy: I would engage students in shuttling between discourses with the hope of developing their empathy with the Other behind or featured in these discourses. My public-speaking class needed to propose policy changes to tackle a social issue. A deep understanding of the Chinese sociopolitical structure and social change following three decades of economic reforms was crucial for effective policy proposals. Therefore, I decided to engage my students in these differing epistemic perspectives. At the end of a meeting with Siwen, I queried about her Weibo post, indicating that someone in the public-speaking class thought *Tiny Times* was a "bad movie." Although she was not in that class, I drew on her thoughts on the movie as a resource in my teaching. Siwen was a slim, petite, and good-looking woman by contemporary Chinese standards with long hair. Dressed in light-colored skirts, she often came to class with a Gucci handbag, a status symbol among middle-class Chinese women. Before the summer program, she spent 30 thousand RMB (5,000 US dollars) on blepharoplasty, creating a double fold in the eyelids to make her eyes appear rounder. Her father was an airport contractor, running gift shops in two midsized airports. Nevertheless, she emphasized that her father was not making easy money, as the airports were located in less developed southwest regions. To run his business, her father had to live separately from her mother for most of the year. The story of Siwen's father is a familiar one these days; market economy has given ordinary Chinese opportunities to become rich through personal strivings. Overall, as second-generation rich (*fuerdai*/富二代), Siwen had constructed a *baifumei* archetype, that is, a light-skinned, rich, and pretty woman (as discussed in chapter 2).

In response to my query, Siwen elaborated her thoughts on *Tiny Times* and attributed the massive criticisms of the movie to a prevailing pathology among the Chinese. In the end, she articulated a cosmopolitan ideal different from that of the Communist Party. Siwen was very articulate, speaking Mandarin Chinese with a distinct Hunan accent. She stated:

SIWEN: 《小时代》怎么说呢？ 中国人现在有一个心态,就是,病态已经,真的就是没有见过世面的人才会那样的。比如说中国,前段时间不是湖南下大雨有个女生冲到井里了嘛,大家开始在悼念了嘛,一听到她爸妈都是官,她爸是,好高啊,是什么书记,书记,然后,然后,她妈又是什么,那个,是官二代嘛,然后他们就说,官二代全家都要死,死得好,活该。

(What should I say about Tiny Times? Chinese people now have a mentality, that is, pathological already. Only those who haven't seen the world will do that. For example, in China, a while ago Hunan suffered a torrential rain and a girl was washed into a pothole. People started paying her condolences. Once they heard that her parents were officials, her father was in a high position, like a secretary, a secretary, and then, then, her mom was something. She was a second-generation kid of government officials. Then people said the entire family should die. They deserved it.)

XIAOYE: 你说有的人这样讲是不是？

(You mean some people said that, right?)

SIWEN: 很多人,太多了中国......还有一个就是波士顿炸弹,然后有个中国女孩死了嘛,然后就有些中国人会说,反正家里有钱,拿着爸妈的钱让你出去玩,出去玩就被炸死了,活该! 就这样子,你知道吗? 然后,然后,他们现在说《小时代》是什么,是什么,炫富。因为当年郭敬明写这本小说的时候就是讲很有钱人的生活,他现在拍成电影了,就是还原他的小说,但是我觉得他那本书就是,它写的就是贵族生活,他们就说什么不现实的,有个老板用个玻璃杯要三千八人民币,我就觉得说,中国人也有人过这种生活啊。贵族就是这样啊,你不能说它这个电影题材是讲贵族的就是超现实的,说它很烂啊。然后就有很多人说炫富啊,现代年轻人腐朽啊,其实那个电影里面也有说奋斗啊。

(A lot of them, too many people in China. . . . There was also the Boston bombing, then a Chinese woman died. Then some Chinese said her family was rich. She spent her parents' money for travel and for fun. She was killed while having fun. She deserved being killed. It was like this, you know? Then, then, now they say Tiny Times is what, what, showing off wealth. When Guo Jingming wrote the novel years ago, it told about the lives of rich people. Now he turned it into a movie and the movie retold the story. But I felt his book is, it talks about the life of rich people. They say the movie is not realistic, a boss uses a glass worthy of 3800 RMB. But I want to say, some people live such lives in China. Rich people are like that. You can't say the movie is surreal or rotten just because it talks about rich people. Then many people say it shows off wealth, young people nowadays are decadent. In fact, the movie also talks about striving for life goals.) (July 19, 2013)

Elaborating her epistemic perspective, Siwen attributes the prevailing resentment of the rich and the powerful (government officials) among the Chinese to their narrow-mindedness. This mentality goes along with their aesthetic aptitude, which apparently has been shaped by socialist realism. They view a high-class lifestyle as unreal and undesirable in artistic representation. Siwen defends her interest and wealth by arguing for a new aesthetics that would accommodate the lived experiences of the rich and the powerful. Nevertheless, Siwen's comments also reveal a sense of corruption and social injustice the wider Chinese population has felt. She seems to disregard or even defend the enormous social and economic disparities that plague China now.

In her criticisms, Siwen articulates an elitist cosmopolitanism. She emphasizes equal human worth and the need to respect people regardless of whether they are poor, rich, have more social power, or live within or outside China. She hints that transnational mobility and a cosmopolitan outlook are necessary qualities for a Chinese middle class. However, this cosmopolitan outlook contrasts ironically with her defense or disregard of socioeconomic differences. In her comments, Siwen shows global knowledge and emphasizes the importance of respecting cultural difference. In her Weibo post, for example, she talks about the expensive props used in Euro-American movies. In the interview, she underscores the need to go beyond one's community to "see the world." She mentions the Boston bombing in spring 2013, an event that took place close to her university, showing her awareness of what happened outside China. She uses her global knowledge to develop an elitist cosmopolitan outlook.

To further discussion on social justice and class relations, with Siwen's consent I shared her remarks with my public-speaking class. Preparing their policy speech at that time, they needed to explain the rationale for a new policy, the key points of the policy, and its practicality. In Michael's

practice speech on improving Chinese cinema, he proposed three policy points related, respectively, to the Chinese government, the movie
industry, and movie viewers. Regarding the viewers, he argued that they
need proper education in movie appreciation and to develop a proper
aesthetics: "We have to change our values in watching movies. We should
value movies as arts rather than entertainment. In order for the audiences to have proper attitude and value, a rudimentary education and
orientation is important. Policy should focus on media and schools." He
continued to view films guided by socialist realism as morally good and
educational. After his speech, the class discussed ways to improve it. On
educating movie viewers, I played the recorded conversation I had with
Siwen to complicate this policy point. Siwen suggests that there are different social classes and therefore diverse lived experiences. For her, a
movie viewer must cultivate tolerance or even appreciation for different
versions of reality, not just the reality artistically constructed based on
the party ideologies for educating the proletarian.

The class first agreed with Siwen on the prevailing resentment of the
rich and the powerful in Chinese society. In the following conversation,
Michael and Chris explored the reasons for such resentment. Michael
first critiqued the sociopolitical mechanism, which had failed to provide
adequate support to the underprivileged. Then he used a recent incident for illustration: after several failed attempts to appeal to the government for help, a disillusioned man performed a suicidal bombing
at Beijing International Airport. Chris interjected, saying that blaming
the government was unfair, a position with which Michael concurred.
Indirectly, the conversation confirmed widespread inequality and injustice in Chinese society. Our classroom discourse was predominantly in
English. Because Siwen made her remarks in Chinese, the class shifted
to Chinese in their response.

MICHAEL: 仇富现象肯定是由于一种社会机制最初的一种不公平,不公平啊
就是源于一种压制和剥削。很多人上访很多年,昨天才发生那个北京机
场爆炸这事情,那个人就是上访多年。然而政府一直都没有管,那你说,
我生活不公平,我今天去跟你抱怨,你是政府,你都不管我,那你让我怎么
办?所以……

(Resenting the rich certainly is due to the initial inequality in the social
mechanism. Inequality comes from a kind of oppression and exploitation.
Many people petitioned the government for help for years. Yesterday a
bombing happened at Beijing International Airport. The bomber had
petitioned the government for years. But the government always ignored
him. Look, I live in inequality and I complain to you. You are the government, and even you do not help me. What else can you expect me to do?
So . . .)

CHRIS: 可是我觉得他们那个对政府的要求太高了，我觉得。就美国政府，美国人才有多少啊?你中国有这么多的问题 . . .

(But I felt they demanded too much from the government, I felt. In terms of the American government, how many people are there in the US [for their government to take care of]? There are so many issues in China . . .)

MICHAEL: 这个是个非常大的问题,非常非常大的问题,中国本身的性质有很大的关系,你不能老骂政府嘛。中国虽然做得不好,但在已有的机制和国情下,已经做得非常好了。

(This is a very serious issue, a very, very serious issue. It has much to do with the nature of China. You can't always blame the government. Although it hasn't done everything well, but given the current [sociopolitical] mechanism and national conditions, the government has done a marvelous job.)

CHRIS: 已经比其他一些发展中的国家好多了。

(Much better than that of other developing countries.)

In this discussion, Michael first adopted the subject position of the socially underprivileged. He took on the persona of the suicide bomber: "Look, I live in inequality and I complain to you. You are the government, and even you do not help me. What else can you expect me to do?" This dialogue indicates that despite their upper-middle-class status, both Michael and Chris were sympathetic to the underprivileged and to the government for doing a challenging job.

As the conversation unfolded, Siwen's comment challenged Michael to modify his position toward those "bad movies" like *Tiny Times*. I managed to lead the class back to Michael's policy point about educating the public on movie appreciation. Michael explained the importance of movies depicting mainstream values in Chinese society. In his view, these values are nearly universal, similar to those portrayed in a majority of US movies: family and the struggles of ordinary people for the betterment of their lives. His sense of mainstream values appears to have been influenced by Communist Party ideologies. In contrast, *Tiny Times* has not depicted those mainstream, universal values.

MICHAEL: 噢,对,因为它的这个题材可能是非常新颖,但它并不属于一种普世的、主流价值观。像美国他们的电影,美国历届好莱坞获得的影片,只有极少的影片是那种属于左派、非主流价值观,大多数都是右派。主流价值观念宣传的是家庭,宣传的是个人奋斗,这种是普世价值观,更值得宣传。比如说断背山这种,在当年比较就是,比较偏离的题材,它只会颁发一种,比如说最佳外语片奖,或者是最佳什么,什么别的,但不把它颁到最主要的奖。所以这是一个,我觉得是,就是,是什么主流就应该打什么旗,不能就是说因为它好、还不错,它是一个事实,所以我们就应该让它成为这个社会上最popular的一种价值观。

(Oh, yes. Although the topic [of *Tiny Times*] may be new, it doesn't represent a universal, mainstream value. Take American movies as an example. Among the award-winning Hollywood movies, only very few have adopted a leftist, non-mainstream value system. Most of them are rightist. Mainstream values promote family, promote personal strivings. These are universal values, more worthy of promoting. Movies like Brokeback Mountain, in the years of their production, deviated from the mainstream values. The Oscars will issue an award, say the Best Foreign Language Film, or the Best something, or the other, but will not issue one of the major awards. So this is an issue, I felt, about raising the right flag for the right mainstream values. We can't say because it's good, not bad, and it reflects reality, we should make it the most popular value in society.)

XIAOYE: 对,所以你对《小时代》的批判大概是这样,是不是?

(Yes. So this is your criticism of Tiny Times, right?)

MICHAEL: 我其实也没有对它什么批判嘛,因为它好不好都是由个人而言,只是它的存在让整个票房非常不合理。对,我主要是说这个,因为我对这个电影没有什么,我自己也觉得它Okay,我自己也看这电影。

(In fact, I didn't criticize it because everyone has his or her views on the movie. But this movie has made box office run in a very reasonable way. Yes, that's what I mainly wanted to say. Because I felt the movie is alright, it is Okay. I watched the movie myself.) (July 23, 2013)

In his comments, Michael backed off from his previous criticisms of *Tiny Times*. While continuously being critical of it for imparting improper values to the youth—"We can't say because it's good, not bad, and it reflects reality, we should make it the most popular value in society"—he did not view the movie as unreflective of reality anymore. His thinking became nuanced, no longer resting on the division between "good movies" and "bad movies." He shifted his perception of movies as black and white to a perception that movies represent mainstream or nonmainstream values. And for him, mainstream values align with Communist Party ideologies, which include understanding and respecting the hard life of the working class, of diaosi. Michael shifted slightly toward Siwen's frame in epistemology and aesthetics: high-class lifestyle is real, and it can be portrayed in Chinese cinema. Another noteworthy epistemic convergence is that the class all agreed with Siwen about the prevailing hate-the-rich sentiment. Siwen viewed it as the root cause of the harsh criticisms against *Tiny Times*.

This class discussion highlights a bifocal tendency among these multilingual students. It is the tendency to see the world through the lenses of home and host culture as part of an interpretive frame stemming from these students' simultaneous, multilayered affiliations across near and distant spaces. The students ostensibly evoked the United States in their deliberation of Chinese social issues. For instance, Chris hailed the Chinese government as performing a praiseworthy job in taking care of a population larger than that of the United States. Michael cited the practice of the US movie industry's promoting mainstream values, a practice he used to gauge Chinese cinema. While Michael's understanding of US cinema may not be accurate, as the movie industry in Hollywood is typically viewed as leftist rather than rightist, the students' ability to turn their comparative gaze to the United States is worth noting here. The students' bifocal tendency is corroborated by a survey conducted by *Foreign Policy*, a US-based news outlet, on 196 Chinese students who have studied at US universities in recent years (Tea Leaf National Staff 2015). The survey indicates that after living in the United States, a majority of the subjects viewed both the United States and China more positively. Their experience in the United States helped them recognize not only the host country's strengths but also the challenges of governing a large country like China. My students' reasoning style may be indicative of the kind of people who, Siwen would say, have seen the world, who are able to view the world from multiple subject positions, positions not completely aligned with that of the Chinese government or of the diaosi either.

The class discussion revealed two distinct cosmopolitan ideals of the rich. Some students seemed to opt for an ideal that is elitist, superficial, and selfish. In Siwen's vision, people live together peacefully and respect each other regardless of their socioeconomic difference; like her, people should become worldly wise through transnational travel. Some students, like Michael and Chris, recognized the importance of Communist Party leadership for achieving the Chinese dream. Showing sympathy for the socially underprivileged, they believed the government could play a key role in helping this group. By extension, they would probably agree with the Chinese dream articulation, in which the betterment of Chinese people's lives is viewed as conducive to and contingent upon world peace and development. Representing distinct cosmopolitan ideals, my students' perspectives on how the government should handle certain social issues naturally differed.

PATHWAYS TO COSMOPOLITAN IDEALS

The class discussion shows that claiming affinity with the diaosi was a popular identity strategy among my students. However, sharing the same strategy did not mean they agreed with each other, nor with the government, on how to handle issues involving the socially underprivileged. Partly due to the emphasis on civic deliberation, the public-speaking class showed enthusiasm in addressing social issues. In their deliberation, my students struggled with a number of questions when addressing a domestic issue: How would they position themselves relative to the Chinese government, which continues to claim alignment with working-class interests? As diaosi sympathizers, would they agree with the government positions on their topics? Otherwise, what other positions could they take?. Historically, government has functioned as a "parent" in Chinese society. In *Great Learning*, one of the Confucian books, those who aspire to civil service are instructed to cultivate themselves first, then to manage the family well, and finally to govern the state and pacify the realm (修身, 齐家, 治国, 平天下). Governing has often been compared to managing a family. Government officials are customarily called *parent-officials* (父母官), meaning they are entrusted to take care of the people like parents would. The parent-official mentality has led to the Chinese government's managing a broad spectrum of matters in people's lives. Despite being imbued with exultations about the Communist government growing up, the students were not afraid to criticize it in their speeches. They often attributed social issues to the malfunctioning of the government—bureaucracy, corruption, and nepotism. They wrestled with the government factor when proposing policies on their topics: What role could the government play in solving an issue? Can government officials be spurred to take actions along with ordinary citizens?

With the imposing presence of the government, the students invariably found themselves weak and lacking in power. Still, they marshalled their linguistic and cultural resources when preparing their speeches. For example, Peter, a business major, addressed the credibility crisis of the Chinese Red Cross Society. In 2011, a series of reports on embezzlement and corruption within or related to the society led people to question its credibility. As a result, fewer people made donations to the society, and more went to private charity organizations like One Foundation. Peter proposed making changes within the society in his policy speech, including creating a centralized management system for relief funds, giving the public access to fund information, and publishing an annual report detailing the society's expenses like the Form 10-K required of companies in the United States. In his inspirational speech, he proposed introducing these changes and inspiring both the society and ordinary citizens to monitor the society. The class reviewed the outline of Peter's inspirational speech when, by accident, he was not present. In the discussion, Danny suggested a radical solution to the society's credibility crisis, representing one position among the students. He proposed that the government close down the society.

> DANNY: If [Peter] wants people to be more hopeful about the Red Cross Society, then he should use the One Foundation as an example. Since a charity can do good things, they can do as good as the One Foundation. So there need a change for, there must be a change in Red Cross Society. But right now, people just don't use faith. But the thing is the whole, the whole Chinese government is having corruption, corruption problem. So unless there is a big change in the government, there's no way people will believe that. So I, me, myself, is really pessimistic about people, people will have faith in the Red Cross Society again as long as it belongs to the government. Because, if I'm correct, the Red Cross Society is not belong to government in any other country. It is a non-profit, independent organization. If I'm correct, I'm not sure, I guess, according to my memory. So charity, charity should not be related to government. We wipe it out and give money to charity like One Foundation, something like that, I don't know. The government officials will against it. But I know, change is radical. And if there's no change, I, me, myself, I am not gonna to believe it.
>
> XIAOYE: So, so here you are really saying that he should even just change his so, so, solution.
>
> DANNY: That's not my suggestion. That's just my solution.
>
> XIAOYE: Okay.
>
> DANNY: I mean, yeah, we can do improvements. We can give public . . . but who's gonna to believe that?
>
> XIAOYE: Okay, okay. So, for his speech, practically he can just stick to his original plan? But, but you personally . . .
>
> DANNY: But it cannot motivate me cause . . . [an eight-second pause] What motivates me is a radical change of mind. . . . If I am coming here and they say, believe the government officials. . . . I don't think anybody's gonna buy it. (August 8, 2013)

As one of the privileged, Danny was concerned about where his charity money would go, a concern widely shared by the rich, indexing a polarizing Chinese society. Both Danny and Siwen seemed to be protective of their wealth and class status. They were both discontented with the government either for standing for the underprivileged or for being corrupt. Danny recognized the government as a key source of the credibility crisis, and he revolted against the sociopolitical structure by refusing to work with it. Danny's position seemed to agree with the ideology of neoliberalism, which advocates reducing government functions and relegating them to the market. His trust in private charity seemed to be shared by the rest of the class, who nodded as Danny was speaking. As diaosi sympathizers, they did not trust the government's ability to fulfill its traditional parental role, particularly in taking care of the socially underprivileged. Their favorable attitude toward private charity might have come from their experience with such organizations in the United States. Danny mentions how the Red Cross Society works in other countries, again evoking a bifocal framing in his thinking.

In contrast to Danny's critical, neoliberal position, Peter took a modest one. While understanding the malfunction of the Chinese Red Cross Society through the lens of government corruption and cognizant of citizens' limited power, Peter was willing to negotiate the political structure. In the afternoon, Peter prepared his PowerPoint slides that would go along with the speech in the public-speaking classroom. Peter and I were the only ones in the classroom. After I showed him Danny's remarks in a video clip, he reasoned with me on the value of the Red Cross Society reforms.

PETER: Danny他讲的是有道理的。因为他说,现在不要讲红十字会了,政府的信任、诚信都有问题, 那你何况就是对红十字会哪。他这是一个很好的点,但是我觉得,我是反过来想,如果红十字会从,在监督之后,对,就是让公民产生了对它的信任,是不是对政府的信任是一个好的一个提高呢?因为红十字会是一个政府的一个分支的机构。

(Danny's comment makes sense. Because he said, we don't need to talk about Red Cross Society now. Even the government is having problem gaining people's trust, so how can the Red Cross Society? He made a good point, but I felt, I reasoned conversely. If the Red Cross Society, working under the suggested supervision, yes, regains the citizens' trust, will this help improve the credibility of the government? Because the Red Cross Society is a government branch.)

XIAOYE: 对。

(Right.)

PETER: 它是,它是跟政府挂钩的,它要通过政府渠道来做很多事情。因为它不象西方,西方是一个完全独立的,但是中国红十字会里面那些立法什么的,法律什么的,与政府挂钩。

(It's, it's connected to the government. It gets many things done through the government. Because it is unlike [the Red Cross Society in] the West, which is completely independent. But in Chinese Red Cross Society, things like law making, laws, are all connected to the government.)

XIAOYE: 对,对,对对对,所以你的想法就是说,通过提高、健全红十字会的运作的话,其实也是……

(Yes, yes, yes. So your thoughts are, improving and strengthening the operations of the Red Cross Society actually is . . .)

PETER: 但是讲这个又偏离我的题目了。

(But discussing this, I will deviate from my topic.)

XIAOYE: 不,等会,等会,你刚才的意思是说通过那个的话也可以增强人民对
于政府的一种信任,公信力是吧?

(No, wait, wait. What you meant just now is that would strengthen people's
trust in the government, the public trust, right?)

PETER: 对。你想,你现在是,大家都对你政府,公众都不说政府,但是突然有
一个机构,比如说很公开, 很公正,然后做得很好的话,那么中国,人民就
会说,啊政府,这个机构却做得不错。通过这个慢慢、慢慢有些改善,所
以你要一块,就是你现在,就是有一大块腐烂的肉,但是你现在从一块慢
慢地开始做,重新建立公民对整个社会的信心。

(Yes. Think about it, you are, people are treating the government, people
don't talk about the government. But suddenly an organization is, say very
transparent, very just, and it does a very good job. Then China, people
will say, aha government, but this organization has done well. We make
improvements slowly, slowly. So you want a piece, that is, now you, that is,
have a big rotten flesh. But you start working on it slowly now, and restore
the citizens' trust of the whole society.) (August 4, 2013)

Compared with Danny, Peter envisioned a more realistic measure to
salvage Chinese citizens' trust of one another. His strategy was to regain
their trust in one segment of the society first. A reformed Red Cross
Society, both transparent and just, can set a positive example for other
government branches and organizations. Peter articulated his strategy
with an awareness of the differences between the Chinese sociopolitical
structure and Western ones. At the same time, he perceived the challenges of the reforms by comparing the Red Cross Society to rotten flesh
waiting to be treated.

Peter's strategy was more realistic because he recognized the omnipresence of the government. By contrast, Danny wanted to entirely rely
on private charity for relief work, which he thought probably would
work in the West. The Chinese government has historically taken charge
of social welfare and relief work; private charity cannot operate indepen-
dently. It needs the cooperation of local government for both efficacy
and efficiency. In their reasoning, both students evoked "the West" as a
reference point, as a frame to understand the work of the Chinese Red
Cross Society. While perceiving different ways the society works in different countries, they recognized that the society's operations had to be
grounded in local sociocultural traditions.

While rejecting Danny's radicalism, Peter took his criticism of the
government into account. In the inspirational speech, the students were

asked to make five rhetorical moves: attention, need, satisfaction, visualization, and action. They first call the audience's attention to the topic, then explain the social issue, introduce their policy points, ask the audience to visualize the consequences of implementing or not implementing the policy, and finally inspire them to take action. Peter wanted to incorporate Danny's criticism in the visualization move to bring the audience to anger. He said the following in our conversation:

我还是要让大家愤怒一下，然后等到最后把Danny的那个丢出来，就说，不要说红十字会，就是整个政府部门也没有，然后我后面要绕过去，我要让，让听众开始，要motivate 听众。我是觉得我们是，我们是作为这个社会的一份子，有责任去做这些事情，不管是我们外面的，还是红十字会内部的都要……

(I still want everyone to feel angry. I will throw in Danny's idea in the end. I will say, not to mention the Red Cross Society, even the entire government lacks [transparency and public trust]. Then taking a detour, I want, want the audience to begin, to motivate the audience. I felt we are, we are members of the society, have responsibility to do these things. We as outsiders or those inside the Red Cross Society must . . .) (August 4, 2013)

In visualization, Peter wanted the audience to imagine, and become angry with, the negative consequences of not implementing his policy. Danny's criticism of the government could help him. Danny emphasized that the government was corrupt and that the people had lost faith in it: "But right now, people just don't use faith. But the thing is the whole, the whole Chinese government is having corruption, corruption problem." Peter would suggest that without implementing the changes in the society he was suggesting, the problems the government faced would persist—its corruption and people's lack of faith in it. Then Peter would present the positive consequences if the suggested changes took place in the society. He wanted these consequences to bring his audience hope. He figured that moving the audience from anger to hope would motivate them to monitor the society.

As it turned out, even Peter's modest measure was stalled by the government. After our conversation, Peter turned on his iPad to prepare his PowerPoint slides. He drafted a speech outline on a piece of paper (see Figure 6.1). He underlined the term "Visualization" with two triangles for emphasis. To the right of the word, he put down "Do not do a bad thing (pictures); do a good thing." He wanted to use images to help the audience see the consequences of not adopting his suggested changes in the society. To search images that showed the ineffectiveness and malfunctioning of the Chinese Red Cross Society, Peter went online. He first opened the Baidu Tupian (百度图片/Baidu Images) page and typed in

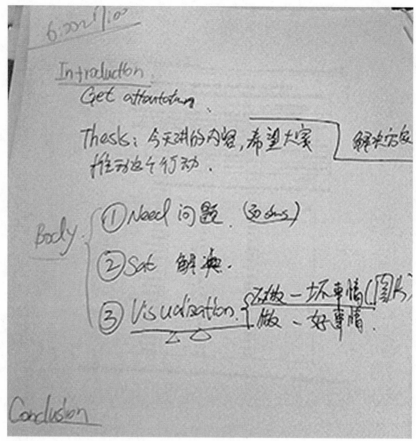

Figure 6.1. Peter's draft outline for the inspirational speech

the search term "红十字会救灾不利的图片" (images showing the ineffectiveness of the Red Cross Society in relief work). He looked through
a dozen images. Some captured the aftermaths of disasters in the United
States and other countries. Very few showed disaster scenes in China.
After about ten minutes, he started talking while gazing at the computer screen: "不好的东西都被屏蔽掉了,看到的都是好的东西,这个东
西太敏感了。对,真没有,看不到" (Negative images have been shielded.
All I can see are good things. The topic is too sensitive. That's right.
There is nothing. I cannot see anything). He then decided to give up his
PowerPoint presentation due to the lack of appropriate images. While
the search term might be the main cause for Peter's inability to find
images he needed, he attributed his failure to government censorship.

He believed Baidu shielded images and texts of sensitive topics. His plan of giving a PowerPoint presentation was crashed by the omnipresence of the government, which oversees Chinese society through both institutional and technological means. The obstacles perceived by Peter are indicative of the challenges ordinary Chinese face when exercising their citizenry duties in public deliberation.

While most of my students chose to be diaosi sympathizers, as demonstrated by Danny and Peter, they articulated different approaches to dealing with the government's inability to take care of the socially underprivileged. Danny rejected the idea of reforming the Chinese Red Cross Society; Peter believed in the worth of working with the political structure. Despite their divergent views, the students embraced civic deliberation inside and outside the classroom. However, as Peter's online research revealed, the government seemed to discourage its citizens from such deliberations by limiting their access to certain types of information. At least, Peter associated his failure in finding the right images to government censorship. This governmental practice goes along with the traditional parent-guardian role the government has adopted. As an overbearing guardian, it has constricted the agency of individuals in amending social ills.

Measured against the goal of cultivating cosmopolitanism, the public-speaking class reveals both possibilities and challenges for the upper middle class. In my teaching, I encouraged the students to address Chinese social issues, particularly those dealing with social injustice. I juxtaposed ideas in class discussions to expose students to multiple perspectives to a social issue. Despite their upper-middle-class status, the students tried to identify with the working class by adopting the diaosi identity strategy. In general, they agreed with the Chinese dream articulated by the party, which promotes a particular version of cosmopolitanism. They seemed genuinely concerned about the socioeconomic disparity in Chinese society and strove to find solutions in their speeches. They deployed their global knowledge to make arguments, to solve local issues. Class discussions encouraged some students, such as Michael and Peter, to learn about other students' positions and modify theirs. The class opened up a space for the students to demonstrate their conscience and to design activism. However, one must ask, did the students truly believe what they preached? Would practicing these speeches only lead them to sophistry, critical thinking, and the general intellectual ability valued in academia? In other words, in addition to accumulating cultural capital, will these students help correct the social injustice they critiqued?

CONCLUSION

After four decades of economic reform, China has become deeply intertwined with the world economy. One consequence of joining global capitalism is the polarization of Chinese society, widening the divide between
the haves and the have-nots. My SIE students were on one side of the
divide. They attended well-equipped K–12 schools designed for city
kids, and they were able to afford North American universities while the
majority of their peers could not. In China's rapid socioeconomic transformation, everyone seems to be on the move. However, not everyone
is moving upward socially. Migrant workers move a lot, from the countryside to the city and from city to city, but they remain secondary class,
the diaosi. In contrast, through global travel, my students accumulated
cultural capital that would lead them to better-paying jobs and a middle-
class status. This social injustice took place right alongside their socialization into the university, a key stepping stone in their upward mobility.

In the summer school, my students constructed discourses related to
social injustice, enriching and redefining global higher education. In
Western and cosmopolitan communication models, they exercised their
citizenry rights to express personal voices. When deciding which higher
education model to pursue, they abandoned the one sponsored by the
Chinese government. In the same manner, when discussing the Chinese
Red Cross Society's credibility crisis, Danny rejected the society due to
its connections with the government. He wanted to close the organization and to rely exclusively on private charity. In contrast, Peter wanted
to engage the society and, by extension, the Chinese government. The
transnational education models provided the students a space to debate
social issues and to exercise their citizenry rights and responsibilities.
Taking place on a Chinese university campus, my students' deliberative
practice solidified a transnational model of education in which they
explored local and translocal issues by drawing on resources from multiple educational traditions.

In their engagement with social issues, the cultural trope diaosi has
deeply mediated my students' reading and writing activities. *Diaosi* first
arose at the lunch table when they were ordering no-frills food items
and playing with domestic-brand smartphones. The term was used in the
context of certain social practices associated with both the working class
and the middle class. The term resurfaced in Siwen's Weibo post on *Tiny
Times*, signifying a particular epistemic perspective on Chinese cinema.
In an interview, she connected the term to a pathological mentality prevalent in Chinese society. Ordinary citizens, including the middle class,
are unsatisfied with their lives; they envy those who are physically and

materially better situated. Perceiving its power, I used the same trope to compose new associations, or transformations, in the classroom. Siwen's critique of the diaosi culture challenged Michael to modify his position in Chinese cinema. Mediating in these literacy practices, diaosi generated an upper-middle-class discourse on identity, social relations, and cosmopolitanism.

In constructing their class identities and subject positions, knowledge of other cultures, particularly Western cultures, figured prominently. Siwen talked about the Boston bombing and the props used in Euro-American movies; Michael commented on the US movie industry; Danny and Peter contrasted the operation of the Red Cross Society in China with that in Western nations. Like a Gucci handbag, the ability to talk about Western cultures became an identity marker. Further, Siwen even argued that Chinese people need a cosmopolitan outlook; that is, they should go beyond their communities and treat the Other with due respect regardless of the latter's socioeconomic background. By making comparisons across cultures and pushing for a cosmopolitan awareness in the Chinese context, the students continued to grow their global and intercultural competences. However, cosmopolitanism as practiced by the students is an elitist, upper-middle-class version. It tends to value knowledge of the Western world rather that of different parts of the world. This version, particularly as practiced by Siwen, sometimes overlooks the socioeconomic disparities in the local context. My students' struggle in developing a true cosmopolitan disposition echoes scholarly concerns about the crushing power of neoliberalism in education (Kubota 2016).

Diaosi is a way of life, a way of looking at this world, a way to compromise with the heightened gap between the haves and the have-nots, between the powerful and the powerless in Chinese society. Resorting to the diaosi discourse was a strategy used by my students to construct identities and positions. Integral to the diaosi culture are gaming practices. Legend has it that the diaosi tend to play online games for long hours. For the SIE students, gaming was indeed an important part of their life. Outside school, gaming became another space in which my SIE students constructed middle-class identities, sensibilities, and relations. More important, their gaming practices were deeply woven into their literacy practices in school. We turn to their games in the next chapter.

7

GAMING LIFE LIKE OUTLAWS

What a lovely morning, everyone.
Here comes the end of our journey. Today is the last day. To our friends and
professor, ah, today will be a day that we will forever remember.
After a whole month of intense nightlife and intense gaming, I want to deliver
my speech.
I want to tell you, my friends, it's time to do less drinking, less smoking, and
less gaming.
You may ask why? And may I ask why do you want to drink? Is it because of me?
You smoke. Is it because of me?
Or what do you feel about the League of Legends?
Ah, do you like first blood?
Do you like penta kill?
Or what do you feel about Chris dragging you to Internet bar 3 o'clock
every day?

(Danny, August 7, 2013)

It was the end of the semester. My public-speaking class lined up to deliver their inspirational speeches, a culmination of six weeks of deliberation on various social issues. Wearing a black baseball cap backward and with his ponytail dancing behind, Danny walked to the podium. After setting down his laptop, with a smirk he joked that it would be far more interesting if he was to persuade everyone to drink rather than not to drink. He went on to say that it would be far more interesting if he used Chinese instead of English. Everyone laughed. He moved on to his scripted speech, occasionally glancing at his ThinkPad screen. Speaking to a room of friends, including classmates and the professor, Danny constructed an engaging opening, as shown in the epigraph. Foregrounding a narrative to which the audience could relate, he called for less drinking, smoking, and gaming. The audience smiled.

DOI: 10.7330/9781607327332.c007

Danny's spirited opening provides a glimpse of the SIE students' life outside the classroom. Danny described it as "intense nightlife and intense gaming." Further, he hinted at his instigation in the students' drinking and smoking. His role comes to better light in a section of the script he skipped in his actual speech.

> Do you miss the tipsy feeling?
> Or did Danny persuade you to drink and drink?
> And how about smoking?
> Is that so cool?
> Do you have so many problems that you need cigarette to anesthetize yourself?
> Or did Danny give you one?

Using a series of rhetorical questions, Danny recreated mesmerizing drinking and smoking scenes among his friends. He skipped this part probably because his instigation could weaken his appeal for less drinking and smoking. He exploited his engagement in these activities to establish his ethos but, wisely, refrained from overkill. Drinking and smoking seemed critical for these students' psychological well-being, as Danny says, "Do you have so many problems that you need cigarette to anesthetize yourself?" In addition to drinking and smoking, gaming was also a part of the students' lives. Danny used the lingo of the online game *League of Legends* ("first blood" and "penta kill") to signify his insider status. Because he was an actant, his funky opening translated and resurrected the deep connections between SIE students' out-of-school lives and their literacy practices in the classroom.

While enchanted by his words, I was startled by a tension. Against the many physical mobilities Danny described was his intercultural inertia. I wondered where the cosmopolitan outlook was that I wanted to foster in the students. Instead of giving voice to the underprivileged, the speech focused on the excess lifestyle of the middle-class students. While Danny called for less smoking, drinking, and gaming, there was no critical reflection upon the social inequality that undergirded the middle-class lifestyle. What Danny had performed was cultural narcissism rather than an outward-looking disposition.

Another tension arose when I tried to evaluate Danny's speech. Listening to him, I was holding an assessment rubric for inspirational speeches (see appendix II). The rubric contains six areas for evaluation (introduction, body, organization, conclusion, delivery, and overall) and lists several points under each. For example, for the introduction, I needed to consider whether Danny had gained the attention and interest of the audience, introduced the topic clearly, related the topic to the

audience, established credibility, and provided a clear thesis and a pre-
view of his main ideas. The rubric translates the general rules of speaking
in North American academia. From a social-constructionist perspective,
a genre embodies recurring social interactions involving actors, rules,
and goals. However, evaluating Danny's speech in the classroom, there
are two obvious issues related to understanding inspirational speech as
a genre. First, the rubric presumes genre-related social interactions, and
hence the uptake of Danny's speech, as primarily taking place within
the classroom. But as an insider to the students' lives, I could see clearly
that most of these interactions resided outside the classroom. Second, in
keeping with Carolyn R. Miller's (1994) criticism of college writing programs in the United States, the public-speaking class "turns what should
be a practical art of achieving social ends into a productive art of making
texts that fit certain formal requirements" (67). The rubric encouraged
students like Danny to game class assignments for better grades rather
than to promote explicit social ends. Setting up epistemic boundaries,
the rubric stopped Danny from moving interculturally.

While several scholars have conceptualized students' academic literacy practices as games (Casanave 2002; Freedman 1994; Swales 1990),
they tend to view such as "game-like situated social practice" taking
place within an academic community (Casanave 2002, 19). The game
metaphor has generally meant students learn about the rules of academic writing, understand the roles they can play, and practice the
skills until they can play the writing game correctly. Further, Anne
Freedman (1994) emphasizes that the academic literacy game consists
not of its rules per se but of the practice of the rules within a discourse
community. Apparently, Danny's speech embodies a dialogical interaction within an academic community. However, his speech also suggests
that speech selection and construction was closely connected to literacy
events outside a typical academic discourse community. While the inspirational speech could be viewed as part of a complex web of interrelated genres, the concept of academic community seems constricting for
understanding the uptake of Danny's speech. One important uptake is
that the speech both portrayed and mediated the process of middle-class
socialization. To understand my students' speeches, I must understand
their socialization outside the classroom and how it intersects with their
academic socialization. I must move from academic community to other
communities, from one single place (classroom) to other places, from
one literacy activity to others.

In this chapter, I continue mapping out the complex links between
my students' literacy practices inside and outside the classroom and the

ways these were bound up in their shifting academic as well as national identities. Whereas the previous chapter focuses on their activities within the bounded walls of the classroom, this chapter extends the analysis through a close tracing of their literate activities across classrooms, bars, restaurants, and social media. Through situated observations of these practices—primarily focused around gaming (video games, television games, board games, drinking games)—this chapter illustrates ways these scenes became densely intertwined with the students' in-classroom presentations. One key finding in examining the students' gaming practices is that their academic socialization inflects the *shanzhai* (山寨) tradition in China. In this tradition, individuals or marginalized communities, who are often portrayed as outlaws, learn the rules and ideas formulated by dominant groups and rewrite them for survival, for resistance, or for creativity. Danny's speech gives one a glimpse of this tradition. Attending to students' gaming practices, this fine-grained analysis points to the ways students' dispositions, literacy practices, and identities are cultivated through weaving and reweaving bits and pieces from near and far-flung spaces. Attention to these translocal practices is conducive to understanding how middle-class mobilities mediate the reproduction of social inequality.

LITERACY NETWORKS

To understand socialization across contexts, we can study how text translates and moves meanings across space and time. Various notions have been proposed in literacy studies to capture the travel of meanings, such as "chronotopic lamination" (Prior and Shipka 2003), "scale jumps" (Blommaert 2008; 2010), "text trajectories" (Silverstein and Urban 1996), "literacy networks" (Leander and Lovvorn 2006), "traffic of texts" (Kell 2011), and "meaning making trajectories" (Kell 2013). These notions emphasize that the meaning of a text or a literacy practice does not stay in one place but rather moves across contexts and spaces. In explaining the notion of "meaning making trajectories," for example, Catherine Kell (2013) highlights the mobility of texts and meanings.

> Literally moving their words, they [people] recontextualise meanings by carrying or sending them into next contexts. Their efforts to make things happen are the thread, which at times becomes "fixed" or "realised" in texts, which then carry the thread across and into new participation frameworks. While most of this projection occurs through written texts, some of it also draws on other modes of communication, so that visual texts, forms of embodied or gestural communication, also transmit and amplify

meanings across contexts and become entwined with the linguistic, at the same time as they link up with material objects. (9)

Kell emphasizes human actors' agency as "the thread," which carries and amplifies meanings in new contexts. Recontextualization takes place not only through verbal but also through embodied and materialistic means. These are exactly the points to be heeded when one tries to understand Danny's speech. He prepared a script on his laptop, carried it into the classroom, and improvised his speech as he read the script. Danny wanted to capture some memorable moments at SIE, to entertain his friends, or to persuade the audience. His efforts materialized in the speech. The meaning of the speech was carried forward through his embodied and gestural communications (wearing a baseball cap backward, smiling at the audience, joking before the speech, and gesturing with his hand).

What resulted from Danny's meaning-making trajectory were agency, engagement, and identity. Danny was able to translate local activities and personal feelings into two different genres (script and speech); he engaged his audience as they listened to him, laughing and smiling; he and his audience fostered identification with certain activities, topics, and feelings. To understand my students' literacy practices in relation to agency, engagement, and identity, Leander and Lovvorn's (2006) concept of "literacy network" can be useful. They argue that "literacy is a form of networking that produces space-time" (293), that is, texts coordinate and structure space-time within a given activity and space-time across diverse activities. Thus, it is critical to understand the configurations, circulation, and translations of texts in relation to other actors in activity. Further, Kevin M. Leander and Jason F. Lovvorn suggest that when different literacy practices organize and constitute space time in unique ways, these relations have consequences for individuals' agency, engagement, and identity.

Viewing literacy as networking with diverse "actants" (Latour 1987, 84), Leander and Lovvorn (2006) seek ways to distinguish literacy practices from one another in ways neither autonomous nor overly situated in particular locales. They propose five dimensions of displacement as an initial way of making distinctions among literacy networks: translation, heterogeneity of space-time representations, movements and positions of texts in circulation, rhythms and speeds of circulation, and network continuity (293). In terms of translation, we can consider "how texts stand in the place of, speak for, or appear to mobilize bodies, objects, and other texts." For space-time representations, we can ask

"what space-times are presented by texts, and how are these representations organized in activity?" To capture the movements and positions
of texts in circulation, we can study "the social-material geography of
texts in activity" and ask whether "texts combine or form hybrids with
other actors in activity." For rhythms and speeds of circulation, we can
examine "the patterns and tempos of movement among texts and other
actors." For network continuity, we can consider how the social-material
relations to texts are more or less extended and continuous (293).

The notion of literacy network provides one way to solve the issue I
faced when trying to understand Danny's speech. The speech was not a
product contained in the classroom, a perspective the assessment rubric
encouraged. Instead, the script and the speech were two of multiple
actants that gave rise to a literacy network. They stood in the place of
and mobilized the students' bodies, their "intense night life and intense
gaming," and their middle-class social relations. This network might
have been connected to other literacy networks inside and outside
SIE. In this chapter, I describe several literacy networks at the summer
school by considering the five dimensions of displacement suggested
by Leander and Lovvorn. Given the characteristics of each literacy network, I cannot give equal attention to all dimensions of displacement
but will highlight those critical for understanding Danny's speech. As my
analysis will illustrate, these networks have transcended the boundaries
between in-school and out-of-school spaces, between the local and the
global, a phenomenon that compels us to reconceptualize space-time in
literacy instruction.

To study the students' literacy networks, I had to follow my students
and other actors. In Actor-Network Theory (ANT), according to Latour
(2005), network does not designate a thing like the World Wide Web or
a guanxi network. Instead it is a method; it indicates the quality of my
chapter. "It qualifies [the text's] objectivity, that is, the ability of each
actor to make other actors do unexpected things. A good text elicits
networks of actors when it allows the writer to trace a set of relations
defined as so many translations" (129).

WEREWOLVES IN CHINESE BARS

Although SIE positioned itself between North American and Chinese
higher education systems, it adopted a parental role in relation to its
students, like a Chinese university. In doing so, it deeply mediated students' socialization outside the classroom. For instance, it organized a
series of extracurricular events. Chinese university students of the same

Figure 7.1. Extracurricular activity posters in the back of a classroom

major and of the same year are typically grouped into classes. They take most of their courses together as a class. Every class has a supervisor who counsels them and organizes intramural activities. These activities can be organized with class, college, or university as a unit. In contrast, in the United States, intramural activities are more commonly organized by chapters of the Greek system or student clubs. During the six weeks of summer school, SIE organized three major social events: singing KTV, a badminton match, and board games. To promote those events, a staff member placed large posters in the back of each classroom (see Figure 7.1). The teaching assistant also came to the class to announce each event, urging the students to sign up. Working in tandem, the posters and the oral announcements translated administrative intentions and styles. Through their poster designs, the student staff brought such intentions down to a local scale. The titles of these events, adopting the style of four-character Chinese idioms, revealed the purposes of the events: K歌之夜 (an evening of KTV), 羽坛争霸 (rivaling in the badminton court), 桌游联谊 (board game for promoting friendship). SIE not only organized but also paid for these events, including rentals, food, and prize money, creating opportunities for the students to network.

Of the three events, the board games attracted the largest crowd. All male students in my public-speaking class went out that evening. The games were held off campus at a place called Station车站桌游吧 (Station Board Game Bar). Two colleagues and I took a taxi to get there. As China is increasingly open to the rest of the world, Western entertainment forms and products have flooded the country, including board games. The same day at lunch, my public-speaking students talked excitedly about 三国杀 (*Killings in the Three Kingdoms*), the game featured in the board-game poster. This is a role-playing game published by a Chinese company in 2008 based on stories from *Three Kingdoms*, a Chinese classic. A board game with online versions, the game itself was inspired by role-playing games from overseas, such as *Bang*.

Off the bustling main street, the bar nestled in a quiet alley. The bar was small but had large windows. At the entrance, a stack of board games sat on a shelf, including *Uno* and *Monopoly*, two North American household games. Some students and the two SIE directors were already there playing on four tables, taking up most of the bar space. I sat down and started playing poker with my colleagues on a spare table. As we were playing, we ordered Cantonese-style dishes for dinner. In a few minutes, my students showed up, and they sat down to play *Werewolves* on a table next to ours. After we played for about an hour, Leon, one of my students, walked in with two bottles of wine. Wine has become the preferred choice over liquor among some Chinese over the last two decades because it broadly symbolizes Western culture and a middle-class taste. A business major at Syracuse, Leon ran a wine business in Guangzhou. His company owns a winery near Toronto, Canada. As the bar did not serve wine, he brought it to share with us, implicitly promoting his business and building a transnational guangxi network. In fact, both drinking wine and playing board games were central to the students' guangxi network.

Although I did not play *Werewolves*, it was important to understand its basic rules, as I would soon play a modified version with my students. *The Werewolves of Miller's Hollow* was designed by two French artists. The story takes place in a small village in the United States haunted by werewolves. Each player is secretly assigned a role—Werewolf, Villager, or a special character such as the Captain, the Hunter, the Witch, the Little Girl, or the Seer. There is also a Moderator who controls the flow of the game. The game alternates between night and day. At night, the Werewolves secretly choose a Villager to kill. During the day, the Villager who was killed is revealed and is out of the game. The remaining Villagers (normal and special villagers alike) then deliberate and vote on a player they suspect is a Werewolf, helped or hindered by the clues the special characters add to the general deliberation. The chosen player is "lynched," reveals their role, and is out of the game. The game rules my students read were a Chinese translation based on the English version in which the artists attribute the origin of the game to a Russian game: "This game is freely based on a traditional Russian Game, also known as 'Mafia' or 'Spies,' which appeared in the Soviet Union in the 1930s" (des Pallieres and Marly 2001). Thus, my students were playing a game that had been translated across cultures and languages. The written instructions structured a particular space-time: the students moved from global, general, and abstract rules to particular roles and scenes in a local bar.

Around 9:30 p.m., my students decided to go to another bar in a pier area where Pearl River Beer Brewery was located (琶醍酒吧街). Relocation to a new place meant the middle-class guangxi network was on the move. To better understand my students' nightlife, I followed them to the pier. As soon as we stepped out of the taxi, we saw people sitting on tables along Pearl River against the shining high-rises in the north shore. Jazz and blues crept out of bars with neon lights. As a group of thirteen, we settled into a corner inside a bar. Sofas were lined up along the walls, forming a square with a large table in the center. The rock music was loud, and the lights were dim. We sat down, and the students ordered six liters of draft beer and a few side dishes. A student also ordered two glasses of Jack Daniels whiskey. The students' accustomedness to drinking suggests alcohol mediated their middle-class "structures of feeling" (Williams 1977, 132) in an important way. As there are no drinking-age restrictions in China, the waiter did not check our IDs. Ordering drinks set the tone for the rest of the night.

Drinking again converged with board games, this time clearly starting a shanzhai practice. As drinks were being served, Danny suggested that we play a game. All students cheered for this idea. With only one set of poker cards at hand, they had to improvise by appropriating features of other games. Inspired by *Werewolves*, which they had just played, the students quickly decided the general theme of the game, that is, killing. They also agreed that there would be townspeople, police officers, killers, and a judge who would be the moderator of the game. However, they debated the number of people suitable for each role. Everyone argued about it based on how they had played other role-playing games, such as *Killing in the Three Kingdoms* or *Werewolves*. Mixing Mandarin and Cantonese, they shouted at each other, partly to fight against the loud music. Changing back and forth between these two languages, these transnational bodies emphasized their local and regional affiliations.

The written instructions for *Werewolves* were carried over, orally, across the bar. They were used to create a new set of rules. The most striking part of the improvisation, as it turned out, was that this role-playing game was transformed into a drinking game. While the students debated the number of people needed for a certain role, Danny, the moderator, summed up their deliberation amidst the loud music and the interjections of other students.

教授,我们来说一下吧, 我们在一个村庄里头,我们在那酒吧里面喝酒,然后
这个酒吧有几个人?十三个人。现在有四个杀手,拿到A's的人就记得自己
是杀手,杀光警察或杀光平民都算赢。单纯的杀人就好了……教授不可以首
杀。我法官……来先干杯。

(Professor, let me explain. We are in a village, drinking in a bar. How many
people are there in the bar? Thirteen. Now there are four killers. Those
who received the A cards must remember they are the killers. When they
kill all policemen or all townsmen, they win. Let's just focus on killing
people. . . . We can't kill Professor in the first round. I am the judge. . . .
Let's have a shot first.) (July 24, 2013)

The improvised story took place in a bar in a village. There were thirteen
people in the bar. Danny concluded his introduction by inviting everyone to have a first shot. The improvised rules connected two literacy networks, moving student bodies, poker cards, and drinking practices from
the board-game bar to this one.

Once the game started, the global, abstract rules turned into specific roles and scenes. A person would be killed every night. On the
first night, Chris was killed. In the daytime, when Chris's death was
announced, he was urged by Danny to have another shot.

CHRIS: 我不知道我为什么变得这么popular了。大家都很喜欢我,很让我
感动。然后我觉得killer应该不是我们这边的这几个人,我刚才在闭眼
的时候,有人在选我。

(I don't know why I have become so popular. All of you liked me, which
really touches me. I feel that the killer shouldn't be among those who sit
on our side [of the wall]. When my eyes were close just now, someone was
selecting me.)

DANNY: 被杀的就要喝,死了就要喝。那好,从Michael开始说。

(The killed should take a shot; the dead should take a shot. Alright, now
our deliberation starts with Michael.)

Joking in his last breath, Chris tried to influence the game by suggesting that the killer was not sitting on his side. Danny urged him to take a
shot as a token of his death. Drinking further played into the students'
ensuing deliberation in identifying a killer. A killer needed to be found
and be lynched. Michael proposed a suspect among the rest of the students by connecting that person to drinking: "大家说家慧吧,她有想喝
酒" (Let's identify Jiahui as the killer because she wants to have a drink).
Jiahui rebelled immediately because she didn't want to die in the beginning of the game. Drinking, as both a theme and a practice, played into
the game in important ways. Not only was the story set in a drinking

context but the playing of the game was mediated by actual drinking. Drinking became a key actant in the local reinvention of a game, a genre that could be traced to the Russian Mafia or the French Werewolves.

In addition to drinking as a variant, the game also included me as a unique character, which enacted a new association, a transformation. In Danny's introduction, he warned the other students that the Professor should not be killed in the first round. Calling me "Professor," Danny reminded the students of the real-life power hierarchy, effectively enjoining a real and a fictional world. This hierarchy was reinforced and appropriated as the game unfolded. When my turn came during the deliberation on who was a killer, I suggested that Michael was. My identity as the Professor influenced the direction of the game.

DANNY: Professor, 你的opinion?

(Professor, what is your opinion?)

MICHAEL: Opinion, 就是informative speech.

(Opinion, is informative speech)

XIAOYE: 我觉得是在那边的三个人。

(I felt like one of the three people there must be a killer).

LEON: 教授讲话,你们不可以讲话。想要零分啊!讲话喝酒, 说一句喝一杯啊。你随便猜一个吧。

(When Professor is speaking, you are not supposed to talk. You want to get a zero? If you talk, you will need to drink. You will take a shot for every sentence you say. [Professor,] you can just randomly pick one.)

XIAOYE: 那我就猜Michael.

(Then I guess Michael is a killer.)

DANNY: 可以,可以,可以。教授说是Michael, Michael 就死了。

(That works, that works, that works. Professor says it is Michael, Michael then dies.)

PETER: 教授说你是, 你就是了。好, 干杯, 干杯。

(Professor says you are, then you are. Alright, bottom up, bottom up.)

In the deliberation, three students managed to guard my authority as the Professor. When some townsmen disagreed with me, Leon threatened them jokingly that they would fail in my class ("You want to get a zero?"). Danny also emphasized the weight of my words ("Professor says it is Michael, Michael then dies"). When Michael wanted to have further say, Peter stopped him by underscoring the power of the Professor ("Professor says you are, then you are"). With the Professor's power, the townsmen successfully "lynched" Michael, eliminating him from the game. My presence added a new character, the Professor, to the game, further modifying the *Werewolves* game rules.

With the players deliberating in a rivalry style, the overall feel of the game was jubilance. The gamers shouted at one another amidst the loud music. Once the dust settled and someone suggested "bottom up," they grabbed their glasses in cheers. Repeatedly, they praised the beer for its tastiness and ordered three more liters. After the Killing game, they moved on to a pure drinking game. Everyone chanted "海盗船长, 嘿修,嘿修" (chief of the pirate ship, *heixiu, heixiu*) or "蒙娜丽莎,嘿修, 嘿修" (Mona Lisa, *heixiu, heixiu*). When someone was being pointed at as the chief of the pirate ship or Mona Lisa, the person as well as those who sat on both sides of them needed to perform certain acts. Anyone who failed would need to take a shot. Then that person started to point at another person amidst the chanting. As we drank more, the game increasingly depended on the participants' quick wit and ability to coordinate limbs. Having had a taste of my students' nightlife, of their shanzhai practice, I excused myself at midnight.

THE VOICE OF CHINA IN THE CLASSROOM

My students' gaming lives extended into school, as did the weaving of their middle-class social networks. They made improvisation and competition important features of their school literacy. They watched television shows featuring contests and improvised such games in my class. In the middle of the semester, we sometimes experienced torrential rains due to typhoons. On those days, my students ordered food and had lunch in the classroom. While eating, they turned on the instructor's computer and watched popular television shows on the wall screen. Their favorite program was the music reality show 中国好声音 (*The Voice of China*). It is a Chinese version of *The Voice*, a popular television show (see also chapter 3) also produced in Britain, Ireland, the Netherlands, and the United States. Initiated in 2012, the Chinese version was anchored by four seasoned Chinese pop singers, who were invited to judge novices singing in the show. Based on their assessment, a singer was accepted, or not, into their training camps. Representing these camps, the pop singers' students then competed against each other on stage. The show was an overnight sensation because it allowed ordinary Chinese to see these master singers on a weekly basis and to witness unknown singers, many of them diaosi, becoming household names.

My students were drawn to the show partly because those novices fueled their imagination for the Chinese dream at a personal level. So focused were they on the show, the students hardly talked to each other while watching. The songs were beautiful and stunning. The stories of the novices were touching and inspiring. The singers came from all walks of life, demonstrating the possibilities of diaosi launching counterattacks in modern-day China. During one lunch break, we watched the rise of several such singers, including a female Chinese student who studied at Virginia Commonwealth University. On stage, blending Chinese and English lyrics, she sang a song originally sung by one of the master singers. However, she did it in a tune different from the original. Even before she finished her song, the four masters all said they liked her voice and invited her to join their training camps. Their ensuing conversation revealed that the singer loved the song so much that with the help of her US friends, she modified the tune by blending elements of African American musical traditions. An ordinary girl who had only sung at home or at parties suddenly won the favor of four master singers, which meant a bright singing future for her. This is, as a Chinese audience might call it, a story of a sparrow turning into a phoenix. Her story inspired the audience, including my middle-class students, who applauded and cheered for her.

Playing and watching competitive games daily, my students transposed them into their school work. They reinvented academic exercises by incorporating some of the games' features, such as the routines, competitiveness, and entertainment. This shanzhai practice became apparent as they got to know each other better toward the end of the semester. To prepare for the inspirational speech, the public-speaking class did a series of exercises. For example, they were asked to produce thirty-second infomercials on a product or a service. They were also asked to give one-minute inspirational speeches on topics of their own choice. For this Motivate Me activity, I gave them the following prompts in a handout:

> Choose 3–4 students to prepare and perform a brief (approximately 1–2 minutes) speech that would aim to convince the class to part with one dollar. Speeches should follow the Motivated Sequence with the appropriate steps: Attention, Need, Satisfaction, Visualization, and Action. (Instructor can supply dollar.)
>
> As speakers prepare in the hallway, remaining members of class in the room can design criteria by which they will evaluate the presentations and award the dollar.
>
> Instructor can guide this discussion, but this type of group

decision-making also works well for illustrative purposes considering the next focus on group communication.

After the speakers present, the remaining class members deliberate to choose who will receive the dollar.

The prompts established the general rules of this exercise. However, my students found ways to modify the rules. For example, when I took 30 RMB (5 US dollars) out of my pocket, they showed no interest to the prize money. They bargained with me, suggesting that the winner should receive bonus points. After some wrangling, I gave in, being dragged into their improvisation. We agreed that the winner would receive three points toward their final grade. Then the class decided the speakers would all speak on the same topic but could take different positions. While everyone was searching for a topic, Danny raised his hand, saying "I found one." He walked to the blackboard and wrote *sugar daddy*. Some students laughed and some were puzzled. Once Danny explained it in Chinese, everyone laughed and accepted the topic. Like *baifumei* (light skinned, rich, and pretty) and *gaofushuai* (tall, rich, and handsome), the term *sugar daddy* indexes wider class shifts, as well as gender inequality, in Chinese society. With the rise of consumerism and the widening of socioeconomic disparities, rich men were often reported as developing extramarital relations with women younger than their wives. They often purchased houses, cars, and other luxurious items for their "little second (wife)" or "little third (wife)," as these women are called these days. Accepting the topic with laughter suggests the students were familiar with this class-gender discourse. They were excited about translating it from a national, general scale level to a local, academic context.

As three speakers stepped outside the room, the rest of the class discussed the evaluation criteria together as judges, effectively transforming the speech genre. At my repeated demand, they decided the speech needed to include the five steps of an inspirational speech, or at least three of them (i.e., satisfaction, visualization, and action). These are the rhetorical moves constitutive of the speech genre as commonly taught in a public-speaking class. Danny proposed that the speaker needed to maintain eye contact and articulate every word. Jackie suggested that the content must be interesting, a criterion that would eventually translate into entertainment and thus reinvent this speech genre.

Once the competition started, the students moved from a national, general level to a local, specific level by infusing a television-contest format into this academic exercise. When they were discussing the order of presentations, Leon joked in Cantonese, "一号佳丽，谁是一号佳丽？"

(Beauty No. 1? Who is beauty No. 1?). His words evoked a beauty contest. Some students laughed, partly at his Cantonese pronunciation of the word *beauty* as *gali*. Danny then followed, jokingly correcting Leon, "欢迎一号男嘉宾" (Welcome, honorable male guest No. 1) in Mandarin. The mixing of Cantonese and Mandarin indexed tensions as the students moved between a national and a local scale level. Peter delivered his speech first, trying to dissuade women from finding a sugar daddy. Then Michael stood up from his seat; with some kind of music in the background, he walked to the podium waving his script like a contestant on television. Smiling at the audience, he said, "各位嘉宾好" (Hello, honorable guests), and Leon quickly interjected, "三位老师好" (Hello, three teachers). Echoing *The Voice of China*, Leon called the student judges "teachers," just as the novice singers called the master singers teachers in the show.

Like the Virginia Commonwealth student, Michael blended in his performance elements from diverse sources. He seemingly wanted to motivate the audience to be tolerant of homosexual practice. Smiling throughout, he delivered the speech with passion. The audience was quiet first but giggled toward the end. They came to realize Michael was not serious at all. He performed a stand-up comedy by appropriating a critical social issue and multiple cultural references from the United States.

> Four scores ago, when our country was still young and wild, we made lots of mistakes. We raise the flag of freedom and ring the bell of liberty from the high of the Rocky to the low of the Ocean Pacific. Meanwhile, we cast intolerable looks on homosexuality. Then, I asked myself, and my country asked itself: Where is the freedom we believe in? We need freedom, from religion to love, from politics to relationship, everything! Yes, everything, because we all do not want to forget what this country is found on. Yes, Philadelphia, freedom, 1776. I have a dream. One day from now on, our despicable look will be found nowhere across the Appalachian mountain, sweep the Mississippi. I have a dream. One day boys and girls, boys and boys, girls and girls, are able to lay in the same bed of pure love passionately, purely, and freely. And I have a dream. One day, black, yellow, white are all able to choose whatever partners they want to choose no matter what gender they are all over the universe. And yes, I have a dream. From today, from now on, nobody, me, she, you, and I, none of us will be afraid to pick up soul dropped on the floor accidently or not accidently. Let homosexuality ring, let liberty ring, for world freedom. God bless you all.

Most obviously, Michael adopted the language styles of two renowned speeches in US history. He starts his speech saying, "Four scores ago, when our country was still young and wild, we made lots of mistakes."

This opening echoes that of the Gettysburg Address, delivered by Abraham Lincoln on November 19, 1863. Lincoln declared, "Four score and seven years ago our fathers brought forth on this continent, a new nation, conceived in liberty, and dedicated to the proposition that all men are created equal." The Gettysburg address was Michael's favorite, as he once told us in class. In the rest of the speech, he imitates Martin Luther King Jr.'s I Have a Dream speech. In addition to his repetitive use of the phrase "I have a dream," Michael also borrowed sentence structures from King. For example, King says, "I have a dream that . . . one day right there in Alabama little black boys and black girls will be able to join hands with little white boys and white girls as sisters and brothers." Michael's says, "I have a dream. One day boys and girls, boys and boys, girls and girls, are able to lay in the same bed of pure love passionately, purely, and freely." Like King, Michael capitalized on the power of repetition, parallelism, and rhyming.

The speech's playfulness was scripted with much thought given to audience and identity. The script Michael read and waved in front of us showed moments of calculation (see Figure 7.2). In the beginning, for example, he first wrote, "When we are still young and wild, we made lots of mistakes." Then, he crossed out "we are" and wrote "Chin(a) is" instead. Next, he crossed out "China" and replaced it with "the US." Finally he chose "our country." Apparently Michael was unsatisfied with the expression "we are," probably not wanting to use "we" twice in one sentence. In search of an equivalent, "China" came into his mind first. However, he soon remembered that homosexual issues would probably be better addressed in the United States. Homosexuality is also a social issue in China, but it has not attracted as much societal attention as in the United States. Therefore, Michael replaced "China" with "the US." After reading the sentence once again, he finally settled on "our country," an expression that could enhance his ethos as a speaker hypothetically speaking to a US audience. Michael's juggling with these expressions reveals the complex world of a multilingual student. He was not fixed in his national identity; instead, he vacillated between China and the United States. In addition, he was also rhetorically skilled, being sensitive to English sounds and the speaker's ethos.

However, while adroit in stitching together these references, Michael showcased the negative side of being an uncritical cosmopolitan. On the surface, he staged sympathy for homosexuality as a social practice in the United States. He understood that gays and lesbians, and by extension, the LGBTQ community, had experienced prejudice for years. Similarly, he showed sympathy for the Chinese working class by adopting a diaosi

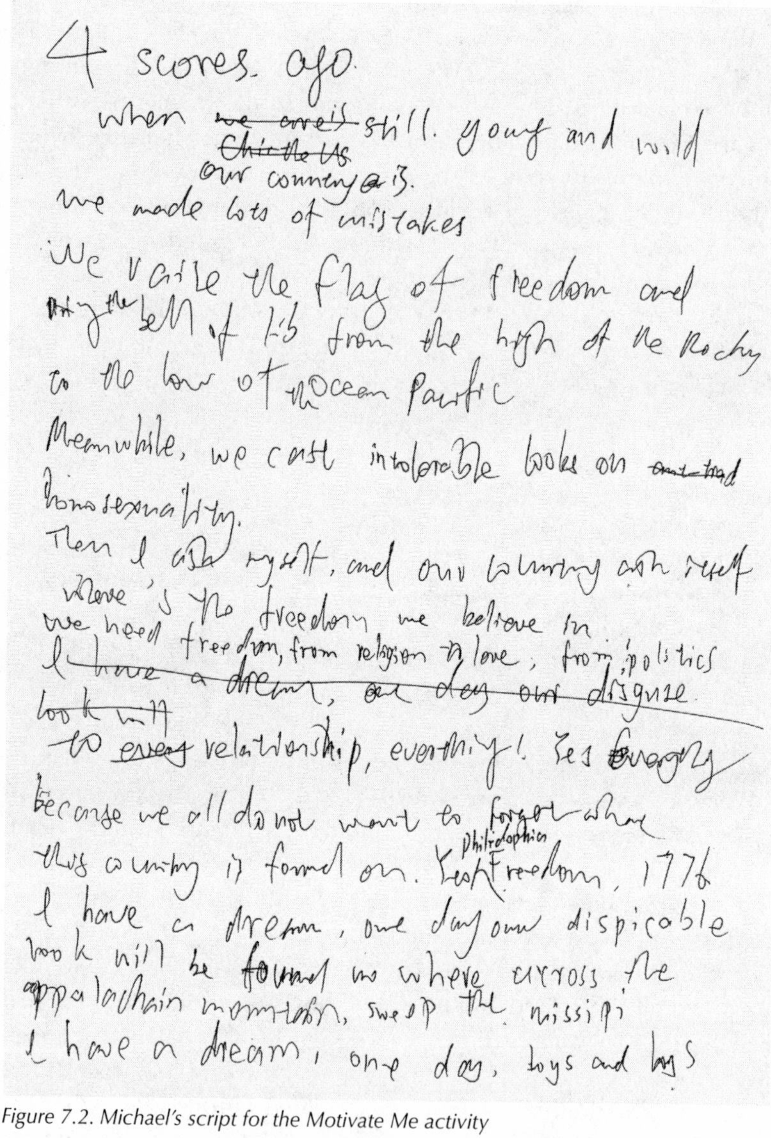
4 scores ago
when ~~we are is~~ still young and wild
~~China the US~~ our country is.
we made lots of mistakes
We raise the flag of freedom and
~~ring the~~ bell of lib from the high of the Rocky
to the low of the Ocean Pacific
Meanwhile, we cast intolerable looks on ~~and that~~
homosexuality.
Then I ask myself, and our country ask itself
where's the freedom we believe in
we need freedom, from religion to love, from politics
~~I have a dream, one day our disguise look will~~
to ~~every~~ relationship, everything! Yes ~~Everything~~
because we all do not want to forget what
this country is formed on. Yes, Philosophical Freedom, 1776
I have a dream, one day our dispicable
look will be found no where across the
appalachain mountain, swept the missipi
I have a dream, one day, boys and boys

Figure 7.2. Michael's script for the Motivate Me activity

identity strategy in his speeches on Chinese cinema. He criticized social inequality and oppression in both nations. Critical on the surface, deep down, Michael's speech on homosexuality was rather facetious and carnivalesque. He called everyone to practice homosexuality: "I have a dream. One day boys and girls, boys and boys, girls and girls, are able to lay in the same bed of pure love passionately, purely, and freely." He did not seem like a member of the LGBTQ community, thus was limited in his understanding of the community's experiences and feelings. He oddly integrated Lincoln's speech with Martin Luther King's, showing insensitivity to their sociohistorical contexts. While this activity was a game show, and it unequivocally helped construct his transnational identity, Michael's cross-border practice stayed at a superficial level. What the audience gained was entertainment rather than a heightened, critical awareness of the topic. Behind the playfulness, one could also read the speech as homophobic. While Michael seemed sympathetic to gay men and lesbians, his carnivalesque description reinforced a negative image of homosexuality.

The third speaker, Chris, infused middle-class "structures of feeling" by projecting the unachievable dreams of the diaosi. Like the first two speakers, he joined the audience to reinforce the genre of television contests. Following Jackie's styled announcement, "欢迎三号男嘉宾" (Let's welcome honorable male guest No. 3), Chris walked to the podium, shaking his upper body and throwing a hand gesture, V. In the background was a Peking Opera tune featuring a battle scene. Facing the audience with a hand in his chest, Chris said, "各位评委你们好, Professor, 你好。我是三号男嘉宾 . . ., 来自山西太原" (Hello, judges. Hello, Professor. I am honorable male guest No. 3 . . . from Taiyuan, Shanxi Province). The audience cheered, clapping their hands. Leon shouted jokingly, "这是客场了" (This is an away game), underscoring the regionality of the show. Once the frenzy was over, Chris started his speech, occasionally glancing at his script.

> Okay, before I get started with my speech. May I ask? Can you close your eyes? And imagine pictures that I am going to describe to you. Now, imagine, you are a person earning ten thousand RMB per mouth. That is already above the average income level. In big cities, even if you don't drink anything, you don't eat anything, you don't spend any money, it will take you several months to buy one square meter of the houses. It takes you forever to own, actually have a home in the city. And now let's cure this nightmare and imagine the pictures that I'm going to describe to you right now.

Chris paused and clicked a button on his IPhone. Piano music, "Pour Chopin," started to circulate in the air. Chris resumed his speech.

> Now, imagine you are in one of the most beautiful beaches in California Malibu. Staying in a fancy convertible R8 and right beside you, there is handsome man, enjoying talking to you on some great topics. Now imagine this life. Please open your eyes. After I describe to you the above pictures, now the chances are in your hand. Life is really short. Live in the best way if you can. And choose a way to achieve your dream. The

easiest way to achieve your dream is, [Chris slammed the podium with a fist] find a sugar daddy. Yes, and finally, finally, [he slammed the podium again] who says sugar daddy is pretty for girls. [He slammed the podium the third time.] There are sugar mothers [he waved one of his hands violently in the air].

The audience cheered crazily, clapping hands and laughing madly. I was quiet, however, not immediately sure what my position was. In the end, Chris won the speech contest.

Chris was favored by the judges because his performance most fully met the entertainment expectation of the television-contest genre. He started off performing the typical verbal exchange between contestants and the audience. He entertained the audience further by acting out funny statements passionately. Chris satisfied some of the criteria established by the judges as well. For example, unlike Michael, who deviated from the topic of sugar daddy, Chris clung to it. He also fully developed the steps of visualization and action. He invited the audience to imagine two different scenes and called them to take action. The scenes catered to the psyche of the Chinese middle class. When they complain about how hard life is in China, they often imagine an easy life in the United States. The California beach scene Chris invited the audience to imagine is not an unfamiliar one among the middle class. It has been infused into the Chinese imagination through US movies and television shows.

However, like Michael, Chris exemplifies uncritical cosmopolitanism in his speech. On the surface, he performed sympathy for the diaosi, who work hard but still cannot afford an apartment in the city. He wanted to find a way to help the downtrodden working and middle classes. But he conformed to the easy-money strategy commonly seen in Chinese consumerism, a strategy that has given rise to new gender and class relations as indexed by the terms *sugar daddy*, *little second*, and *little third*. Instead of critiquing and transforming these relations, Chris promoted them, thus reproducing social inequality. Responding favorably to his speech, the students uncannily accepted the message. In the end, Chris's cross-border literacy practices commodified women and perpetuated a money-worshipping ideology in the shifting Chinese society.

Together, the contestants and the audience turned a school literacy exercise into an entertainment program. The handout and the evaluation criteria mobilized the students' bodies and texts. In performing their speeches, they translated these written rules and speech scripts. The speeches restructured space-time in notable ways. The handout represented global, general knowledge and skills required by the textbook and the instructor. In articulating the evaluation criteria and constructing individual speeches, the students moved from a global, general level to a local, specific level. The written texts were embedded in the activity and formed hybrids with other immediate and distant actors—the students, *The Voice of China* program, the Gettysburg Address, the I Have a Dream speech, and the piano music "Pour Chopin." The students' deep engagement with this literacy exercise could be explained by their relation with space-time as well as the hybrids formed by texts and other actors. They were able to bring the exercise to a local level by enabling the formation of the hybrids.

The students' failure to exercise critical cosmopolitanism in their speeches can be attributed to reasons at two levels. At the surface level, I should be blamed for my nonaction throughout this exercise. I gave in to the students when we were formulating rules. Once the students took control of this exercise, they added entertainment as a key assessment criterion. After Michael's speech, I could have stopped the class to critique it. However, while recognizing his insensitivity in handling his topic, I realized he was improvising a stand-up comedy. I was torn between censoring insensitive speech and encouraging rhetorical creativity. Throughout the semester, sometimes I introduced my "correct" thinking by critiquing the students on a certain topic, but they always found ways to subvert my authority through playful improvisations. This was a perpetual tension I struggled with while teaching this group of students.

At a deeper level, there was profound ethnocentrism in the class, which was counter to the development of critical communicators. Growing up as members of the Han, the ethnic majority in China, the students and I were insensitive to race, sexual, and gender issues. In Maoist China, through various political campaigns, class divisions were smoothed out and racial and gender equality was achieved to a great extent, at least based on the official discourse. After China rejoined global capitalism following the Cultural Revolution, racial, class, and gender difference became increasingly prominent. However, under Communist ideologies, school education has tended to evade those issues or treat them as issues of the past, thus students do not get the chance to explore them in the contemporary context. Government-controlled media also tend to soften their reports on these issues in Chinese society. As Michael's speech script showed, owing to government propaganda and the influence of traditional values, the Chinese tend to associate those issues more with the United States than with China. Living in the United States, while our sensitivities to those issues improved, we continue to view them as more problematic in the United States.

LEAGUE OF LEGENDS ACROSS CITIES

Gaming meant more than entertainment for my students. It is pivotal in their lives and structured them, enabling them to develop social networks and foster strategies to meet everyday challenges. The students in my English-writing class loved games as much as my public-speaking students did. In an interview, Siwen revealed to me how she had navigated the transnational education marketplace as a student, as a gamer. She had played online games ever since high school. The games became deeply interwoven or "knotted" into her academic life. She started gaming higher education by negotiating its rules in high school. We talked about how she had entered the university and survived her freshman year.

XIAOYE: TOEFL之外,你还有其他成绩吧,如高中成绩呀, 等等?

(Besides TOEFL, did you have other test scores, such as your high school grades, and so on?)

SIWEN: 都自己填啊。

(I just filled out the high school transcript myself.)

XIAOYE: 所以随便填。

(So you did it at your will.)

SIWEN: 基本上出去的人还都在重点高中啊,如果我们学校的物理平均分是 50分,我考个四五十分,我总不能拿这个成绩去吧。假如说我们去学校 拿资料,盖章什么的,老师就给你那个抬头,就自己打印,自己添成绩,自己 盖章,章都自己盖的。

(Most of the students studying abroad graduated from key high schools. If the average score for Physics was 50 points in my school, and if I scored somewhere between 40 and 50 points, I could not show this score in my application. When we went to our high school to pick up the paperwork, like getting some documents stamped, our teacher would give us the letterhead. Then I printed out the transcript form, filled in my grades, and stamped the transcript with the school seal. I stamped it myself.)

XIAOYE: 对,对,噢。那这样一个问题就是说,你到那边学习,不会觉得很吃 力吗? 因为别人认为你的起点会更高一些?

(I see, I see, oh. Then, there is an issue: When you studied there [in the US], didn't you find the schoolwork challenging? Because other students thought you were academically better positioned in the first place?)

SIWEN: 对啊,但是,其实就是,还是英语不好吧。如果换成中文,因为我上的 是经济的课嘛,经济书都有翻译成中文的。

(Yes, I did. But, in fact, it was because of my poor English. If we had switched to Chinese, because I mainly took economics courses, and most of the textbooks had Chinese translations.)

XIAOYE: 你看中文书,其实还是很容易看懂的。

(Chinese translations were easy for you to understand.)

SIWEN: 看中文书秒杀啊。我上课其实,经济课我只有交作业和quiz、考试的时候去,其他的时候我都不去。然后,然后,我就自己在家里。

(Reading Chinese translations is SecKill. In fact, I only went to class when I needed to turn in homework or to take quizzes or exams. I didn't go the other times. Then, then, I stayed at home.)

XIAOYE: 自学?

(You studied by yourself?)

SIWEN: 对啊,就自己看看书,就可以了,我就考,照样考个A啊.

(Right. I studied the books by myself. That's good enough. I scored As in exams.)

Siwen clearly understood the game of transnational higher education. US universities generally require TOEFL scores, high-school transcripts, and recommendation letters for international-student admissions. In contrast, their Chinese counterparts admit students primarily based on college entrance-exam scores. Students' extracurricular achievements are increasingly valued by Chinese universities these days, but high-school transcripts and recommendation letters are seldom required. Therefore, Chinese high schools are not prepared to provide official transcripts to universities. Siwen's school, therefore, let students make up their own transcripts. Siwen seemed to have mastered the game at the university as well. Her economics courses seemed to value homework and exam scores rather than class participation. Reading the Chinese translations of her textbooks, she found the coursework easy and achieved top grades. English was the only roadblock.

The academic game rules Siwen mastered are no secret to US universities. There is plenty of journalism on how Chinese international students participate in test-taking schemes, forge high-school transcripts and recommendation letters, and survive US university courses through outsourcing course assignments (see chapter 1). Our study of Chinese international students at Michigan State shows how "scumbags of learning" and "lords of learning" clung together, forming an underground economy of academic survival. Siwen was forced to forge her high-school transcripts, she claimed, because the US education system does not neatly match the Chinese one. With this knowledge, US universities sometimes are suspicious about Chinese applicants' credentials. For the same reason, they cast doubts on the credits transferred from SIE and other summer schools. To survive and prosper in transnational education, US universities, and summer programs like SIE, Chinese international students like Siwen are involved in this catch-me-if-you-can game.

Invariably, Siwen's gaming the education systems and my public-speaking class's reinventing the werewolf game and the Inspire Me speech index the shanzhai (山寨) tradition in Chinese society. *Shanzhai* literally means "fortified mountain village," often referring to an alternative system or practice designed to resist and subvert the establishment. Shanzhai stories have long enjoyed popularity in the Chinese imagination. For instance, in the classical fictional tale *The Journey to the West*, the Monkey King, based in Flower and Fruit Mountain, fights against the Heavenly army with his magical power; in *Three Kingdoms*, southern states Shu and Wu marshal intrigues to defeat the central government; in *Water Margin*, 108 Robin Hood-style heroes, based in Liang Mountain, plot uprisings against the Song government. A key shanzhai practice is to master the rules of a system and then subvert it by rewriting the rules, as Siwen and the public-speaking class did. This practice is commonly seen in world history when the marginalized fight against the center, or the oppressed against the oppressor. Over the last three decades, for instance, China was often criticized by the West for violating intellectual property rights, human rights, and other international regulations. These violations took place because shanzhai practice could not be fully contained. And this practice is vital for individual and national survival in an unjust world system. For my middle-class students, shanzhai practice was critical for their upward mobility, as some studies show fair play might block key paths to success in certain careers (DiSalvo and Bruckman 2010; Harrell and Harrell 2009).

Sharing with me her strategies in the academic game, Siwen inadvertently called my attention to her online gaming experience. She used the term 秒杀 (SecKill) to refer to the ease of understanding her textbooks in translation. Originating from online games, SecKill literally means killing an enemy in a split second. Now widely used in sports, stock-market investment, online shopping, and other contexts, the expression means a strategic move that leads to a decisive win or result. When Siwen did not go to class, according to her, she played online games sometimes. At the end of the interview, I asked her whether I could observe her playing a game. She was puzzled by my request. After I explained to her my interest in understanding SIE students' literate lives outside school, she agreed to let me watch her. A few days later, after class, she told me she was going to her 首胜, or "first blood," of the day, and that I could join her.

As we were walking to an Internet café, Siwen started typing on her IPhone. She was using WeChat to invite her friends in Changsha, her hometown, to play games with her. We walked along the same street where my public-speaking students and I often had lunch. I was surprised to discover that Siwen actually stayed in a budget hotel right above the Internet café. She chose to live close to the SYSU campus and to her gaming world. It was dim inside the café, with desktop computers lining up in more than ten rows. Behind the monitors were young men and women staring at the big screens. We walked over to a counter in the middle of the café, and Siwen showed an employee her ID card. The Chinese government tries to keep tabs on people in the virtual world by requesting ID cards in Internet cafés. Siwen was given an access code for using any of the spare computers. We picked one and sat down.

WeChat conversations continued to mobilize bodies and objects. Siwen wanted to check to see whether her friends had arrived at an Internet café. She used WeChat again, this time on a desktop. One of her friends had forgotten his picture ID and was trying to borrow one from strangers on the street. This is another instance in which institutional power was subverted by ordinary citizens. Siwen found borrowing a stranger's ID card "ridiculous" (逗逼) and started laughing both online (with the help of emoticons) and offline (vocally). She then invited her friends to have dinner with her over the weekend in Changsha. Watching her typing, I understood the gist of the conversation, but not every word. Siwen and her friends invented expressions phonetically based on Changsha dialect, a variety of Hunan dialect. The dialogue about having dinner on the weekend, for example, was filled with dialectal expressions, which I mark in bold below.

SIWEN: 好久不见**野别列**。回来一起**恰饭**啊哈哈哈

(I haven't seen Ye for a long time. I will have dinner with you guys after I go back, hahaha.)

FRIEND: 你直接约**撒**

(You invite him yourself.)

FRIEND: **宝**吧

(You are crazy.)

SIWEN: 我又**冒**他联系方式!

(I don't have his contact information!)

SIWEN: **宝**什么**咯**!

(Why crazy?)

FRIEND: qq塞

(Use qq.)

SIWEN: 冒的列!!

(I don't have it.)

SIWEN: 就那么几个伢子

(Just a few guys)

SIWEN: 你又不是不晓得。我喊了你你就喊他咯。国多屁话咯

(You know what you are supposed to do. I call you and you call him. So much shit.)

FRIEND: 看喊得到咯

(So let's see whether he will come.)

SIWEN: 。。。。。什么意思咯

(What do you mean?)

SIWEN: 他还扮翘??

(He is pretentious??)

SIWEN: 你们还要好久哦。。我先大乱斗一把啦。。。

(How long will it take you guys? I will play a fight first.)

Changsha dialect shows up in both content words and sentence-ending sounds. Based on a Mandarin translation Siwen sent to me later, the content words include 恰饭 (eat), 宝 (crazy), 冒 (not to have), 伢子 (guys), 晓得 (know), 国多 (so much), and 扮翘 (pretentious). Sentence-ending sounds include 列 (lie), 撒 (sa), 咯 (ge), 塞 (sai), and 哦 (oh). In addition to these dialectal expressions, the dialogue blended two terms from the online world. "qq" means QQ, a China-based instant-messaging program. 大乱斗 refers to a gaming mode in the online game *League of Legends*, that is, ARAM-Howling Abyss-Normal All Random. Together with the online lingo, the dialect performed communal, identity functions. Siwen used it to connect with friends back home, more than four hundred miles away. Not being able to speak the dialect, I had difficulty grasping the subtleties of the conversation and was thus excluded from her hometown friend network. More broadly, the WeChat texts translated Siwen's intentions to reconnect with her friends and to have fun. They mobilized people and objects (cellphones, ID cards, computers) in two distant places.

As her friends were not online yet, Siwen started a game with other gamers. It was *League of Legends* (*LOL*), a multiplayer battle arena game. As the game was loading onto her client, she explained to me the rules. Players form into two teams of five Champions. There are more than a hundred different Champions from which to choose. Each player begins at opposing sides of a map near a building called a Nexus. A battle is won when either team's Nexus is destroyed. To destroy a Nexus, each team must work through a series of Turrets placed along a path, referred to as a Lane, to each base. Along the way, each player gains levels from killing the opposing team's Champions and Minions (nonplayer characters controlled by the computer that regularly spawn and attack the other team) and defeating neutral monsters. Completing objectives rewards players with gold, which is used to purchase items, making their Champions stronger.

Siwen chose to play the game on a China-based server. According to her, she had played it on a US-based server when she was in the United States. Now that she was in China, playing the game on a China-based server could help avoid lag. Lag for even split second could be fatal for a Champion. Playing the game on a US-based server, Siwen would have had to use English, the system language, and to interact with English-speaking players. When Siwen was moving the curser and hitting the keyboard, she did not just control her avatar. She also typed quickly in a dialogue window, which displayed both her team discussions and the system updates on major events unfolding in the game. The window provided a means for the team members to discuss strategies and coordinate actions. In a few minutes, Siwen's team seemed to be losing.

When the game was over, Siwen sat back to relax. But soon, she revealed to me how heavily online games had mediated her life across cities. She opened an IE browser to book her train ticket for going back to Changsha the next day. She interacted with the railway ticket-booking system and made her selections (place, time, train number, price). She also called to order Chinese-food delivery because she planned to play games for the next few hours. Then she walked out of the café and, in a few minutes, came back with her train ticket and a box of fried squid for a snack. She picked up her ticket at a travel agency next door. With the help of the Internet and her cellphone, the Internet café became a hub of her mobile life.

Soon Siwen's friends were online and ready to play. They chatted in the dialogue window, trying to figure out one another's user names. Then the team moved into a discussion on assignments and fighting strategies. Siwen proposed that they not gank before reaching level 6 and that she would be a jungler, roaming in the jungle and killing the neutral monsters. Popularized by the success of *World of Warcraft, gank* comes from *gang kill.* A gang kill occurs when a group of players attacks single ones and kills them with relative ease. *Jungle* refers to any area of the map that is not a Lane or part of either team's base. However, her proposal to be a jungler was challenged by a teammate.

> 同学: 画你的JB (Draw your JB)
>
> 同学: 当模特咯 (You act as a model)
>
> 同学: 6J以前不gank (Don't gank before 6J)
>
> 同学: 还是说不要打野 (Or we don't need juggling)
>
> 同学: 要不要打野啊!!!!!!!!!!(Do we need juggling or not!)
>
> 真特么骚、: 换个打野 (Someone else can be the juggler)
>
> 同学: 不。我这个好 (No, I can do it)
>
> 爽: 上路不要来送双buff啊 (Don't do double buff)
>
> 同学: 特别## (Especially # #)
>
> 真特么骚、: 废物 (Garbage)
>
> 同学: niubi (Stong)
>
> 同学: 那就6J前不gank (Alright, we don't gank before 6J)
>
> 同学: 你们慢慢啊 (Take your time)
>
> 同学: 哈哈 (Haha)
>
> 真特么骚、: AP狼人记得 (Do you remember AP werewolves?)
>
> 同学: No!!!!!(No!)
>
> 同学: 我玩狼人要你叫?、(Do I need you to call me how to play a werewolf?)
>
> 同学: 教?(teach?)

In this exchange, the two (同学 and 真特么骚、) challenged each other jokingly, a signifying practice also found in other gaming contexts and other cultures. After Siwen proposed that she would be hunting down the monsters in the dark jungle, one of her (male) friends suggested that someone else could play this role. Further, he reminded her of the magic attack tactics of the werewolf, the fictional character she chose to play.

Central to their signifying practice was the use of profanity. Siwen's friend contested her, probably because Siwen started the exchange with a filthy word. She joked that she wanted to paint this friend's JB, or 鸡巴 (*ji-ba*), meaning "penis." Later, Siwen used 牛逼/屄 (*niubi*), meaning "cow's genitalia," to refer to the strength of her Champion. But the gaming system recognized its inappropriateness, turning the Chinese characters into hashtags (##). Therefore, Siwen had to retype the expression phonetically as *niubi.* Later, Siwen told me that using dirty words was a common practice among *LOL* players. English-speaking players often use expressions, such as, in her words, "what the fuck, fucking noob, and shut up." When she was playing *LOL* in the United States, Siwen told me, her roommate found her taking on an entirely different persona. The gaming system also played a role in the signifying practice. It censored the gamer language. In the contestation with her friend, thus, Siwen adopted shorthand (JB) and alternative spelling (*niubi*) to resist censorship.

In addition to using profanity and resisting censorship, the gamers used expressions only comprehensible to *LOL* players. Although these expressions had Chinese translations, Siwen and her friends tended to use English. In the above dialogue, for example, these expressions include "gank," "buff," and "AP." They did use Chinese translations though, such as "打野" (jungling). Some expressions blended Chinese and English, such as "6J," "双buff," and "AP狼人." "6J" comes from 6 ji or 6 级, meaning level 6. "双buff" comes from *double buff*. "AP狼人" means "AP werewolf," or werewolf with attack power (AP) versus attack damage (AD).

The series of texts Siwen produced reveal several features of her literacy practice. First, she developed a cosmopolitan style of Chinese in her texts, a style that clearly defied national and cultural boundaries. She blended elements from Changsha dialect and *LOL* lingo (in both Chinese and English) with Standard Chinese, elements signifying her identification with both local and translocal communities. Second, Siwen's texts coordinated actions—going to the Internet café, playing *LOL*, and purchasing train tickets. Produced across different technological platforms (cellphone, computer, WeChat, and *LOL* dialogue window), these texts translated Siwen's strong desire to network in local and translocal spaces. Third, these texts enabled Siwen to constantly move between the global, general level and the local, specific level in space-time. Often, she articulated her (game) plans in these texts and then took actions subsequently online or offline.

Soon the team moved into the battlefield in their avatars, or Champions. The signifying practice continued for a minute or two when the team members were buying their equipment. As the game unfolded, the dialogue started to focus on coordinating actions.

HOTPOT LITERACY

Finally, we came to the end of the game, not *LOL* but the SIE summer program. After six weeks of intensive reading, writing, and discussion, both my classes came to their final assignments. After delivering their inspirational speeches, my public-speaking class proposed having a farewell dinner together, a common practice at Chinese universities. They wanted to go to 海底捞 (Haidilao), a popular hot-pot chain restaurant, near the subway station Kechun. Shortly after 6 p.m., Danny called me. After a two-hour wait, he had secured a table.

Danny waited for me at the restaurant entrance wearing an apron like a chef. Walking to our table, we elbowed through customers waiting for a hot-pot table in a large bright waiting area. Sitting around small tables, they were playing board games or eating free snacks. We sat down at a square table with other students. A big pot with water was set inside a big hole carved out in the middle of the table. Not far away from us was a large shining stainless table serving several-dozen sauces as well as fruits and snacks. An employee pushed a button on the wall, and soon water started to boil in our pot. She then poured a bag of sauce into it. The familiar spicy and numbing aroma filled the space. Everyone was given an IPad to select menu items. In a few minutes, the employee pushed a cart to our table with our orders, which included shrimps, sliced beef, cow stomach, pig lung, tofu, and vegetables. There was light music in the background, and I was impressed by the modern setup of the restaurant. In my memory, smaller and often greasy hot-pot restaurants seldom used fancy technologies.

In addition to modern technologies and elegant interior design, the restaurant brought traditional art forms to the clients. As we were eating and chatting, sounds of traditional Chinese opera came from afar. Holding a small record player, an ancient Chinese figure with a painted face mask and a colorful robe came close to our table. With a colored fan in hand, he trotted in small circles and performed acts in a traditional opera style. As he was making a circle, he suddenly struck the fan in front him. His face transposed into an entirely different one, showing a different emotion. He walked briskly toward me, struck his fan, and changed his face again. I was startled, but everyone applauded. This was the famous face-changing technique in Sichuan Opera, a technique used to depict one's changing emotions. It was my first time witnessing this magnificent technique. Bringing high-class art forms to the masses seemed to be a marketing strategy. Combining new technologies, modern interior design, and traditional arts, the restaurant transformed the hot-pot experience/expression.

After dinner, while we were leaving the restaurant, Danny asked me to listen to Kanye West's rap song "Dark Fantasy." He handed me his Xiaomi smart phone, which enacted new associations of texts, songs, and bodies. The rap and the students' chatter reverberating in my ears, I could feel the music but could not hear the lyrics. The song was related to Danny's inspirational speech delivered that morning. After his speech, as Danny was sitting down, he had asked Michael, who sat next to him, whether Michael had recognized that his speech pattern was borrowed from West. Then he had started singing, moving both hands higher and higher: "Can we get much higher, so hiiiigh." And then he said, gesturing toward the speech script on his computer screen with both hands, "This song, 这一整段都是从他那,类似的,不一样" (This song, the entire passage comes from him, similar but different). Upon arriving in my hotel room, I googled the song. I listened to it as well as to Danny's speech. The song starts with a narrative, retelling writer Roald Dahl's poetic rework of "Cinderella." West begins his verse saying that he fantasized about the story back in Chicago, and then he moves into topics such as decadence and hedonism. Drinking is at the center of his lyrics. In Danny's speech, like West, he starts with a narrative on the students' nightlife, which we hear in the epigraph to this chapter. In the section where he explicitly references West, he "raps" too, painting his dark fantasy.

> Listen to yourself
> Listen to your body
> Your liver is failing
> Your lung is failing
> Your body is slowing
> Your brain is not as fast as before
> Your eyes cannot see
> Even if you get a big house . . .
> If you get a pretty girl, you can only see her in a blurred world
> Drinking a shot of whiskey, flowing to throat, into your liver
> Smoking one pack of cigarette, the nicotine being absorbed, think of your lungs
> Playing a whole night of online gaming, imagine how radioactive you become
> You are a walking dead, waking up with feeling of lethargic
> Heads are pounding
> Throats are drying
> Drug addiction
> Fainting children, our future children
> And what is the problem?
> You ask me, "Can we get much higher?"

In his rapping, Danny painted some dreadful scenarios resulting from excessive drinking, smoking, and gaming. Using rhetorical strategies such as repetition and rhyming, he "rapped" with passion while smirking. He borrowed from West's lyrics: "Can we get much higher?" But when Danny said, "You ask me, 'Can we get much higher'?" he insinuated that the whole class was involved in drinking and smoking. Did he sincerely try to persuade the audience not to drink, not to smoke, and not to play games? Or did he deliver the speech as part of a heavy drinking game?

How to understand my students' speeches as part of their academic socialization was the lingering challenge for me. I could have done so using the assessment rubric as a guide. However, doing so, I would have focused on their reading, writing, and speaking within the classroom, on the audience response, and on whether the students had acquired the conventions related to oral communication. I would have arrived at a narrow understanding of the students' emergent academic identities. Tracing several literacy networks as I wrote this chapter, I came to perceive the speeches as part of a game, an academic exercise integral to middle-class socialization. It is a game about reading, writing, and speaking across ecological systems, national borders, cultural discourses, and physical spaces. It is a game not so different from a hot-pot dinner, a game in which the students marshal ingredients and sauces based on context and purpose to create different tastes, meanings, experiences, and identities. This game has always been a shanzhai practice in which students actively learn the topics, ideas, and rules of academia and rewrite them for survival, resistance, or creativity. In the process, they transformed, and are also transformed by, the game.

It is critical to recognize that Danny drew on multiple literacy networks to perform identity work in his speech. Obviously, he referenced the drinking and online games in which he participated. He appropriated the genre of inspirational speech to create a competitive show. His speech was a build-up from the practice speeches the class had produced. He was also inspired by the rap performance "Dark Fantasy" from a distant place. He threaded these networks together to create meanings, to perform his identity. Thus, his identity was contingent, contested, fluid, and multidimensional—an international student, an upper-middle-class man, a drinker, a gamer, and a transnational rap fan. He achieved his agency, being able to educate, excite, and please his audience because they identified with certain aspects of his identity work. This identity work is full of contradictions. While performing hot-pot style literacy, for instance, Danny revealed multiple contradictions—an upper-middle-class upbringing with empathy for the working class, a decadent lifestyle with wariness of its dangers, an obsession with art while being submerged in mundane consumer practices. Danny wrestled with these contradictions in his speech, in his literacy practices inside and outside the summer program.

In addition to gaming, my students' cosmopolitan language style also threaded through their literacy networks. As I have proposed elsewhere (You 2016), we can understand our everyday language practice as cosmopolitan. While various institutions and individuals try to impose linguistic norms, we tend to break them in actual language use by negotiating and crossing the boundaries between styles, between genres, between dialects, and between languages. We cross these boundaries when trying to engage interlocutors of different communities. By doing so, we seek identification between us, thus taking on different identities. My students' cosmopolitan language style, critical to their identity work, mediated their middle-class socialization in important ways. For example, the public-speaking students referred to each other by their English names inside and outside the classroom. English names indexed their membership in an Anglo-American-educated professional community. The communal practice also included frequent code switching and mixing. Students often switched between English and Chinese discourses (code switching) with ease, as when they discussed Siwen's remarks on the movie *Tiny Times*. They mixed elements from different language systems at the sentential level (code mixing), as they did when explaining the term diaosi to me or when playing the werewolves drinking game. Siwen did so too when conversing with her friends on WeChat and in the *LOL* dialogue window. The students' cosmopolitan styles allowed them to flow fluidly from one literacy network to another or to inhabit multiple networks simultaneously. Some of their cosmopolitan styles, such as the use of English names and switching between English and Chinese discourses, are highly valued in the professional world. Practicing these styles across literacy networks was the students' way of accumulating cultural capital.

Understood in the framework of literacy networks, my students' meaning-making practices can offer implications for a transnational pedagogy, or a pedagogy conceived from a transnational perspective. First, as Leander and Lovvorn (2006) suggest, the conventional demarcation between in-school and out-of-school spaces does not match students' literacy practices in space-time. While students are aware of the boundaries of these physical spaces, they draw on resources of diverse origin to construct meanings, often spanning these spaces. Forcing physical-space distinctions in students' literacy work may negatively affect their agency, engagement, and identity. Second, the SIE students' literacy practices suggest that to understand their in-class reading and writing practices, the teacher must view these in a network with other actants. The teacher should step outside the classroom and be an ethnographer in their students' communities, treading between being an insider and an outsider. Third, if a teacher adopts the literacy-network perspective, they can no longer evaluate their students' work as purely cognitive achievements or communications isolated within the classroom or within an academic community. Instead, evaluation should turn into seeking understanding of and appreciation for students' meaning-making strategies across activities and spaces. Fourth, literacy networks are critical for students' middle-class socialization, though they often reproduce social inequality. Understanding students' literacy networks provides educators an opportunity to intervene in the students' socialization process. While cultivating a cosmopolitan disposition and an aspiration for social justice in students proves to be challenging, understanding their literacy networks provides a basis for strategic educational intervention. In the age of globalization, such intervention is an imperative for cultivating global citizens.

CONCLUSION

In this conclusion, we return to a scene on the bridge over the Red Cedar River at Michigan State University. The following is an image of the rock at MSU painted with the message "Support the Hong Kong China Democracy" that was part of a protest during the umbrella revolution (Figure 8.1). During this time period, there was a series of sit-in street protests against Beijing in Hong Kong's main economic district in opposition to what the protesters claimed was the capital's refusal to grant open elections by 2017. The protests and tensions spilled onto the MSU campus, where Hong Kong students engaged in a demonstration at the campus rock on the National Day of China. By two o'clock that same day, however, the message on the rock had been replaced with a Chinese national flag. Mainland students posted more than sixty photos on the CSSA (Chinese Student and Scholar Association) web page along with hundreds of messages. In this manner, the political tensions and battles on the campus became layered and sedimented into the MSU landscape.

With tensions ripe and reports of Mainlanders refusing to speak to Hong Kongers in classes, a second-year student studying journalism from the city of Yiwu outside Shanghai decided to cover the various sides of the political debate as part of a communications course. While striving to maintain objectivity and report on both sides of the issue, she felt personally angry and hurt by the public display against China over the unlawful British colonization of the mainland's territory. Her own positon was indexed in the second paragraph of her article, where she included a quote from a roommate's WeChat. The passage read,

> Like most Chinese students, Xu Lin felt angry and hurt. She posted before and after pictures of the rock on WeChat. "So-called 'wear yellow for Hong Kong', if you guys ultimately must occupy the rock to distribute these thoughts, I want to ask: What kind of 'democracy' are you looking for?" she wrote in a post on WeChat. "Only spoiled kids scold their mother. Happy national Day! To all Chinese people with backbones."

The next paragraph explained that more than twenty Chinese students—friends who had been surveyed on social media across the

DOI: 10.7330/9781607327332.c008

Figure 8.1. Hong Kong student protest at campus rock

United States and China for the article—firmly agreed with this sentiment. The text suggested that most Hong Kong citizens were also against the demonstration and that the noise and commotion from the protest came from a vocal minority. Though the author tried to present the side of the Hong Kong students, this section appeared toward the bottom of the story, so less space was devoted to their side of the debate. The marginalization of the Hong Kong side points to wider tensions she experienced while writing it. During an interview with the student organizer of the protest from the Hong Kong Student Association, the author held her tongue to hide her own perspective. She also expressed defiance against Western bias in the press, which was implicitly critical of the Chinese government.

As the scene illustrates, she was complexly entangled among an array of competing narratives. Because she firmly aligned herself against the protest movement, one might understand her struggle to write an "objective" news report as bound up in a wider struggle. Trying to write the story was linked to the development of a bifocal perspective, that is, learning to view the world from multiple points of view. In this fashion, the production of the article was bound up in the construction of her identity. As a Chinese student engaged in writing English journalistic pieces, Steve (one of the coauthors of this book) instantly recognized her writing talent and approached her about participating in the study. He imagined her as an ideal candidate, an international student engaged in traversing languages and cultures in her in-school and out-of-school literacies. As a staff writer for the Chinese student publication *Nebular* (chapter 2), she was further related to the social web of actors that had become core to Steve's research. However, his second interview with her about her coverage of the umbrella-revolution article was a tense affair. Afterwards, he received an e-mail response to his request for follow-up information, including a microblog post in WeChat called "Moments" from her roommate, which she had used in the article. The e-mail is partially quoted here:

> . . . The moment was deleted and I cannot find that. And I don't know whether [roommate] wants to talk [about] it or not. Actually, I don't want to talk about it either, I don't know why you are so curious about it and it makes me feel like you just concern about the negative part of my articles. To write this news makes me feel pain and angry, and to talk about it also makes me pain and angry. And you keep asking, it really makes me upset. I hope I didn't show angry and impatience on my face, if I did so, wish you can understand that I did not meant to do that. I throw all the notes, deleted all the record of this news, and I cannot provide any other materials, so sorry.
> . . . I am so busy these days, and I don't think I have time to talk with you any more, because of my intern[ship].
> Anyway, nice to talk to you.

The e-mail about the exchange shows the student was upset and had felt interrogated. She had been unnerved by the gaze of a Western English-speaking professor who probed about this sensitive topic related to Chinese national sovereignty. Not fully comprehending the delicate nature of the situation, Steve had crossed social lines. In the process, the case study of this student was firmly finished before it had ever started. In this instance, the unexpected breakdown and tensions indexed a wider set of tensions in relation to the social field in which the actors were located. While serving to foreground the significance of students' national and collective identities, this story ultimately remains fragmented and part of a wider unfinished thread. At the end of Paul Prior's (1998) study on disciplinary practices of graduate students, he turns to Andrew Pickering's (1995) notion of "mangle of practice." The mangle of practice points to the gap between the narratives traditionally used to represent research methods in formal academic settings and the much more messy realities that often unfold on the ground. We present this story as a way to avoid purifying our research and suggest the ways it was full of struggles, breakdowns, and loose ends. This story points to the wider challenges of engaging in cross-cultural and global research.

As the research unfolded, numerous other fault lines and tensions emerged as the researchers encountered literacies and activities turning up in unexpected places. Indeed, Steve and Xiqiao encountered a rich underground economy that was widespread on the MSU campus and difficult to access or document. This economy included students engaged in a range of hidden literacy practices, such as those of the Director (see chapter 2), who leveraged his social capital at the school to start a rich network of businesses that ultimately extended back to China. Central to the interviews with him were social and political tensions, including the recognition that many of his businesses were not officially permitted based on his student-visa status. As indicated, we moreover were disconcerted to find the profile picture of this student, who had literally served as the poster child for the MSU diversity initiative, openly displaying a Nazi flag in the background. Such findings presented us with a number of ethical questions and uncertainties. Should we put a picture of him in this book with a Nazi flag in the background? What were the ethical implications and potential consequences for him? Though he signed an IRB form, was he fully aware of what he had agreed to and did he recognize the nature of what the Nazi flag signified? On the other hand, what were the ethical implications of not discussing this story? Shouldn't the public and wider academic community be made aware of such wide disjunctures? Often the tensions we experienced left us with few clear or straightforward answers.

In key respects, our research frameworks were disrupted in parallel with the traditional norms, standards, and ways of thinking, doing, and being at the university. Much research in education on third spaces and underground literacy practices identifies these acts as forms of resistance to a dominant educational order that attempts to regulate and marginalize such activities. These studies traditionally take up a social justice perspective with the wider aim of shifting students from deficit positions. In observing the literacy practices of the Chinese international students, however, our findings are more complex and fail to neatly fit into these well-worn tropes. In some cases, for example, the students were linguistically and culturally marginalized but economically privileged. In addition, we had evidence of students gaming the academic system on standardized tests and in the classroom itself. In response, the university was implementing policies of containment in an effort to regulate the students and tame a problem it had manufactured. In mapping out this interplay, our aim has not been to judge the students but instead to understand these struggles as part of a wider political and economic struggle through which the higher education system is being globally transformed. These struggles are on display in pictures of rooms of students in China hooked to IV fluid bags while studying long hours for the state-sponsored educational exam, and in images of throngs of parents pressed against fences outside the schools while the students take their exams. These scenarios quickly demonstrate the significant pressures within the society to get into a top university while revealing how educational regimes have infiltrated almost all aspects of the students' and their families' lives. Given these scenes, the extent to which some are willing to go in order to enter into a US university is not surprising. In the context of wider social and historical shifts, many citizens are not far removed from the Cultural Revolution or periods of economic hardship.

Moreover, as insiders at the university, we were not divorced from this process but were deeply part of this dynamic and shifting landscape. Our study not only documents this messy process but is also bound up in its representation and production. With these caveats in mind, we continue to map out shifts in the wider global eduscape through bringing together more fully some of the threads in each of the case studies. In making these moves, our aim is to extend our tracing of people and things across space-time and to uncover ways this process is bound up in the construction of a wider transnational social field in higher education. Aihwa Ong (1999) defines transnationalism as a process unfolding through space or across lines, as well as the changing nature of something (4). With respect to this definition, our study has not only set out to focus on the complex movements of actors and things across near and distant spaces but also on the changing nature of the spaces themselves. We have focused on the ways students learn to invent the university as part of a complex and jointly mediated process involving the tying and untying of texts, tools, actors, and objects. Studying how actors weave and are woven into wider social systems, we have furthermore focused on how the world grant university is being reinvented.

Our mobile-literacies approach makes visible a transnational social field in which educational spaces are products of multiple relations that mediate the complex flow of students, pedagogies, ideologies, policies, and practices—co-constituting mobility systems in the making—across dynamic and changing pathways. It is through tracing these complex and shifting pathways that we have unmasked power geometries shaping and shaped by mobile practices of actors and objects. This stance does not solely foreground power per se but rather power relations. This stance is grounded in that notion that power is not concentrated in single locales but is instead exercised relationally in interactions with other places. In bringing together the various connections and linkages across our sites, our studies foreground that it may well take a village to study a village or ecological system of learning (Lemke 2000). Yet the inclusion of multiple researchers as part of our multisited approach has added an element of complexity, as manifested in shifting voices, orientations, unfinished threads, and ways of representing our work. Similar to the reconfiguration of the higher education landscape, these disjunctures are bound up in wider sets of tensions related to studying global complexity.

Core to the reconstruction of the higher education landscape is the shift to the world grant university. Intertwined with this social imaginary is the dual character of the university: that is, on one hand the world grant extends rhetorics of the public good to a global scale, while on the other it imagines ways to colonize new international markets. These two competing narratives have led to a range of tensions, struggles, and contradictions being played out on the fly and on the ground. On the MSU campus, for example, the university continues to espouse rhetorics of diversity and cross-cultural exchange even as many of its admissions policies are creating a structure that is fostering a sense of division and social segregation. On the Sun Yat-sen campus, one also finds contradictions embedded in competing and contradictory narratives of the public and private sphere. Even as the Chinese Communist party continues to espouse notions of national and educational sovereignty, the increasing number of for-profit educational enterprises is bound up in the production of a Western marketplace model. These contradictions materialize in the location of the for-profit SIE school on the margins of the Guangzhou campus, indexing the school's movement onto the fringes of the national educational system. In this fashion, public and private spheres of activity are deeply inscribed into the local landscape. Further complicating this shifting network, or knotwork, the Chinese summer schools are in competition with each other while simultaneously positioned in relation to national education systems at home and abroad.

Bound up in this struggle are HEIs' efforts to maintain their borders and boundaries through policies of containment. Bureaucratic levers of the state are used to regulate and control the educational social field through admissions, credits, certifications, degree requirements, transcripts, and other instruments of managerial control. On the MSU campus, these regimes were materialized in everything from curricular structures to residence-hall housing structures. Operating across a range of scales, these microphysics of power were further inscribed into the Sun Yat-sen campus infrastructure, such as in the Great Firewall (i.e., China's blockage of outside digital networks) that limited students' abilities to receive online textbooks or locate websites that had been removed. Co-constituting wider regimes of mobility, these relational networks regulated social and geographic movement in and across the higher education landscape.

Part of a wider and contested field, the students mobilized complex sets of grassroots literacies and resources to resist and subvert this system. Situated in social and historical contexts, the act of shanzhai, or copying, in the twelfth century was a noble political act of resistance bound up in a broader struggle against authoritarian regimes. In this context, the emergence of copycat North American-style summer programs might be viewed as a challenge to a dominant hegemonic educational apparatus. While shanzhai products have the reputation of low quality, the strategy in China has resulted in the success of multibillion-dollar tech companies who have used this strategy to enter the market and reinvest their earnings to improve the products' quality and reputation. Shanzhaiism is, in fact, a philosophical concept meaning "innovation with a peasant mind-set." In this fashion, shanzhai might be understood as a way to achieve social and class mobility. On a more local level, acts of copying by students such as Siwen, who fabricated her own high-school transcript, might be understood as part of a social, economic, and class struggle. This process often entailed the marshalling of tightly bundled and distributed relationship webs (*renji guanxi wang*). Through networking and knotworking, students inflected, resisted, and appropriated educational policies and practices aimed at disciplining the student body. These transnational networks frequently spun off into nonacademic contexts extending across various regions of the world. The construction and movement through these webs of activity were further bound up in the production of wider geographies of difference. In this fashion, building relationship webs was a means of accumulating social and mobile capital.

Through tracing the complex and messy circulation of actors and objects across our various field sites, our mobile-literacies approach renders visible how wider policies, discourses, ideologies, signs, and symbols were recontextualized in local spatialized practices. Offering ethnographically informed accounts of global connections, our tracing of transnational flows, or scapes, has attended to a number of intertwined areas. We have articulated some of the key ways various flows of actors and objects have moved in and across our various sites. (See also appendix I.)

- Policies. We traced educational policies and their social effects at the SIE school and on the MSU campus. With international study largely regulated and controlled by nation-states, the controversy surrounding the SIE program called attention to national policies of containment. Mapping out this struggle, we traced the social effects on the Guangzhou campus in e-mails, staff-room meetings, academic trade journals, and classroom interactions. We further attended to the impact of these policies on the MSU campus, where students debated the merits of enrollment in Chinese summer schools. In this fashion, we traced the enforcement, maintenance, and enactment of policies as they were negotiated across near and far-flung contexts.

- Physical structures. We followed the development and expansion of the SIE model as an MSU business school student copied it by starting her own competing program, SCP, in China. Connecting our field sites, we traced the circulation of social and material structures as they complexly traveled across borders.

- National discourses. We traced national discourses, such as the Chinese dream, and how they were materialized in political slogans, popular media, student performances, and academic trajectories. For example, the Chinese dream framed oral presentations presented by students at the SIE school; the dream discourse further mediated the narratives in *Nebular* and the literate trajectory of MSU student Yisi Fan, who decided to pursue her dream of becoming a writer.

- Social and class identity markers. We traced the circulation of social-identity markers related to socioeconomic status. Xiaoye's study, for example, traced how *diaosi* as a key marker of social and class identity was performed, contested, appropriated, and maintained through situated moments of activity, as students engaged in social debates linked to the construction of the national imagination. At the center of these debates were deep ambivalences toward social and class shifts in Chinese society, as these tensions were manifested in everyday practices inside and outside academic spaces. Constellations of related concepts such as *baifumei* (white, rich, and beautiful) and *gaofushuai* (tall, rich, and handsome) further were taken up, resisted, and transformed across varied contexts, ranging from elite social gatherings in New York City to speech performances and activities in the SIE program in Guangzhou. Linked to wider regimes of mobility, these social imaginaries were literally embodied in the case of Siwen, whose physical appearance and dress conformed to this identity type. Further illustrating how these labels were deeply embodied was the bare-chested figure on the *Nebular* cover with terms such as "second-generation rich" inscribed on his abdomen.

- Educational identity markers. We traced the circulation of identity markers linked to educational status, such as the social matrix of terms that socially and geographically positioned students in Xiqiao's classroom. These identity markers literally shaped how the students organized themselves in the physical classroom and in their digital networks, as these areas became deeply intertwined. These socially prescribed categories further circulated across others contexts, such as in the case of Yisi, who sought to have others "carry" her in her course work. These terms continually shaped and were shaped in the context of everyday mobile literacy practices.

- Popular media. We traced the circulation of media such the popular television talent show, *The Voice of China*, as international-student contestants from NYU and other universities were interviewed in *Nebular*. The student-run magazine further brokered business arrangements with the producers to help market an international season. Part of a global mediascape, Xiaoye's students watched episodes over lunchtime during typhoon season in the SIE classroom, and discourse from the show was recontextualized in student inspirational speeches. Bound up in an interlocking set of rhetorical and ideological practices, dream discourses framed the show's premise, indexing how these tropes were deeply overlapping and multidimensional.

Attending to these interlocking threads of activity, we have reconceived the relations between physical mobility, social mobility, virtual mobility, and educational mobility. Taken together, these mobilities form part of a fluid and complex web knotted into wider social and historical trajectories shaping and shaped in the context of everyday practices. These mobile practices (Nordquist 2017) are mediated by face-to-face and digital practices in institutionally sanctioned and non-sanctioned spaces. In short, we have looked at the complex circulation and movement of people and things across classrooms, barrooms, and online chatrooms. We have further attended to the ways constellations of texts, tools, actors, objects, and histories coordinate this activity. Finally, we have attended to ways these constellations are themselves on the move as they are continually configured and reconfigured. Through tracing the ways these constellations of terms, tropes, texts, and textual practices are taken up across contexts, we reveal the dynamic, emergent, and deeply contested nature though which wider flows, or scapes (Appadurai 1996), are rewoven in and across a transnational social field.

Turning more specifically to pedagogical implications, instructors may ask what our findings mean for working with international and multilingual students. Broadly, our study offers a framework to better understand the dynamics and complexities of teaching and learning in a space in which national identity, social class, culture, and language are increasingly entangled. This framework provides key insights into a rich underground set of literacies and practices that remains invisible to educators. To reiterate Li's (2006) key question, how can we teach if we do not know who we are teaching? Our study provides a glimpse into this population's lifeworlds. Central to this move is a less bounded approach that attends to the complex intersections inside and outside the classroom as students traverse a range of near and far-flung spaces. Moreover, our mobile-literacies framework argues for not merely attending to cultural differences but for attending to the power and structural relations mediating these social and linguistic divides. The question, as the studies show, is not whether to change or not, as global complexities have made such changes largely inevitable. The question rather becomes how to negotiate these changes as part of a process Li (2006) refers to as a "pedagogy of reciprocity." This is an orientation that understands teaching as a complex site of negotiation between educators and students, as both jointly reconfigure and acquire different practices, values, understandings, and ideologies.

We educators/researchers developed creative and liberatory pedagogies that leveraged students' linguistic and cultural assets, but these moves were far from perfect. As Xiqiao's classroom illustrates, for example, even cultural insiders and Chinese speakers may encounter complex sets of student resistance. Moreover, the cultivation of bifocal and cosmopolitan lenses is often a messy and highly uneven process, as indexed by the student delivering his inspirational speech who drew on various bits and pieces from the emancipation proclamation, MLK's I Have a Dream oratory, and LGBTQ rights discourses. As the speech demonstrates, the process is partial and deeply fragmented. It furthermore suggests that without a complex and deep understanding of social and historical contexts of both home and host cultures, there is a danger of reproducing social and class inequalities even as instructors attempt to confront them. Uncovering these complications, the study does not offer straightforward answers or clear-cut solutions to these knotty problems. Rather, it presents a broader framework for approaching these issues and working toward reciprocal pedagogies as part of a complex negotiation between students and instructors.

Pointing to the highly uneven, long-term, and complicated nature of students' literate trajectories, Xiaoye decided to consult with one of his focal participants, Siwen, in July 2016, three years after the SIE Guangzhou program. At the time of the Skype conversation, Siwen was doing her hair in a salon in Changsha, her hometown. She had just returned from the United States after graduation. They recalled their days at SIE and discussed what Siwen had achieved thereafter. Talking about Guo Jingming and his *Tiny Times* movie series, Siwen said she always liked his movies. When asked about her Weibo comments about *Tiny Times* written three years before, Siwen was unwavering about them: the 2013 movie was realistic because it was based on Guo's original novel and because there are rich people in China who lead luxurious lives, as depicted by Guo. Talking about negative reports on Chinese international students in the United States, she felt some Chinese people's resentment of the rich had not receded in three years' time. However,

Siwen did change. In the ensuing years, she realized the importance of immersing herself in US academic culture. She tried to stay away from other Chinese students in the classroom and actively sought out opportunities to interact with US students, who seemed to understand teacher expectations better than did Chinese students. She gained more from working with them in group work. She enhanced her English and graduated with a 3.2 GPA, improved from 2.0 her freshmen year. Before graduation, she found a sales-associate job in a department store in Washington, DC. However, as the company would not support her H-1 visa application, she could only work in the United States for a year. Her parents encouraged her to work for their family business instead because she would hardly make ends meet working as a sales associate. Siwen could not decide whether to return to the United States or not.

The vignette points to Siwen's complex trajectory. In the discussion, which she participated in from a hair salon, she still maintained her staunch defense of the wealthy and their right to live extravagant lifestyles. In this respect, she had not developed a more critical stance toward the increasing class and social divisions in a rapidly shifting Chinese society. At the same time, she had tried to integrate more fully into US culture and had successfully graduated. She had furthermore located employment working in the Macy's cosmetics department as a sales associate. The position itself suggests how the wider social imaginary perpetuated in popular media such as *Tiny Times* was manifested in her career and lifestyle choices. Unable to sustain this lifestyle, she was nevertheless forced to return home and work for the family business after a year because of work visa laws and the fact that she was not able to make ends meet on her own as a sales associate. In this fashion, she was negotiating multiple and competing mobility regimes linked to immigration laws, global imaginaries, and economic systems. Now residing in China, she still struggles with whether to remain or to return to the United States. This complex back-and-forth movement—across social, geographic, and imagined spaces—is part of an ongoing struggle bound up in the development of her identity. As her story illustrates, this process is highly uneven, fragmented, messy, and deeply knotted into multiple strands of activity.

As our case studies have illustrated, it is to these "messy circulations and plural geographies" (Leander, Phillips, and Taylor 2010, 335) that we need to more fully turn in order to capture global complexity. Central to these transformations is a need to reconfigure our teaching and research frameworks through fine-grained attention to moments of everyday literate practice and to link these moments to wider semiotic chains of activity. Part of a more holistic framework, this focus necessitates imagining translingual writers (and other actors) as knotworkers continually tying and untying an array of texts, tools, actors, and objects distributed across near and far flung spaces. In the context of twenty-first-century higher education, this mobile-literacies orientation is increasingly critical, as both writing studies and higher education are increasingly knotted into wider globalized networks of activity.

APPENDIX 1
Methodological Appendix

CONNECTING SITES

Adopting a flat ontology, our research methods incorporated three steps (Latour 2005): localizing the global, redistributing the local, and connecting sites. In this section, we detail more fully the third move and how we connected our disparate field sites. Tracing activity in and across our separate studies, we searched for key themes and patterns. Critically, as part of our holistic framework, we traced semiotic, social, and physical structures across the field sites. Attending to how they were recontextualized, we further conceptualized these structures as stabilized-for-now constellations or repeated knots of activity.

To identify how actors (or actants) and objects traveled across our sites, we engaged in a process of constant comparison while identifying analytic themes and social practices. For example, in Steve's study of the student publication *Nebular* (chapter 2) he found Communist artwork in the tradition of socialist realism in the magazine, with the texts and images critiqued through repurposing. Socialist realism is a style of realistic art developed in the Soviet Union that spread to other Communist nations and glorified the working class and Communist values. In Xiaoye's study of his classroom (chapter 6), he found this trope surface in a debate over whether Western popular culture and media were valuable or "real." Embedded in this discussion were underlying tensions related to social, cultural, and economic shifts in a globalizing Chinese society. These issues were compared to the ones in the *Nebular* text. In this fashion, we established links across our sites while attending to the ways they were localized in each setting. As part of a more connective approach, we conceptualized these disparate locations as part of a wider social assemblage, or knotwork, in the making. Table A1.1 details the themes across our various sites.

DOI: 10.7330/9781607327332.c009

Table A1.1. Key Themes

		Ch 1 (Steve)	Ch 2 (Steve)	Ch 3 (Steve)	Ch 4 (Xiqiao)	Ch 5 (Xiaoye)	Ch 6 (Xiaoye)	Ch 7 (Xiaoye)
Socialist Realism			x				x	
Video Gaming			x					x
Internet language	Gender						x	
	Class	x		x		x		
	Education		x	x				
Facework (Mianzi)				x	x			
The Chronicle of Higher Education						x		
Dream Discourse				x		x		x
Poaching of American Popular Media/Culture				x	x	x	x	x
Voice of China			x					x
Technologies (WeChat)			x	x	x			x
Guanxi			x	x	x			x
Entrepreneurship			x	x	x			x
Shanzhai		x	x			x		x
May 4th Movement			x	x				
For-Profit Chinese Summer Schools			x			x		x
Automobiles (Social Class Marker)		x	x		x			

Below we provide more methodological details about our individual studies.

CHAPTER 1

The data gathered in this chapter are largely grounded in semistructured interviews with seventeen administrators, three instructors, and four students. The aim was to understand key ways the influx of international students was impacting departments and units across MSU. In many instances, administrators were selected after being recommended or verbally referenced in the context of another interview or conversation. These intertextual connections were used to establish a network of associations, as I (Steve) traced the complex relationships among people, units, and departments. In most instances, meetings were audio recorded, subsequently reviewed, and selectively transcribed. These interviews were further supplemented with conversations with other faculty and administrators who intersected with the Chinese international-student population and with observations in the context of my everyday work as a faculty member in the writing program. This activity included serving on first-year-writing committees and participating in faculty meetings where issues surrounding international students arose. Moreover, one key site was a faculty learning community (FLC) I attended three times during the fall 2016 academic semester. The FLC brought together faculty and staff from across the university to engage in dialogue related to the international-student community. The instructors selected for the study all participated in these meetings. The students selected for the study were linked either to Project Explore or the Intercultural Aide program. As such, they offered insights into university programs designed to integrate the international-student population into the wider student population. Finally, the analysis was supplemented with attendance at a range of university functions, such as the global fest, a half-day multicultural workshop called Asian Invasion, international-student coffee hours, pedagogical workshops for international students, and three showings of local documentaries on the Chinese international-student population. I furthermore asked a research assistant residing in Beijing over the summer of 2016 to observe an orientation for incoming first-year students.

These methods were coupled with the collection of artifacts. Often, these were provided in the context of the interviews: for example, a sample of a student report for MAP-works (a system to monitor student progress) or an informational brochure listing the new admissions criteria at the Eli Broad College of Business. I also collected and reviewed other university artifacts, such as a set of instructional videos sponsored by the Office of International Student Services to orient students to the university before their arrival. And finally, with the help of a Chinese-speaking research assistant, I examined Chinese signs around campus and a wide range of social media posts.

To analyze the data, I traced the relationships among the different spaces, sites, people, stories, and artifacts as I attempted to construct a dense web, or network, of connections. As part of a reflective process, I focused on key questions related to the unexpected, asking what made something unexpected and why. I further posed question related to social change and shift and the university, asking who/what was changing and to what extent? Using a grounded theoretical approach, policies of containment emerged as a dominant analytic theme serving as a way to make sense of and organize the data.

CHAPTER 2

Situating this chapter in a broad social context, my overall study included observations of a wide range of student activities and practices in and across the campus. My understanding of guanxi as a widespread cultural practice emerged through tracing the activities of key informants (including Yisi, described in chapter 3), in-depth interviews with twenty-six students on their academic and nonacademic language and literacy practices (including eight entrepreneurs), semistructured interviews with Chinese student organizations (MSUwe54, Chinese Student and Scholar Association, China Entrepreneur Network), and rhetorical analysis of student social media sites and online publications. It is within this broader context that I selected the two focal participants for the case studies, as they served as telling cases that foregrounded key social dynamics that emerged across other social spaces.

I conducted a total of four interviews with Zi'an and two with the Director. All were audio recorded, and the final one with Zi'an was video recorded. In keeping with a grounded theoretical approach (Charmaz 2014), interviews were transcribed and coded. As part of a recursive process of open and more focused coding, guanxi served as a sensitizing concept for making sense of the data. In the case of the Director, I further triangulated the analysis with stories about him from participants in the wider study and in-depth analysis of his Renren social media site, where he documented his university life over a period of three years. I also triangulated the analysis with the review of his WeChat blog entries, which offered a rich account of his activity after his return to China. In the case of Zi'an, I supplemented the interviews with stories from Yisi about their work together on *Nebular* and Humans of East Lansing. With the assistance of Chinese-speaking research assistants, I also conducted rhetorical analyses of his publications; twenty-two individual articles were translated with the aid of a research assistant and thematically coded. Finally, I reviewed his WeChat microblog, in which he documented his activities managing *Nebular*.

CHAPTER 3

From 2013 to 2014, I met with Yisi on a weekly and sometimes biweekly basis, in total approximately thirty-six times, with interviews

audio and often video recorded. I further took notes during these meetings and documented key quotes, stories, and interactions. I then selectively reviewed and transcribed tapes. Towards the end of the first academic year, we began to use a screen-capture program to record her in
situ writing. Interviews typically lasted between one and three hours. I
collected notes, jottings, and tests from all her courses. I further regularly reviewed her Weibo, WeChat, and Ren Ren social media accounts.
Yisi additionally provided me with other texts including her personal
diary and fictional stories. I spent more than ty hours reviewing her
Chinese materials with a research assistant. I ther continued to meet
with Yisi on a semiregular basis through 201 s I began to focus more
on her journalistic and professional writing in parallel with her increasing engagement in these areas.

CHAPTER 4

In my (Xiqiao) study, data was collected during the course of six
months (September 2013 to March 2014) in and out of a bridge writing
course entitled Preparation for College Writing (PCW). Recruitment of
the participants was carried out in two sections of PCW I taught in fall
2013. A survey of multilingual and multimodal literacies was adminis-
tered to students. Close to 90 percent of the students were of Chinese
origin, all of whom indicated they participated in WeChat study groups
at the university. Based on the survey responses, I invited thirty-six
Chinese students to participate in one-time semistructured group interviews (in groups of three). Semistructured group interviews with the
cohort were conducted from September 2013 through January 2014.
Taking a constant comparative approach, I used these interviews to
develop a grounded theory of students' literacy experiences and identities during their first year of college. The bulk of the data with Yan
was collected between September 2013 and January 2014, although I
continued to conduct follow-up interviews until April 2014 with Yan
and Lee. Data consist of semistructured interviews about their literacy
histories and WeChat activities, observations of Yan's activities in the
classroom and seven episodes of Lee's WeChat tutorials, collection of
Yan's writing samples and artifacts, and recordings of her activities in
an informal WeChat study group she created, which included thirteen
other Chinese students in the class. All interviews were conducted in
Mandarin and translated into English, except when the original transcription provided evidence of the participant's language use. Interview
data was translated and transcribed through the coordinated effort of

an undergraduate research assistant and the researcher, who were both bilingual in English and Chinese. Interview data and chatting records allowed me to get a glimpse of how expert students actively constructed their identity as an expert.

CHAPTERS 5–7

Most of the empirical data for chapters 5–7 were collected between June 30, 2013, and August 9, 2013, when SIE summer school in Guangzhou was in session. Further data were gathered from students through phone interviews and e-mails until June 2016. The participants include twelve students, ten faculty members, and two administrators.

During the summer session, adopting a mobile ethnographic approach, I (Xiaoye) gathered data from multiple sources. First, following my students, I audio recorded their interactions in classrooms, restaurants, bars, and an Internet café. I attended faculty meetings, banquets, and sightseeing trips and recorded instructor and administrator conversations on those occasions. The audio recordings, eighty-two total, cover more than one hundred hours. Second, I video recorded class discussions and student presentations, as well as a student playing online games in an Internet café. The twenty-five video recordings cover more than fifteen hours. Third, I gathered artifacts inside and outside the classroom. I collected students' essay and speech drafts, notes, and online postings. I took pictures of scenes in the classroom, on the SYSU campus, and in bars and an Internet café, as well as on the streets outside the SYSU campus. Fourth, I gathered e-mails, online postings, and print advertisements used by SIE for internal and external communications.

As soon as I completed a recording, I listened or watched it at the end of the day. In the meantime, I took notes in Chinese to record the time the recording was made, the subject matters discussed and the times they were discussed in the recording, and the important human and non-human actors at the scene. I did this almost every day during the summer session. Through reviewing the notes recursively, I searched for key actors and themes. Halfway through the semester, key actors and themes emerged. This type of information came to inform my teaching, allowing me to take some of these themes, such as diaosi, *Tiny Times*, the Chinese dream, online games, and foods as materials for eliciting class discussions. Further, key human actors who emerged in the data became focal students in my participant observations. I followed these students into restaurants, bars, and an Internet café to further observe their interactions with the social and material worlds.

In chapter 5, echoing the thematic structure of chapter 1, I sought to understand and delineate how the US education system intersects with the emerging international-education market in China as embodied by the SIE summer school. Perceiving myself and other teachers and students as knotworkers, I searched in my recording notes and artifacts for moments of disruption, examples of translation (Latour 2005), and scenes of association between the two activity networks. These moments, examples, and scenes constitute the interlocking nodes between the networks. I identified a bulletin board on the SYSU campus, container trucks pulling into a student residence compound, a *Chronicle of Higher Education* article, and the SIE academic dean's visit as such nodes for close examination. The human and non-human actors mediated the formation of a transnational higher education social field, of which SIE was a part.

In chapter 6, after identifying diaosi as a key term used by my middle-class students for their identity work, I decided to usher this term into my public-speaking class as part of my teaching. I watched out for moments in my students' reading and writing activities when issues of Chinese social class were broached. I strategically called my students' attention to the term diaosi and used it to elicit discussions grounded in their class assignments. In data analysis, I focused on how the term and the discussions it provoked mediated students' reading and writing processes in the classroom, making the students confront the socioeconomic disparities in China. I paid particular attention in the data to deciphering the subject positions my focal students constructed in relation to the Chinese lower working class and the Chinese dream propagated by the Communist Party.

In chapter 7, after identifying gaming as another key theme in the student discourse in the middle of the semester, I decided to further understand how games mediated the students' literacy practices inside and outside the classroom. I followed them into bars and an Internet café, places where board games and online multiplayer games were played. I observed how games were played, I played them sometimes, and I discussed them with my student gamers. In data analysis, I first sought moments when a game (such as *The Werewolves* or *League of Legends*) was actually played and when game discourse and strategies entered classroom writing and speaking activities. Next, I identified the specific terms and strategies used in a game. Then, I searched for moments in the classroom discourse or in student speech drafts where these terms and strategies seemed to have been deployed. Finally, looking beyond those moments, I connected students' literacy activities inside the classroom and their gaming activities outside the classroom to understand their identity work. Through comparing their gaming styles across contexts, I identified shanzhai practice as a uniting theme, not only as a strategy of the students' academic socialization but more broadly as a strategy of their middle-class socialization.

After data analysis, I drafted the chapters. I showed them to the focus students for member checking. With their feedback, I revised my narratives and analyses.

APPENDIX II
Motivational Speech Evaluation

Speaker:_____ Topic:_____

Category	Rating and Comments				
Introduction	Very Good	Good	Average	Poor	Unsatisfactory
15%					
• Gained attention and interest					
• Provided clear thesis and preview of main ideas					
Body	Very Good	Good	Average	Poor	Unsatisfactory
25%					
• Distinct and well-supported main points					
• Adequately explained Need, Satisfaction, and Visualization steps of the Motivated Sequence					
• Fitting language for topic, audience, and speech purpose					
• Adapted message to audience					
• Met assignment criteria for motivational speech					
Organization	Very Good	Good	Average	Poor	Unsatisfactory
10%					
• Assembled parts of the Motivated Sequence into a coherent whole					
• Used clear transitions					
Conclusion	Very Good	Good	Average	Poor	Unsatisfactory
10%					
• Summarized and drew out key points					

Continued on next page

DOI: 10.7330/9781607327332.c010

Continued

Conclusion	Very Good	Good	Average	Poor	Unsatisfactory
• Presented a memorable call to action					
• Left an impact					

Delivery	Very Good	Good	Average	Poor	Unsatisfactory
25%					
• Appeared well practiced and extemporaneous					
• Conveyed enthusiasm					
• Maintained consistent eye contact					
• Varied oral style through volume, rate, pauses, and inflections					
• Avoided verbal fillers					
• Used effective gestures and stance/posturing					
• Avoided distracting mannerisms					

Overall	Very Good	Good	Average	Poor	Unsatisfactory
15%					
• Typed outline follows guidelines of MMS, is well organized, and grammatically correct					
• Adapted message to audience, held interest					
• Challenging, civically engaged topic with new information					
• Passionate about the topic					
Time:					

Time (minutes)	4:00–6:00	6:00–7:00	7:01–7:30	7:31–8:00	Beyond 8:00
Grade penalty	Requirement	Grace period	–5 points	–10 points	–15 points

REFERENCES

Adey, P. 2010. *Mobility*. New York: Routledge.

Agar, M. 1994. *Language Shock: Understanding the Culture of Conversation*. New York: William Morrow.

Anson, C. M., and C. Donahue. 2015. "Deconstructing ting Program Administration' in an International Context." In *Transnational Writi Program Administration*, edited by David S. Martins, 22–47. Logan: Utah State University Press. https://doi.org/10.7330/9780874219623.c001.

Appadurai, A. 1996. *Modernity at Large: Cultural Dimensions of Globalization*. Minneapolis: University of Minnesota Press.

Ayash, N. B. 2014. "U.S. Translingualism through a Cross-National and Cross-Linguistic Lens." In *Reworking English in Rhetoric and Composition: Global Interrogations, Local Interventions*, edited by B. C. Horner and K. Kopelson, 116–28. Carbondale: Southern Illinois University Press.

Bakhtin, M. M. 1981. *The Dialogic Imagination: Four Essays by M.M. Bakhtin*. Edited by M. E. Holquist, translated by C. Emerson and M. Holquist. Austin: University of Texas Press.

Bartholomae, D. 1986. "Inventing the University." *Journal of Basic Writing* 5 (1): 4–23.

Barton, B. F., and M. S. Barton. 1993. "Ideology and the Map." In *Professional Communication: The Social Perspective*, edited by N. R. Blyler and C. Thralls, 49–78. Newbury Park: SAGE.

Barton, D., and M. Hamilton. 1998. *Local Literacies: Reading and Writing in One Community*. London: Routledge. https://doi.org/10.4324/9780203448885.

Baynham, M., and M. Prinsloo. 2009. *The Future of Literacy Studies*. New York: Palgrave Macmillan. https://doi.org/10.1057/9780230245693.

Bazerman, C. 2004. "Intertextuality: How Texts Rely on Other Texts." In *What Writing Does and How It Does It: An Introduction to Analysis of Texts and Textual Practices*, edited by C. Bazerman and P. Prior, 167–200. Mahwah, NJ: Lawrence Erlbaum.

Berry, P. W., G. E. Hawisher, and C. L. Selfe. 2012. *Transnational Literate Lives in Digital Times*. Logan: Computers and Composition Digital Press/Utah State University Press.

Black, R. W. 2009. "Online Fan Fiction, Global Identities, and Imagination." *Research in the Teaching of English* 43 (4): 397–425.

Blommaert, J. 2005. *Discourse: A Critical Introduction*. Cambridge: Cambridge University Press. https://doi.org/10.1017/CBO9780511610295.

Blommaert, J. 2008. *Grassroots Literacy: Writing, Identity and Voice in Central Africa*. New York: Routledge.

Blommaert, J. 2010. *The Sociolinguistics of Globalization*. New York: Cambridge University Press. https://doi.org/10.1017/CBO9780511845307.

Blommaert, J. 2013. *Ethnography, Superdiversity, and Linguistic Landscapes: Chronicles of Complexity*. Bristol: Multilingual Matters.

Bourdieu, P. 1977. *Outline of a Theory of Practice*. Cambridge: Cambridge University Press. https://doi.org/10.1017/CBO9780511812507.

Bourdieu, P. 1986. "The Forms of Capital." In *Handbook of Theory and Research for the Sociology of Education*, edited by J. Richardson, 241–58. New York: Greenwood.

Bourdieu, P. 1991. *Language and Symbolic Power*. Cambridge, MA: Harvard University Press.

Brandt, D. 2001. *Literacy in American Lives*. Cambridge, MA: Cambridge University Press. https://doi.org/10.1017/CBO9780511810237.

DOI: 10.7330/9781607327332.c011

Brandt, D, and K. Clinton. 2002. "Limits of the Local: Expanding Perspectives on Literacy as a Social Practice." *Journal of Literacy Research* 34 (3): 337–56. https://doi.org/10.1207/s15548430jlr3403_4.

Brooks, R., and J. L. Waters. 2011. *Student Mobilities, Migration and the Internationalization of Higher Education.* New York: Palgrave Macmillan. https://doi.org/10.1057/9780230305588.

Bruna, K. R. 2007. "Traveling Tags: The Informal Literacies of Mexican Newcomers in and out of the Classroom." *Linguistics and Education* 18 (3–4): 232–57. https://doi.org/10.1016/j.linged.2007.07.008.

Burawoy, M. 2000. *Global Ethnography: Forces, Connections, and Imaginations in a Postmodern World.* Berkeley: University of California Press.

Burnett, S. A., and J. Huisman. 2010. "Universities' Responses to Globalization: The Influence of Organizational Culture." *Journal of Studies in International Education* 14 (2): 117–42. https://doi.org/10.1177/1028315309350717.

Butler, M. 2013. "Chinese Summer Program's Credits Are Not for Sale." *Chronicle of Higher Education,* January 30. http://chronicle.com/blogs/letters/chinese-summer-programs-credits-are-not-for-sale/.

Callero, P. L. 2009. *The Myth of Individualism: How Social Forces Shape Our Lives.* Lanham, MD: Rowman & Littlefield.

Canagarajah, A. S. 2006. "The Place of World Englishes in Composition: Pluralization Continued." *College Composition and Communication* 47 (4): 586–619.

Canagarajah, S. 2013. *Translingual Practice: Global Englishes and Cosmopolitan Relations.* New York: Routledge.

Cardon, P., and J. Scott. 2003. "Chinese Business Face: Communication Behaviors and Teaching Approaches." *Business Communication Quarterly* 66 (4): 9–22. https://doi.org/10.1177/108056990306600402.

Casanave, C. P. 2002. *Writing Games: Multicultural Case Studies of Academic Literacy Practices in Higher Education.* Mahwah, NJ: Lawrence Erlbaum.

Cendrowski, S. 2016. "China Spreads the Wealth Around." *Fortune* (December 15): 139–44.

Charmaz, K. 2014. *Constructing Grounded Theory.* Los Angeles, CA: SAGE.

Chen, B. H. 2014. "'学霸'热该降降温了" [It's time to cool the lord-of-learning heat]. *China Education Daily,* April 8.

Chen, J. 2013. "陈俊宏:我对"中国梦"的理解" [Chen Junhong: My understanding of the "Chinese Dream"]. 人民网 [people.cn]. May 8. http://theory.people.com.cn/n/2013/0508/c49150-21401869.html.

Cheng, C. 1986. "The Concept of Face and Its Confucian Roots." *Journal of Chinese Philosophy* 13 (3): 329–48. https://doi.org/10.1111/j.1540-6253.1986.tb00102.x.

"China's Losers." 2014. *Economist,* April 19, 39–40.

Chinese Film Association Theoretical Commentary Committee. 2008. *2008中国电影艺术报告* [A report on Chinese film art, 2008]. Beijing: Zhongguo dianying chubanshe.

"Chinese Students Built 'Chengguan Gang' in the US, Violation and Fight." 2015. ["中国留学生在美国成立'城管帮'恐吓打人."] 头条新闻 [*Chinese Headline News*], February 2015. http://weibo.com/1618051664/C2qDt3txn?type=comment#_rnd1499720161189.

Clarke, I., T. B. Flaherty, N. D. Wright, and R. M. McMillen. 2009. "Student Intercultural Proficiency from Study Abroad Programs." *Journal of Marketing Education* 31 (2): 173–81. https://doi.org/10.1177/0273475309335583.

Cresswell, T. 2010. "Towards a Politics of Mobility." *Environment and Planning. D, Society & Space* 28 (1): 17–31. https://doi.org/10.1068/d11407.

des Pallieres, P., and H. Marly. 2001. *The Werewolves of Millers Hollow.* Thiercellieux: Lui-Même.

Dingo, R. 2012. *Networking Arguments: Rhetoric, Transnational Feminism, and Public Policy Writing.* Pittsburgh, PA: University of Pittsburgh Press.

Dingo, R., R. Riedner, and J. Wingard. 2013. "Toward a Cogent Analysis of Power: Transnational Rhetorical Studies." *JAC* 33:517–528.

DiSalvo, B., and A. Bruckman. 2010. "Race and Gender in Play Practices: Young African American Males." In *Proceedings of the Fifth International Conference on the Foundations of Digital Games (FDG 2010)*, Monterey, California, June 19–21, 2010, 56–63. https://doi .org/10.1145/1822348.1822356.

Donahue, C. 2009. "'Internationalization' and Composition Studies: Reorienting the Discourse." *College Composition and Communica* 61 (2): 212–43.

Dreier, O. 1999. "Personal Trajectories of Participation across Contexts of Social Practice." *Outlines: Critical Practice Studies* 1 (1): 5–32.

Duffy, J. M. 2007. *Writing from These Roots: Literacy in Hmong-American Community*. Honolulu: University of Hawaii Press.

EIC Education. 2014. "中国低龄留学生研究报告" [y on Chinese students studying abroad at an early age]. http://www.eic.org.cn/s /eic_research_report_2014/.

Emerson, R. M., R. I. Fretz, and L. L. Shaw. 1995. *Writ nographic Fieldnotes*. Chicago: University of Chicago Press. https://doi.org/10.72 cago/9780226206868.001.0001.

Encyclopedia. 2013. "屌丝" [Diaosi]. Baidu. http://baike.baidu.com/view/5642513.htm.

Fischer, K. 2015. "Navigating NYU's 'Island' in China." *Chronicle of Higher Education*, September 18, A23.

FlorCruz, M. 2014. "China's 'Diaosi': Growing 'Loser' Population Sheds Light on Chinese Youth." *International Business Times*, December 4. http://www.ibtimes.com/chinas-diaosi -growing-loser-population-sheds-light-chinese-youth-1734575.

Fong, V. L. 2011. *Paradise Redefined: Transnational Chinese Students and the Quest for Flexible Citizenship in the Developed World*. Stanford, CA: Stanford University Press.

Foster, D., and D. R. Russell, eds. 2010. *Writing and Learning in Cross-National Perspective: Transitions from Secondary to Higher Education*. New York: Routledge.

Fraiberg, S. 2010. "Composition 2.0: Toward A Multilingual and Multimodal Framework." *College Composition and Communication* 62 (1): 100–26.

Fraiberg, S., and X. Cui. 2016. "Weaving Relationship Webs: Tracing how IMing Practices Mediate the Trajectories of Chinese International Students." *Computers and Composition* 39:83–103. https://doi.org/10.1016/j.compcom.2015.11.005.

Freedman, A. 1994. "Anyone for Tennis?" In *Genre and the New Rhetoric*, edited by A. Freedman and P. Medway, 43–66. London: Taylor and Francis.

Gee, J. P. 1996. *Social Linguistics and Literacies: Ideology in Discourses*. London: Taylor and Francis.

Gee, J. P. 2005. *An Introduction to Discourse Analysis: Theory and Method*. New York: Routledge.

Gillespie Group. 2015. "Midtown家 Creative Living." Accessed July 15, 2015. http:// midtownlansing.com/features/.

Giroux, H. 2010. "Rethinking Education as the Practice of Freedom: Paulo Freire and the Promise of Critical Pedagogy." Truthout. January 1. http://www.truth-out.org /archive/item/87456:rethinking-education-as-the-practice-of-freedom-paulo-freire -and-the-promise-of-critical-pedagogy.

Glaser, B. G., and A. L. Strauss. 1967. *The Discovery of Grounded Theory: Strategies for Qualitative Research*. Chicago: Aldine.

Greenholtz, J. 2000. "Assessing Cross-Cultural Competence in Transnational Education: The Intercultural Development Inventory." *Higher Education in Europe* 25 (3): 411–16. https://doi.org/10.1080/713669273.

Guerra, J. C. 1998. *Close to Home: Oral and Literate Practices in a Transnational Mexicano Community*. New York: Teachers College Press.

Guerra, J. C. 2008. "Cultivating Transcultural Citizenship: A Writing across Communities Model." *Language Arts* 85 (4): 296–304.

Guerra, J. C. 2015. *Language, Culture, Identity and Citizenship in College Classrooms and Communities*. New York: Routledge.

Hammer, M. R., M. J. Bennett, and R. Wiseman. 2003. "Measuring Intercultural Sensitivity: The Intercultural Development Inventory." *International Journal of Intercultural Relations* 27: 421–43.

Harley, J. B. 1988. "Maps, Knowledge, and Power." In *The Iconography of Landscape: Essays on the Symbolic Representation, Design and Use of Past Environments*, edited by D. Cosgrove and S. Daniels, 277–312. Cambridge: Cambridge University Press.

Harley, J. B. 1996. "Deconstructing the Map." In *Human Geography: An Essential Reader*, edited by J. Agnew, D. Livingstone, and Alisdair Rogers, 422–33. Oxford: Blackwell.

Harrell, S. V., and D. F. Harrell. 2009. "Exploring the Potential of Computational Self-Representations for Enabling Learning: Examining At-Risk Youths' Development of Mathematical/Computational Agency." In *Proceedings of the 8th Digital Arts and Culture Conference (DAC 2009)*, Irvine, CA, December 12–15. http://groups.csail.mit.edu/icelab/sites/default/files/pdf/VeeragoudarHarrell&Harrell_DAC2009.pdf.

Harris, J. D. 2012. *A Teaching Subject: Composition since 1966*. Logan: Utah State University Press.

Harvey, D. 2006. *Spaces of Global Capitalism*. London: Verso.

Harvey, D. 1996. *Justice, Nature and the Geography of Difference*. Oxford: Blackwell.

Hawisher, G. E., C. L. Selfe, Y. H. Guo, and L. Liu. 2006. "Globalization and Agency: Designing and Redesigning the Literacies of Cyberspace." *College English* 68 (6): 619–36.

Hay, M. 2015. "Nazi Chic: The Asian Fashion Craze That Just Won't Die." Vice. February 12. https://www.vice.com/en_us/article/nazis-chic-is-asias-offensive-fashion-craze-456.

He, L. 2016. "Transnational Higher Education Institutions in China: A Comparison of Policy Orientation and Reality." *Journal of Studies in International Education* 20 (1): 79–95. https://doi.org/10.1177/1028315315602931.

Heath, Shirley Brice. 1983. *Ways with Words: Language, Life, and Work in Communities and Classrooms*. New York: Cambridge University Press.

Hesford, W. S. 2006. "Global Turns and Cautions in Rhetoric and Composition Studies." *PMLA* 121 (3): 787–801. https://doi.org/10.1632/003081206X142887.

Hesford, W. S., and E. E. Schell. 2008. "Introduction: Configurations of Transnationality: Locating Feminist Rhetorics." *College English* 70 (5): 461–70.

Hirsch, E. D. 1987. *Cultural Literacy: What Every American Needs to Know*. New York: Houghton Mifflin.

Ho, D. 1976. "On the Concept of Face." *American Journal of Sociology* 81 (4): 867–84. https://doi.org/10.1086/226145.

Holton, R. 2009. *Cosmopolitanisms: New Thinking and New Directions*. Basingstoke: Palgrave Macmillan. https://doi.org/10.1007/978-1-137-03837-1.

Horner, B., Min-Zhan Lu, J.J. Royster, and J. Trimbur. 2011. "Language Difference in Writing: Toward a Translingual Approach." *College English* 73 (3): 303–21.

Huang, Y. 2006. "Collectivism, Political Control, and Gating in Chinese Cities." *Urban Geography* 27 (6): 507–25. https://doi.org/10.2747/0272-3638.27.6.507.

Hvistendahl, M. 2013. "China's Publication Bazaar." *Science* 342 (6162): 1035–39. https://doi.org/10.1126/science.342.6162.1035.

Institute of International Education. 2014. *Open Doors 2014: Report on International Educational Exchange*. https://www.iie.org/Who-We-Are/News-and-Events/Press-Center/Press-releases/2014/2014-11-11-Open-Doors-Data.

Ivanič, R. 1998. *Writing and Identity: The Discoursal Construction of Identity in Academic Writing*. Philadelphia, PA: John Benjamins. https://doi.org/10.1075/swll.5.

Jamieson, K. M. 1975. "Antecedent Genre as Rhetorical Constraint." *Quarterly Journal of Speech* 61 (4): 406–15.

Johnstone, C. L., and K. M. McCullough. 2008. *The Art of the Speaker: Effective Oral Communication in Everyday Life*. University Park: Pennsylvania State University, Department of Communication Arts and Sciences.

Kang, Y. K. 2015. "Tensions of Local and Global: South Korean Students Navigating and Maximizing US College Life." *Journal of Composition and Literacy Studies* 3 (3): 86–109. https://doi.org/10.21623/1.3.3.6.

Kell, C. 2009. "Literacy Practices, Text/s and Meaning Making across Time and Space." In *The Future of Literacy Studies*, edited by M. Baynham and M. Prinsloo, 75–99. New York: Palgrave Macmillan. https://doi.org/10.1057/9780230245693_5.

Kell, C. 2011. "Inequalities and Crossings: Literacy and the Spaces-In-Between." *International Journal of Educational Development* 31 (6): 606–13. https://doi.org/10.1016/j.ijedudev.2011.02.006.

Kell, C. 2013. "Ariadne's Thread: Literacy, Scale and Meaning Making across Space and Time." Working Papers in Urban Language & Literacies 118. https://www.kcl.ac.uk/sspp/departments/education/research/Research-Centres/ldc/publications/workingpapers/abstracts/WP118-Ariadnes-thread-Literacy,-scale-and-meaning-making-across-space-and-time.aspx.

Kimmel, K., and S. Volet. 2012. "University Students' Perceptions of and Attitudes towards Culturally Diverse Group Work: Does Context Matter?" *Journal of Studies in International Education* 16 (2): 157–81. https://doi.org/10.1177/1028315310373833.

Kinginger, C. 2008. *"Language Learning in Study Abroad: Case Studies of Americans in France."* Special issue, *Modern Language Journal* 92 (1).

Knobel, M., and C. Lankshear. 2007. "Remix: The Art and Craft of Endless Hybridization." *Journal of Adolescent & Adult Literacy* 52 (1): 22–33. https://doi.org/10.1598/JAAL.52.1.3.

Kubota, R. 2016. "The Multi/Plural Turn, Postcolonial Theory, and Neoliberal Multiculturalism: Complicities and Implications for Applied Linguistics." *Applied Linguistics* 37 (4): 474–94. https://doi.org/10.1093/applin/amu045.

Lam, W. S. E. 2009. "Multiliteracies on Instant Messaging in Negotiating Local, Translocal, and Transnational Affiliations: A Case of an Adolescent Immigrant." *Reading Research Quarterly* 44 (4): 377–97. https://doi.org/10.1598/RRQ.44.4.5.

Lam, W. S. E., and D. S. Warriner. 2012. "Transnationalism and Literacy: Investigating the Mobility of People, Languages, Texts, and Practices in Contexts of Migration." *Reading Research Quarterly* 47 (2): 191–215. https://doi.org/10.1002/RRQ.016.

Latour, B. 1987. *Science in Action*. Cambridge, MA: Harvard University Press.

Latour, B. 1999. *Pandora's Hope: Essays on the Reality of Science Studies*. Cambridge, MA: Harvard University Press.

Latour, B. 2005. *Reassembling the Social: An Introduction to Actor-Network-Theory*. Oxford: Oxford University Press.

Leander, K. 2003. "Speaking and Writing: How Talk and Text Interact in Situated Practices." In *What Writing Does and How It Does It: An Introduction to Analysis of Texts and Textual Practices*, edited by Charles Bazerman and Paul Prior, 167–200. Mahwah, NJ: Lawrence Erlbaum.

Leander, K. 2008. "Toward a Connective Ethnography of Online/Offline Literacy Networks." In *Handbook of Research on New Literacies*, edited by J. Coiro, M. Knobel, C. Lankshear, and D. J. Leu, 33–66. New York: Lawrence Erlbaum.

Leander, K. M., and J. F. Lovvorn. 2006. "Literacy Networks: Following the Circulation of Texts, Bodies, and Objects in the Schooling and Online Gaming of One Youth." *Cognition and Instruction* 24 (3): 291–340. https://doi.org/10.1207/s1532690xci2403_1.

Leander, K. M., N. C. Phillips, and K. H. Taylor. 2010. "The Changing Social Spaces of Learning: Mapping New Mobilities." *Review of Research in Education* 34 (1): 329–94. https://doi.org/10.3102/0091732X09358129.

Leander, K. M., and D. Wells Rowe. 2006. "Mapping Literacy Spaces in Motion: A Rhizomatic Analysis of a Classroom Literacy Performance." *Reading Research Quarterly* 41 (4): 428–60.

Leander, K. M., and M. Sheehy. 2004. *Spatializing Literacy Research and Practice*. New York: Peter Lang.

LEAP (Lansing Economic Area Partnership). 2015. Home. Accessed June 12. http://globallansing.com.

Lee, A., R. Poch, M. Shaw, and R. Williams. 2012. *Engaging Diversity in Undergraduate Classrooms: A Pedagogy for Developing Intercultural Competence.* ASHE Higher Education Report 38 (2). San Francisco, CA: Jossey-Bass.

Lefebvre, H. 1991. *The Production of Space.* Translated by Donald Nicholson-Smith. Oxford: Blackwell.

Leki, I. 1991–1992. "Building Expertise through Sequenced Writing Assignments." *TESOL Journal* 1 (2): 19–23.

Lemke, J. L. 2000. "Across the Scales of Time: Artifacts, Activities, and Meanings in Ecosocial Systems." *Mind, Culture, and Activity* 7 (4): 273–90. https://doi.org/10.1207/S15327884 MCA0704_03.

Leonard, R. L. 2013. "Traveling Literacies: Multilingual Writing on the Move." *Research in the Teaching of English* 48 (1): 13–39.

Leonard, R. L., K. Vieira, and M. Young. 2015. "Special Editors' Introduction to Issue 3.3." *Literacy in Composition Studies* 3 (3): VI–XI.

Leung, T. K. P., and R. Chan. 2003. "Face, Favor, and Positioning—a Chinese Power Game." *European Journal of Marketing* 37 (11/12): 1575–98. https://doi.org/10.1108/03 090560310495366.

Levitt, P., and N. G. Schiller. 2004. "Conceptualizing Simultaneity: A Transnational Social Field Perspective on Society." *International Migration Review* 38 (3): 1002–39. https://doi .org/10.1111/j.1747-7379.2004.tb00227.x.

Li, G. 2006. *Culturally Contested Pedagogy.* Albany: SUNY Press.

Lin, Y. 2014. "中学生"学习外号"多达十余种" [More than ten learning nicknames for middle-school students]. *Beijing Youth Daily,* January 2. http://epaper.ynet.com/html /2014-01/02/content_33628.htm

Lu, X. 2000. "The Influence of Classical Chinese Rhetoric on Contemporary Chinese Political Communication and Social Relations." In *Chinese Perspectives in Rhetoric and Communication,* edited by D. R. Heisey, 3–24. Stamford, CT: Ablex.

Lucas, S. 2013. "English Public Speaking and the Cultivation of Talents for Chinese College Students." *Chinese Journal of Applied Linguistics* 36 (2): 163–82.

Luke, C. 2006. "Eduscapes: Knowledge Capital and Cultures." *Studies in Language and Capitalism* 1 (1): 97–120.

Ma, S. M. 2015. "The Forked Tongue of Chinese-English Translation at MSU (Mandarin-Speaking University?), circa 2015." *Journal of Intercultural Inquiry* 1(1): 6–27.

Marcus, G. E. 1995. "Ethnography in/of the World System: The Emergence of Multi-sited Ethnography." *Annual Review of Anthropology* 24 (1): 95–117. https://doi.org/10.1146 /annurev.an.24.100195.000523.

Marcus, G. E. 1998. *Ethnography through Thick and Thin.* Princeton, NJ: Princeton University Press.

Martins, D. S., ed. 2015. *Transnational Writing Program Administration.* Boulder: University Press of Colorado.

Massey, D. 1994. *Space, Place and Gender.* Minneapolis: University of Minnesota Press.

Massey, D. 2005. *For Space.* London: SAGE.

McCarthy, L. P. 1987. "A Stranger in Strange Lands: A College Student Writing across the Curriculum." *Research in the Teaching of English* 21 (3): 233–65.

McMurtrie, B., and L. Farrer. 2013. "Chinese Summer Schools Sell Quick Credits." *Chronicle of Higher Education,* January 14. http://chronicle.com/article/Chinese-Summer -Schools-Sell/136637/.

McNamara, T. M. 2016. "Dreams and Disappointments: Chinese Undergraduates and Investment in the US Writing Classroom." PhD diss., University of Illinois at Urbana-Champaign. https://www.ideals.illinois.edu/bitstream/handle/2142/92790/MCNA MARA-DISSERTATION-2016.pdf?sequence=1.

Mei, J., and D. B. Qin. 2015. "Data on Chinese International Student Adaptation." Paper presented at the *MSU Neighborhood Data Summit,* East Lansing, MI. https://drive

.google.com/file/d/0BzqmHLP1NTPaQi1xQ0lsM0tocURfRm10aE1VNnJOc01BSE
sw/view?pref=2&pli=1.

Meinhof, U. H. 2009. "Transnational Flows, Networks, and 'Transcultural Capital': Reflections on Researching Migrant Networks through Linguistic Ethnography." In *Globalization and Language in Contact: Scale, Migration, and Communicative Practices*, edited by J. P. Collins, S. Slembrouck, and M. Baynham, 148–69. New York: Continuum.

Meyers, S. V. 2014. *Del Otro Lado*. Carbondale: Southern Illinois University Press.

Miller, C. R. 1994. "Rhetorical Community: The Cultural Basis of Genre." In *Genre and the New Rhetoric*, edited by A. Freedman and P. Medway, 67–78. London: Taylor & Francis.

Ministry of Education. 2006. "教育部关于当前中外合作办学若干问题的意见" [Ministry of Education on several issues in Chinese-foreign cooperation in running schools]. http://www.crs.jsj.edu.cn/index.php/default/news/index/1.

Ministry of Education. 2007. "教育部关于进一步规范中外合作办学秩序的通知" [A notice on further regulating Chinese-foreign cooperation in running schools]. http://www.crs.jsj.edu.cn/index.php/default/news/index/18.

Ministry of Education. 2009. "中外合作办学评估方案(试行)" [A plan for assessing Chinese-foreign cooperation in running schools, a trial version]. http://www.chinade grees.cn/xwyyjsjyxx/xwbl/zcfg/gzzd/264671.shtml.

Ministry of Education. 2015a. "硕士及以上中外合作办学机构与项目(含内地与港台地区合作办学机构与项目)名单" [A list of approved graduate level Sino-foreign cooperative education institutions and programs, including the mainland and Hong Kong and Taiwan cooperative education institutions and programs]. http://www.crs.jsj.edu.cn/index.php/default/approval/orglists/1.

Ministry of Education. 2015b. "本科中外合作办学机构与项目(含内地与港台地区合作办学机构与项目)名单" [A list of approved undergraduate level Sino-foreign cooperative education institutions and programs, including the mainland and Hong Kong and Taiwan cooperative education institutions and programs]. http://www.crs.jsj.edu.cn/index.php/default/approval/orglists/2.

MSU China Working Group. 2005. *The China Concept Paper*. Accessed July 15, 2015. http://www.isp.msu.edu/globalencounter/china/docs/China%20Concept%20Paper.pdf.

MSU Office of the Registrar. 2014. "Geographical Students of Students: Other Countries." Michigan State University. Accessed December 18, 2015. https://www.reg.msu.edu/RoInfo/EnrTermEndRpts.asp?ts=42323.

Muchiri, M. N., N. G. Mulamba, G. Myers, and D. B. Ddoloi. 1995. "Importing Composition: Teaching and Researching Academic Writing Beyond North America." *College Composition and Communication* 46 (2): 175–98.

National Bureau of Statistics. 2014. "统计局:2013年全年城镇居民人均总收入29547元" [National Statistics Bureau: The average disposable income for city and town dwellers reached 29547 yuan in year 2013]. http://sn.people.com.cn/n/2014/0120/c340887 -20436713.html.

National Center for Education Statistics. 2013. "Projections of Education Statistics to 2021." (40th ed.). (NCES 2013–008). Washington, DC: U.S. Department of Education.

Nespor, J. 2004. "Educational Scale Making." *Pedagogy, Culture & Society* 12 (3): 309–26. https://doi.org/10.1080/14681360400200205.

Newkirk, T. 1996. "Seduction and Betrayal in Qualitative Research." In *Ethics and Representation in Qualitative Studies of Literacy*, edited by P. Mortensen and G. E. Kirsch, 3–16. Urbana, IL: NCTE.

Nordquist, B. 2014. "Composing College and Career: Mobility, Complexity and Agency at the Nexus of High School, College and Work." PhD diss., University of Louisville.

Nordquist, B. 2017. *Literacy and Mobility: Complexity, Uncertainty and Agency at the Nexus of High School and College*. New York: Routledge.

Norris, S., and R. Jones. 2005. *Discourse in Action: Introducing Mediated Discourse Analysis*. New York: Taylor and Francis.

O'Brien, A., and C. Alfano. 2015. "Tech Travels: Connecting Writing Classes across Continents." In *Transnational Writing Program Administration*, edited by David S. Martins, 48–71. Logan: Utah State University Press. https://doi.org/10.7330/9780874219623.c002.

Ong, A. 1999. *Flexible Citizenship*. Durham, NC: Duke University Press.

Ong, A., and D. Nonini. 1997. *Empires: The Cultural Politics of Modern Chinese Transnationalism*. New York: Routledge.

Pahl, K., and J. Rowsell. 2006. *Travel Notes from the New Literacy Studies: Instances of Practice*. Clevedon: Multilingual Matters.

Pennycook, A. 2012. *Language and Mobility: Unexpected Places*. Bristol: Multilingual Matters.

Pickering, A. 1995. *The Mangle of Practice: Time, Agency, and Science*. Chicago, IL: University of Chicago Press. https://doi.org/10.7208/chicago/9780226668253.001.0001.

Pratt, M. L. 1991. "Arts of the Contact Zone." *Profession* 91: 33–40.

Prior, P. 1998. *Writing/Disciplinarity: A Sociohistoric Account of Literate Activity in the Academy*. New York: Lawrence Erlbaum.

Prior, P. 2004. "Tracing Process: How Texts Come into Being." In *What Writing Does and How It Does It: An Introduction to Analysis of Texts and Textual Practices*, edited by Charles Bazerman and Paul Prior, 167–200. Mahwah, NJ: Lawrence Erlbaum.

Prior, P. 2008. "Flat Chat? Reassembling Literate Activity." Paper presented at Writing Research Across Borders, Santa Barbara, CA, February 22–24. http://www.semremtoo.org/Prior/home/PRIOR_FlatChat2008.pdf.

Prior, P., and J. Julie. 2010. *Exploring Semiotic Remediation as Discourse Practice*. Houndmills: Palgrave Macmillan.

Prior, P., and S. Schaffner. 2011. "Bird Identification as a Family of Activities: Motives, Mediating Artifacts, and Laminated Assemblages." *Ethos* 39 (1): 51–70. https://doi.org/10.1111/j.1548-1352.2010.01170.x.

Prior, P., and J. Shipka. 2003. "Chronotopic Lamination: Tracing the Contours of Literate Activity." In *Writing Selves/Writing Society: Research from Activity Perspectives*, edited by Charles Bazerman and David R. Russell, 180–238. Fort Collins, CO: WAC Clearinghouse and *Mind, Culture, and Activity*.

Qi, X. 2011. "Face: A Chinese Concept in a Global Sociology." *Journal of Sociology* 47 (3): 279–95. https://doi.org/10.1177/1440783311407692.

Rao, S. 2007. "现实主义电影发展及其现代化转换" [The evolvement of realist cinema and its modernization turn]. 光明日报 [*Guangming Daily*], May 15. http://www.gmw.cn/01gmrb/2007-05/15/content_606063.htm.

Reynolds, N. 2007. *Geographies of Writing: Inhabiting Places and Encountering Difference*. Carbondale: Southern Illinois University Press.

Rizvi, F. 2009. "Global Mobility and the Challenges of Educational Research and Policy." In *Globalization and the Study of Education*, edited by T. S. Popkewitz and F. Rizvi, 268–89. Malden, MA: Blackwell. https://doi.org/10.1111/j.1744-7984.2009.01172.x.

Roozen, K. 2009. "From Journals to Journalism: Tracing Trajectories of Literate Development." *College Composition and Communication* 60 (3): 541–72.

Roozen, K., and J. Erickson. 2017. *Expanding Literate Landscapes: Persons, Practices, and Sociohistoric Perspectives of Disciplinary Development*. Logan: Computers and Composition Digital Press/Utah State University Press.

Rosow, S. J. n.d. *Globalization and Corporatization of the University: A Report on the Changing Structure of the University*. United University Professions. http://uupinfo.org/research/GlobalizationReport07.pdf.

Rounsaville, A. 2015. "Taking Hold of Global Englishes: Intensive English Programs as Brokers of Transnational Literacy." *Journal of Composition and Literacy Studies* 3 (3): 67–85. https://doi.org/10.21263/1.3.3.5.

Rouse, R. 1992. "Making Sense of Settlement: Class Transformation, Cultural Struggle and Transnationalism among Mexican Migrants in the United States." In *Towards a*

Transnational Perspective on Migration: Race, Class, Ethnicity and Nationalism Reconsidered, edited by N. Glick Schiller, L. Basch, and C. Blanc-Szanton, 25–52. New York: New York Academy of Sciences. https://doi.org/10.1111/j.1749-6632.1992.tb33485.x.

Russell, D. R., and A. Yañez. 2003. "'Big Picture People Rarely Become Historians': Genre Systems and the Contradictions of General Education." In *Writing Selves/Writing Society: Research from Activity Perspective*, edited by Charles Bazerman and David R. Russell, 331–62. Fort Collins, CO: WAC Clearinghouse.

Schiller, N. G., and N. B. Salazar. 2013. "Regimes of Mobility Across the Globe." *Journal of Ethnic and Migration Studies* 39 (2): 183–200. http://dx.doi.org/10.1080/136918 3X.2013.723253.

Scollon, R., and W. Scollon. 2003. *Discourse in Place: Language in the Material World.* New York: Routledge. https://doi.org/10.4324/9780203422724.

Scollon, R., and W. Scollon. 2004. *Nexus Analysis: Discourse and the Emerging Internet.* New York: Routledge.

Shahjahan, R. A., and A. J. Kezar. 2013. "Beyond the 'National Container': Addressing Methodological Nationalism in Higher Education Research." *Educational Researcher* 42 (1): 20–29. https://doi.org/10.3102/0013189X12463050.

Sheff, D. 1999. "He's Got Guanxi!" *Wired*, February 1. https://www.wired.com/1999/02 /bofeng/.

Sidhu, R. 2006. *Universities and Globalization: To Market.* Mahwah, NJ: Lawrence Erlbaum.

SIE. 2013. SIE History. Accessed July 1, 2013. http://summer.sieschool.org/about/sie _history/.

SIE. 2015. SIE International Summer Sessions. Accessed July 1, 2013. http://summer .sieschool.org/en/.

Silverstein, M., and G. Urban, eds. 1996. *Natural Histories of Discourse.* Chicago, IL: University of Chicago Press.

Simon, A. K. 2009. *Embracing the World Grant Ideal: Affirming the Morrill Act for a Twenty-First-Century Global Society.* http://worldgrantideal.msu.edu/_files/documents/monograph .pdf.

Simon, L. A. K. 2010. "World Grant Universities: Meeting the Challenges of the Twenty-First Century." *Change: The Magazine of Higher Learning* 42 (5): 42–46. https://doi .org/10.1080/00091383.2010.502876.

Simon, L. A. K. 2013. "From Land-Grant to a 'World-Grant' University: Musings of a State University President." *International Educator* 22 (5): 49–51.

Singh, M., F. Rizvi, and M. Shrestha. 2007. "Student Mobility and the Spatial Production of Cosmopolitan Identities." In *Spatial Theories of Education*, edited by K. Gulson and C. Symes, 195–214. London: Routledge.

Smith, P. S., and L. E. Guarnizo. 1998. *Transnationalism from Below.* New Brunswick, NJ: Transaction.

Sobré-Denton, M., and N. Bardhan. 2013. *Cultivating Cosmopolitanism for Intercultural Communication: Communicating as Global Citizens.* New York: Routledge.

Soja, E. W. 1996. *Thirdspace: Journeys to Los Angeles and Other Real-and-Imagined Places.* Cambridge, MA: Blackwell.

Soja, E. W. 2004. Preface to *Spatializing Literacy Research and Practice*, edited by K. M. Leander and M. Sheehy, ix–xv. New York: Peter Lang.

Soria, K. M., and J. Troisi. 2014. "Internationalization at Home, Alternatives to Study Abroad: Implications for Students' Development of Global, International, and Intercultural Competencies." *Journal of Studies in International Education* 18 (3): 261–80. https://doi.org/10.1177/1028315313496572.

Spinuzzi, C. 2003. *Tracing Genres Through Organizations: A Sociocultural Approach to Information Design.* Cambridge, MA: MIT Press.

Spinuzzi, C. 2008. *Network.* Cambridge, MA: MIT Press. https://doi.org/10.1017/CBO9780 511509605.

Starke-Meyerring, D. 2015. "From 'Educating the Other' to Cross-Boundary Knowledge-Making: Global Networked Learning Environments as Critical Sites of Writing Program Administration." In *Transnational Writing Program Administration*, edited by David S. Martins, 307–31. Logan: Utah State University Press. https://doi.org/10.7330/9780874219 623.c013.

Stecklow, S., and A. Harney. 2016. "Chinese Education Giant Helps Its Students Game the SAT." *Reuters*, December 23. http://www.reuters.com/article/us-college-china-testing -exclusive-idUSKBN14C1G7.

Sternglass, M. S. 1997. *Time to Know Them: A Longitudinal Study of Writing and Learning at the College Level*. Mahwah, NJ: Lawrence Erlbaum.

Street, B. V., ed. 1993. *Cross-Cultural Approaches to Literacy*. Cambridge: Cambridge University Press.

Suárez-Orozco, C., and M. M. Suárez-Orozco. 2001. *Children of Immigration*. Cambridge, MA: Harvard University Press.

Sun, X. 2004. "How to Walk Down the Road of Chinese-Foreign Cooperation in Running Schools." *China Education Daily*, July 7. Accessed July 1, 2015. http://www.jyb.cn/gb /2004/07/07/zy/5-zszk/1.htm.

Swales, J. M. 1990. *Genre Analysis: English in Academic and Research Settings*. New York: Cambridge University Press.

SYSU Office for International Students' Affairs. 2012. 中山大学SIE国际暑期学校正式开学 [SYSUSIE summer school officially started]. Accessed July 2013. http://iso.sysu.edu .cn/tzyxx/102187.htm.

Tardy, C. M. 2015. "Discourses of Internationalization and Diversity in US Universities and Writing Programs." In *Transnational Writing Program Administration*, edited by David S. Martins, 243–62. Logan: Utah State University Press.

Tea Leaf National Staff. 2015. "Do Years Studying in America Change Chinese Hearts and Minds?" *Foreign Policy*, December 9. http://foreignpolicy.com/2015/12/07/do -years-studying-in-america-change-chinese-hearts-and-minds-china-u-foreign-policy -student-survey/.

Thaiss, C., G. C. Bräuer, P. Carlino, L. Ganobcsik-Williams, and A. Sinha, eds. 2012. *Writing Programs Worldwide: Profiles of Academic Writing in Many Places*. Fort Collins, CO: WAC Clearinghouse and Parlor.

Thrift, N. 2006. "Space." *Theory, Culture & Society* 23 (2–3): 139–46. https://doi.org/10.1177 /0263276406063780.

Tsing, A. L. 2005. *Friction: An Ethnography of Global Connection*. Princeton, NJ: Princeton University Press.

Tyre, P. 2016. "How Sophisticated Test Scams from China Are Making Their Way into the U.S." *The Atlantic*, March 21. https://www.theatlantic.com/education/archive/2016/03 /how-sophisticated-test-scams-from-china-are-making-their-way-into-the-us/474474/.

University Committee on Faculty Affairs. 2013. *Faculty Instructional Experiences with International Students at Michigan State University: A Survey Conducted by the University Committee on Faculty Affairs (UCFA)*. Accessed February 27, 2017. http://fod.msu.edu/sites /default/files/page_media/ucfa_international_students_survey_final_results.pdf

Urry, J. 2003. *Global Complexity*. Cambridge: Polity Press.

Urry, J. 2007. *Mobilities*. Malden, MA: Polity.

Vertovec, S. 2004. "Migrant Transnationalism and Modes of Transformation." *International Migration Review* 38 (3): 970–1001. https://doi.org/10.1111/j.1747-7379.2004 .tb00226.x.

Vertovec, S. 2009. *Transnationalism*. New York: Routledge.

Vieira, K. 2011. "Undocumented in a Documentary Society: Textual Borders and Transnational Religious Literacies." *Written Communication* 28 (4): 436–61. https://doi.org /10.1177/0741088311421468.

Vieira, K. 2016. *American by Paper: How Documents Matter in Immigrant Literacy*. Minneapolis: University of Minnesota Press. https://doi.org/10.5749/minnesota/9780816697519.001.0001.

Walvoord, B. E., and L. McCarthy. 1990. *Thinking and Writing in College: A Naturalistic Study of Students in Four Disciplines*. Urbana, IL: NCTE.

Wang, Y., and L. Miao. 2014. 中国留学发展报告 [Annual report on the development of Chinese students studying abroad]. Beijing: Shehui kexue wenxian chubanshe.

Wang, Z., ed. 2014. *Revolutionary Cycles in Chinese Cinema, 1951–1979*. New York: Palgrave Macmillan. https://doi.org/10.1057/9781137378743.

Wardle, E. 2007. "Understanding 'Transfer' from FYC: Preliminary Results of a Longitudinal Study." *WPA: Writing Program Administration* 31 (1–2): 65–85.

Wargo, J. M., and P. I. de Costa. 2017. "Tracing Academic Literacies across Contemporary Literacy Sponsorscapes: Mobilities, Ideologies, Identities, and Technologies." *London Review of Education* 15 (1): 101–14. https://doi.org/10.18546/LRE.15.1.09.

Wasserstrom, J. N. 2014. "The Elusive Chinese Dream." *New York Times*, December 26. https://www.nytimes.com/2014/12/27/opinion/the-elusive-chinese-dream.html?_r=0.

Waters, J. L. 2006. "Geographies of Cultural Capital: Education, International Migration and Family Strategies between Hong Kong and Canada." *Transactions of the Institute of British Geographers* 31 (2): 179–92. https://doi.org/10.1111/j.1475-5661.2006.00202.x.

Waters, J. L. 2012. "Geographies of International Education: Mobilities and the Reproduction of Social (Dis)advantage." *Geography Compass* 6 (3): 123–36. https://doi.org/10.1111/j.1749-8198.2011.00473.x.

Wertsch, J. V. 1991. *Voices of the Mind: A Sociocultural Approach to Mediated Action*. Cambridge, MA: Harvard University Press.

Wetzel, D. Z., and D. W. Reynolds. 2015. "Adaption across Space and Time: Revealing Pedagogical Assumptions." In *Transnational Writing Program Administration*, edited by David S. Martins, 93–116. Logan: Utah State University Press. https://doi.org/10.7330/9780874219623.c004.

Wilhelm, I. 2010. "Falsified Applications Are Common Among Chinese Students Seeking to Go Abroad, Consultant Says." *Chronicle of Higher Education*, June 14. http://www.chronicle.com/article/Falsification-Is-Common-Among/65946/.

Wilkins, S. 2016. "Transnational Higher Education in the 21st Century." *Journal of Studies in International Education* 20 (1): 3–7. https://doi.org/10.1177/1028315315625148.

Williams, R. 1977. *Marxism and Literature*. Oxford: Oxford University Press.

Williams, T. R. 2005. "Exploring the Impact of Study Abroad on Students' Intercultural Communication Skills: Adaptability and Sensitivity." *Journal of Studies in International Education* 9 (4): 356–71. https://doi.org/10.1177/1028315305277681.

Wimmer, A., and Glick N. Schiller. 2002. "Methodological Nationalism and Beyond: Nation-State Building, Migration and the Social Sciences." *Global Networks* 2 (4): 301–34. https://doi.org/10.1111/1471-0374.00043.

Wood, D. 2010. *Rethinking the Power of Maps*. New York: Guilford Press.

Wortham, S. 2006. *Learning Identity: The Joint Emergence of Social Identification and Academic Learning*. New York: Cambridge University Press.

Xian, J. P. 2014. "不可轻视'学霸学渣'的"标签效应" [Don't underestimate the "label effects" of "lord of learning and dregs of learning"]. people.cn. http://edu.people.com.cn/n/2014/0113/c1053-24104354.html.

Yancey, K. B., L. Robertson, and K. Taczak. 2014. *Writing across Contexts: Transfer, Composition, and Cultures of Writing*. Logan: Utah State University Press.

Yang, D. T. 2016. *The Pursuit of the Chinese Dream in America: Chinese Undergraduate Students at American Universities*. Lanham, MD: Lexington Books.

Yang, R. 2008. "Transnational Higher Education in China: Contexts, Characteristics and Concerns." *Australian Journal of Education* 52 (3): 272–86. https://doi.org/10.1177/000494410805200305.

Yi, Y. 2007. "Engaging Literacy: A Biliterate Student's Composing Practices beyond School." *Journal of Second Language Writing* 16 (1): 23–39. https://doi.org/10.1016/j.jslw.2007.03.001.

Yin, R. K. 2003. *Case Study Research: Design and Methods*. Thousand Oaks, CA: SAGE.

You, X. 2010. *Writing in the Devil's Tongue: A History of English Composition in China*. Carbondale: Southern Illinois University Press.

You, X. 2016. *Cosmopolitan English and Transliteracy*. Carbondale: Southern Illinois University Press.

You, X., and X. You. 2013. "American Content Teachers' Literacy Brokerage in Multilingual University Classrooms." *Journal of Second Language Writing* 22 (3): 260–76. https://doi.org/10.1016/j.jslw.2013.02.004.

Yu, Q. 2014. 学霸引领校园正能量. ["Lord of learning" leads positive energy on campus] Language Planning.

Zamel, V., and R. Spack, eds. 2004. *Crossing the Curriculum: Multilingual Learners in College Classrooms*. Mahwah, NJ: Routledge.

ABOUT THE AUTHORS

STEVEN FRAIBERG is an assistant professor in the Department of Writing, Rhetoric, and American Cultures at Michigan State University where he is affiliated with the Jewish Studies and Global Studies in the Arts and Humanities programs. His research is focused in the areas of language, culture, and globalization. He has published in *College Composition and Communication, Computers and Composition, Technical Communication Quarterly, Kairos,* and *Israel Studies Review.*

XIQIAO WANG is a fixed-term assistant professor in the Department of Writing, Rhetoric and American Cultures at Michigan State University. Her research has been published in *Journal of Adolescent and Adult Literacies* and *Composition Studies.*

XIAOYE YOU is an associate professor of English and Asian studies at Pennsylvania State University and Yunshan Chair Professor at Guangdong University of Foreign Studies. He studies multilingual writing, comparative rhetoric, and cosmopolitan English. His first monograph, *Writing in the Devil's Tongue: A History of English Composition in China,* won the 2011 Conference on College Composition and Communication (CCCC) Outstanding Book Award. His recent book, *Cosmopolitan English and Transliteracy,* argues for the ethical use of English in everyday life and for cultivating global citizens in English literacy education.

INDEX

Page numbers in italics indicate illustrations.